INFORMATION and BEHAVIOR: SYSTEMS of INFLUENCE

COMMUNICATION

A series of volumes edited by:
Dolf Zillmann and Jennings Bryant

INFORMATION and BEHAVIOR: SYSTEMS of INFLUENCE

Richard A. Winett
*Virginia Polytechnic Institute
and State University*

LAWRENCE ERLBAUM ASSOCIATES, PUBLISHERS
1986   Hillsdale, New Jersey   London

Lawrence Erlbaum Associates, Inc., Publishers
365 Broadway
Hillsdale, New Jersey 07642

Library of Congress Cataloging-in-Publication Data

Winett, Richard A. (Richard Allen), 1945–
    Information and behavior.

    Includes index.
    1. Mass media—Psychological aspects. 2. Mass media—Social aspects. I. Title.
HM258.W52 1986   302.2′34   85-20653
ISBN 0-89859-690-4

Printed in the United States of America
10 9 8 7 6 5 4 3 2 1

To my parents, Arthur and Belle, for their love and strength.

Contents

Preface

This book tries to integrate theory, research, values, and action in the study and application of information interventions. A multilevel framework—behavioral systems—which is an amalgamation of principles from social learning theory, communication, social marketing, and behavior analysis is developed. It is used throughout the book to conceptualize, plan, and implement information interventions. A research approach emphasizing experimental field studies is offered as a natural accompaniment to behavioral systems.

These concepts and methods are relatively unique in communication and information theory and application. The dominant approach in these disciplines has been, and remains, a cognitive one. Often, what has been measured are perceptions, memory, and attitudes investigated within circumscribed settings. The alternative presented in this book is to first understand behavior in context (i.e., in relationship to group, organizational, community, and institutional systems of influence), plan information interventions with this understanding, and implement and evaluate the effects of these interventions on key behaviors in the natural environment.

Any book about human change takes value positions. It goes with the territory. However, often the value positions are implicit, not recognized, and not overtly stated. I have tried to avoid that mistake by being explicit about the value positions of this book. The overwhelming asymmetry of power and influence between the corporate structure (i.e., the multinationals and large national firms) and consumers is a starting point for much of the discussion in chapters about television, new media, health, and consumer policy. A consistent conclusion is that there is a need for government intervention on the side of the consumer in order to make the marketplace truly competitive. In other words, the balance between the large corporate structure and consumers has been so disorted by the mid-1980s that renewed government intervention is the key to restoring a major goal of our economy—competition.

This is not a popular idea at this time. Deregulation and the free market are supposed to be the miraculous answer to the problems of our over-regulated society. I do not believe that this "miracle" has occurred. In particular, myths and problems with communication (and regulatory) policy (e.g., information remedies, access to media), form the backdrop for several chapters. It is hoped that by being explicit about values and politics, this book can help to counter some prevailing beliefs and policies.

The action objective of this book pertains to the development and implementation of effective information for consumer, health, and prosocial purposes. It is argued that for a variety of conceptual, strategic, methodological, and political reasons, most consumer and prosocial efforts have not been effective. This has been the case so often that many in the communication field and in government conclude that information is not effective (i.e., "information cannot change behavior"). A number of examples in this book are used to dispell this belief. Information that is expertly designed, follow communication, social learning, and behavior analysis principles, seeks realistic changes, and is properly targeted, can be quite effective. The major tasks for action are appropriate information design and regulatory change that can provide access for more diverse media images and messages.

These starting points—theory, research, values, and action—are detailed in the introductory chapter. Every chapter then uses these points in its discussion. An attempt is also made to "always look at the data." In some chapters (e.g., prosocial television), this works quite well. For example, in that chapter, it is possible to examine a number of prosocial efforts and assess which variables are effective and which are ineffective for behavior change. Other chapters (e.g., new media) are more speculative. There simply is not the wealth of studies available to make very definitive conclusions. In those chapters, the reader is forewarned and urged to bear with the speculations.

Finally, I feel that all the chapters fit together and are cross-referenced, but yet may have a separate flavor about them. After reading the introduction, any chapter can be read, although the present order appears to be the most logical one.

ACKNOWLEDGMENTS

A number of people, in different ways, have contributed to the development and completion of this book. Len Krasner, my mentor at Stony Brook from 1967 to 1971, has remained a continuing influence. Not surprisingly, the overall perspective of this book is similar to his own work. My friend, Robin Winkler, has also over a long period of time always reminded me to put my values and professional work together. John Kagel, an economist, showed me the importance of some of my earlier work for economic and regulatory theory and policy. John has had a major influence on the success of my career.

The Learning Resource Center at Virginia Tech has provided the expert means to implement some of my ideas on information and television. Without the Center, none of the studies that I have done could have been properly formulated, much less implemented. All of these projects have been generously supported since 1979 by the National Science Foundation. I also want to acknowledge the fine work of students in these projects: Joe Hatcher, Rick Fort, Ingrid Leckliter, Fred Fishback, Anne Riley, Susie Love, Donna Chinn, Brian Stahl, Kathryn Kramer, Bruce Walker, Steve Malone, and M. K. Lane.

Jennings Bryant, one of the editors of this series, provided encouragement, specific feedback, and suggestions on earlier chapter drafts which is much appreciated. The word processing craft of Trevia Moses, Linda Southard, and Abby Box is also acknowledged and appreciated.

Richard A. Winett

INFORMATION and
BEHAVIOR:
SYSTEMS of INFLUENCE

1 Introduction: A Behavioral Systems Framework for Information and Effects

GOALS AND PERSPECTIVE

This book has two basic goals. The first goal is to present how information is formed, used, channeled, and delivered in a number of different contexts and systems with varying impacts. By way of example, these diverse arenas include television and prosocial programs; the conveying of health information by physicians to patients; community information campaigns; government originated information to remedy market failures, and computer-mediated networking for long-distance therapeutic interactions. The second goal is to present these diverse applications within one framework so that there is continuity between the different subjects and chapters. The framework is "behavioral systems," which is an emerging, rather than fully developed, approach (Wahler & Graves, 1983; Winkler & Winett, 1982). Thus, this book is also an attempt to further evolve and show the viability of this framework.

The behavioral systems approach presented here is different from its predecessors, for example, Kantor's interbehavioral psychology (Morris, Higgins, & Bickel, 1982), or more contemporary operant-systems perspectives (Wahler & Graves, 1983), or behavioral ecology (Willems, 1974). I make no claim for precise theoretical explications of the approach in this book, or for exact definitions and boundaries. Instead, I purposely use the term *framework* to suggest its current status. This framework is an amalgamation of social learning, communication, and behavior analysis principles overlayed by social marketing concepts and variables. The framework is useful for understanding behavioral effects, and most useful for developing strategies for behavior change and evaluating impacts. The framework, its concepts, principles, and strategies, are presented later in this chapter, throughout subsequent chapters, and then are brought together in the last chapter. At this point, behavioral systems is described as a perspective.

It is hoped that this book will be contributory in providing one alternative to the dominant, cognitive approach in communication, information processing, and now, diverse computer applications. Obviously, a cognitive approach should be relatively dominant in these fields. It would be absurd to describe information processing and communications without addressing cognitive processes—attention, memory, internal decision making, and heuristic systems. However, what is missing in most contemporary expositions is a balance of internal and external variables in conceptualization, research, and application. For example, as is shown, most consumer behavior studies leave us with a consumer lost in thought; rarely do we see the flow through from stimuli, cognitive processes, to actual purchases. Studies of computer-mediated interaction have rarely asked one simple question: "What does the person do with this experience *outside* of the computer situation?"

This lack of balance is depicted in Fig. 1.1. The person and cognitive processes are supreme. The conceptualization of problems, the research enterprise, and public policy recommendations, for the most part, revolve around person-centered variables. The figure, the person, is important; the ground, the context, is not. In psychology, this has been characterized as the study of asocial individuals (Sarason, 1981). This perspective has been dominant in American psychology and economics, although at various junctures it has been seriously challenged on different fronts (e.g., Bronfenbrenner, 1979; Galbraith, 1973).

The purpose of this book is not to resort to the equally untenable blackbox, stimulus-response paradigms or one-step communication approaches that tend to error on the other side by ignoring person variables. However, to restore balance,

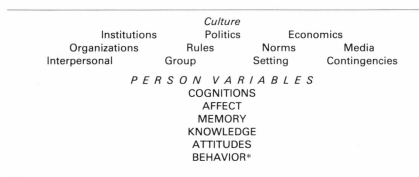

FIG. 1.1.   Schema of a cognitive framework.+
+ The hallmark of the approach is the interrelationships of the person variables. Factors external to the person, particularly high-order factors, are deemphasized.

   *Behavior is rarely measured in real-life contexts. Laboratory methods are often used.

CULTURE

INSTITUTIONS   POLITICS   ECONOMICS
ORGANIZATIONS   RULES   NORMS   MEDIA
INTERPERSONAL   GROUP   SETTING   CONTINGENCIES

Person Variables
Cognitions
Affect
Memory
Knowledge
Attitudes
Behavior*

FIG. 1.2. Schema of the behavioral systems framework [+]
*Behavioral measurement in real-life contexts is emphasized. Field experiments are often used.
[+] The hallmark of the approach is multilevel analysis. At this point, the systems framework is more contextual. Note how higher order factors are emphasized compared to the cognitive approach.

---

often stimuli, modality, channel, system, i.e., the independent variables and context, are emphasized at the expense of person-centered dependent variables, except for behavioral outcomes. This emphasis is depicted in Fig. 1.2. Thus, I readily push this particular perspective in demonstrating its applicability to diverse issues and problems in information and behavior. The point of emphasizing person or context is a dialectical one and, perhaps, the pull will be too much on the side of context. If this work is effective, it might require a balancing response in the other direction.

BIASES

This book has several other biases (the word is used advisedly), for which I make no apology, but rather prefer to be simply candid about them. I have always tried to emphasize in my work, as others have done (e.g., Rappaport, 1977), that the behavioral sciences cannot pretend to be politically neutral in how research topics are chosen, or how and what is investigated within these topics. Wittingly or unwittingly, we are always involved in these value decisions. Many of the positions taken here can be characterized as neoliberal; some readers on the further extremes of the political spectrum may have more descriptive terms for these positions. For example, I favor strong federal government interventions in the marketplace that will take us beyond illusions of a free-market and help restore competitiveness to the marketplace (particularly, with regard to very large corporations; LeDuc, 1982). This position is best shown in the chapters on consumer behavior and prosocial television. It would be wonderfully consistent with free-market principles if consumers were effectively informed about un-needed products; if there was more real choice (diversity) on what to view on TV; and if access to expensive media was less centralized.

Thus, there is a concern with equity issues and more equal access to re-sources. This is most apparent in chapter 5 on new media, and to some extent in chapter 6 on health. Finally, there are holdovers from my 1960s days—some distrust of high technology and hyperbolic claims of innovations, particularly those that portray all effects as positive; and a lack of reverence for some institutions, e.g., the medical establishment. Integrating ideological concerns with technological advances is a third goal here and, thus, the reader is consid-ered forewarned.

A behavioral systems perspective may neglect some person-centered, depen-dent variables, but it does not neglect one such variable—behavior. We will always be asking the question, ''What was the immediate and longer term behavioral effect?'' For example, how do children who frequently view violent TV programs behave; or, how does this type of information from the physician affect a patient's health behaviors; or, how much was the sale of low-sodium products increased through this multimedia campaign? That these types of ques-tions should be asked seems obvious; that data are rarely available to answer such questions is less obvious. For example, it appears that for advertising and other prosocial campaigns, there are reams of data on exposure, comprehension, rec-ognition, recall, attitudes and, perhaps, even self-reports of decisions and behav-ioral intentions (McGuire, 1981). Almost always lacking are actual behavioral data or real representations of behavior, e.g., observations of consumers, sales data, health records. This is true for several reasons. If a model emphasizes cognitive processes and person variables, there will be less attention paid to behavioral outcomes. Further, if a model assumes some relatively linear rela-tionship between exposure, comprehension, liking, attitude change, and so on through to behavior change, i.e., ''a hierarchy of effects model,'' then tapping preliminary variables in the chain may be seen as sufficiently convincing. A final reason is based on how research is conducted. Collecting real behavioral data is difficult, time-consuming, and sometimes expensive. It is made next to impossi-ble to have real behavioral data if there is no real behavioral data to collect!

At the same time that attention is focused on information modalities and behavioral outcomes, another, hopefully positive bias is to try to understand influences not only at the level of behavioral outcome, but also at a level or two above the behavioral level. For example, how violent television programs influ-ence children is dependent on their viewing habits, age, and skills, but also on family factors (group level). At the same time, the question has to be asked, ''Why is there so much violence on television and what can be done about it?'' This question is directed toward the controlling forces of commercial television in our free-enterprise system (institutional level). Likewise, in trying to under-stand patient behavior, physician behavior must be understood, as well as incentives and disincentives in our health care system that influence both parties. Thus, attempts will be made at multilevel analyses for understanding behaviors and practices, for designing interventions, and for evaluating impacts.

A final bias is the type of research approach seen as appropriate to the behavioral systems framework. It appears that the behavioral sciences' commitment to real world research (e.g., Bronfenbrenner, 1979) was short-lived. Thus, one of the biases of this work is to heavily favor field studies, and to attempt to redirect some work away from the confines of the laboratory.

TYPES OF RESEARCH EMPHASIZED

A good deal of the research in many of the fields represented here have excessively relied on analog laboratory research. There is nothing inherently wrong with laboratory research, just as there is nothing inherently good about field research. Perhaps an example here can illustrate the problems and strengths of laboratory research used to address issues in information processing, communication, and consumer behavior. The general issue is how information framing and channel of delivery affects choice. Let us say that the topic is adoption of physical fitness activities that can be phrased or couched in how much you have to gain or lose by adoption or nonadoption (Kahneman & Tversky, 1984). The message, in turn, can be primarily delivered through print media (i.e., words) or through more visual and graphic depictions of the activities to be adopted.

This is fairly typical (and, much less an analog than some studies) of an elegant 2 × 2 experimental design. It can be made even more elegant by random assignment of people to different conditions, with people, perhaps segmented by education level (now a 2 × 2 × 2 design). Perfect control of the length and content of the different messages can be achieved. All messages can be delivered on a TV screen in a laboratory and data collection can be done at several points in time after the message presentation. Diverse and sophisticated variables tapping recognition, recall, comprehension, attitude change, and even behavioral intention can be used and can contribute to the study's internal validity. Perhaps, also, its external validity (how much the results can be generalized to other contexts, i.e., "the real world") can be enhanced by keeping messages to a length that is representative of Public Service Announcements (PSA's), and by embedding messages in television programs. If all these refinements were made in the design, the experiment would be more than typical and elegant. It would be an excellent experiment and of far better quality than most that have been done. Much can be learned from this study that could be valuable to the general field of communication and, more specifically, for health promotion campaigns.

However, the mistake that is often made is assuming that because of the elegance and rigor of the design and measures generalization can be made with a high degree of confidence. The worst mistake is to assume that reported attitude change and reported behavioral intentions will actually be related to real life behavior. There is no assurance that the person showing a change in attitude toward exercise and intention to jog regularly actually will do so. McGuire (1981) has called this the "distal measure fallacy." Measurement is most frequently done early in a causal chain with the fallacy being that early measures (e.g., memory) are closely linked to later measures (e.g., behavior).

Figure 1.3 depicts a simple flow-through model for long-term purchase behaviors. Whereas few researchers would agree to the close, linear relationship between variables suggested by the arrows, curtailing measurement early in the chain implies such relationships. Indeed, the only way to know if information stimuli promote long-term behavior change is to measure behavior over time.

The experiment that was previously described on information framing and channel and exercise behavior could be improved by taking behavioral measures over time, such as unobtrusive observations of exercise. However, this is rarely done. In addition, even if such measures were available, the specialness of the laboratory setting would preclude confidently affirming that messages similar to the effective ones in the experiment delivered through PSA's on network TV will have a similar behavioral effect. This may or may not happen.

The experimental example used is somewhat unusual in that it is less of an analog than many of the laboratory studies that have been conducted. Nonetheless, the problems in generalizing both its stimuli and results to the real world are apparent. It is unclear if the procedures will work until they are tried. The laboratory study may be a good first step in a series of studies to develop effective health promotion messages, but it is assuredly not the last step. If these statements seem strong, and call into question the use and pervasive influence in communication and related fields of cognitive laboratory studies (virtually following an advertising paradigm; Flay & Cook, 1981), it is because that is exactly the intention.

Not all laboratory studies are conducted as a prelude to behavior change programs or campaigns. Rather, many are conducted to understand basic processes. If understanding context is endemic to understanding basic processes, then some laboratory studies fall short because of inattention to creating, or at least simulating, real life contexts.

The alternative advocated here is the field study, but not just any kind of field study. Using survey techniques and asking representative citizens which (actual) PSA's they recognize, recall, or like best, or even think influenced their behavior, may introduce more reality into the research process. However, this would be done at the expense of rigor and the ability to delineate cause–effect relationships. The ideal approach is the field experiment in which representative consumers in their own homes would be (potentially) exposed to different types of PSA's, perhaps, representing similar conditions to the laboratory experiment. This can be accomplished with split-cable systems (Robertson, Kelley, O'Neill, Wixom, Eirwirth, & Haddon, 1974). Again, it would be important to use measures that tapped cognitive processes, but also initial and long-term behavior change measures must be used. Studies in the behavioral tradition generally use frequent measurement of the target behavior, rather than simply having pre- and post-measures. The behavioral measures (e.g., percent cars speeding) need also to be linked to more direct policy measures (e.g., traffic accidents; Flay & Cook, 1981). Thus, field experiments are not easy to do, but they can and should be done (Fairweather & Tornatzky, 1977).

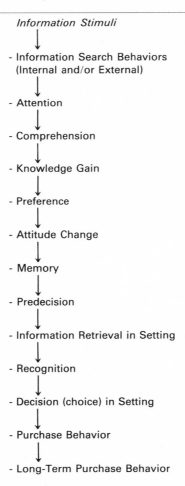

FIG. 1.3.   Schema of a flow-through model from information stimuli to long-term purchase behavior.*

*Many studies in consumer behavior have only tapped top variables (e.g., knowledge, preference, attitude, predecision) relatively early in this chain. Few consumer behavior studies have actually studied purchase behaviors.

What is advocated is a research approach that may use laboratory and survey research techniques to develop and refine ideas and procedures (i.e., "formative research"; Palmer, 1981), but where the proof of the pudding is the field experiment. A caveat here is that the field experiment may not and usually cannot answer all questions. Field experiments may have to be done in a long series to sufficiently answer questions (Flay & Cook, 1981; Hersen & Barlow, 1983), or questions raised in field experiments may be reverted back to laboratory or survey studies (Winett & Ester, 1982). After refinements, another field experiment may be done.

It should also be clear what is and is not advocated. Poorly controlled field experiments usually are without much value. Field experiments also do not guarantee external validity. For example, if a research person visited homes to make sure families watched the special health PSA's, it would be difficult to conclude that ordinarily delivered PSA's will have the same effects as these. If it is believed that setting and context are critical, then the field experiment must reflect this position. Thus, a common mistake of the field experiment may be overgeneralization, or overstating the case. This may occur when reality is not adhered to in the field, with reality being one of the major reasons for doing field experiments in the first place!

One central question is why field experiments are not done more frequently if they potentially represent the best approach? The reasons have to do with costs, logistics, time, and illusions and traditions in science. A good field experiment can be expensive, although not excessively so. In fact, in many of the areas discussed here, field experiments can be done without great costs. However, as I can well-attest, it is difficult and takes special care to maintain acceptable scientific rigor in the field. This is particularly true as far as assuring random assignment of individuals, households, or other units to different conditions, and maintaining no contamination between conditions. The time involved may be more than laboratory studies, although this may not always be the case. However, much time to set up field experiments will not be spent with professional peers. Considerable time may be spent with community groups and individual citizens, business, media, education leaders, and field staff. Such interactions may or may not be rewarding to the behavioral scientist and may not be seen as scientific work by evaluative peers.

The illusion is that other methods can be used to assess impacts of particular stimuli, procedures, or technology. Until an independent variable is tried under representative conditions, there really is no true way to accurately assess such impacts.

Although it is the contention that the field experiment is the ultimate answer, it is apparent that there simply are some questions that can never be addressed in a true field experiment. For example, it is ethically and practically impossible to have a situation where an experimenter would control all of a child's television viewing from birth. However, various quasi-experimental designs (Campbell,

1969), which essentially do not require random assignment to conditions, have been developed and are receiving increased use.

Traditions and pressures in scientific disciplines appear to militate against field experiments. Work in a laboratory is seen as theoretical, scientific, and hence, prestigious. Work in the field is only applied, unscientific, and not prestigious. Field experiments can be difficult to set up, may take a long time to conduct, and therefore, are somewhat risky. Although standards may be changing to once again emphasize quality (Hayes, 1983), academic/scientific advancement in the last 2 decades, in many cases, focused on quantity of publications. This also appears partly to be a response to market forces, i.e., an oversupply of behavioral scientists leading to more difficult criteria (read, quantity) for advancement. Focusing on field experiments may not be the best way for a beginning behavioral scientist to prosper, unless it is clear that quality will be the evaluation criterion.

The conception that field experiments are somehow not really science and are atheoretical still pervades. In the case of sloppy field experiments, or where the only concern is evaluation, or in some research in advertising (Harris, 1983), this is true. However, equating all laboratory-based research with science, and field research with nonscience is clearly unwarranted. In the 1970s, for example, at the National Science Foundation (NSF), through the Research Addressed to National Needs (RANN) program, there seemed to be a consensus that scientific approaches in the behavioral sciences could be meshed with applied concerns. This program was phased out, and its mission spread to diverse programs in the NSF. In a few years, this spread was also effectively phased out. It is, for the most part, back to business as usual, which may be true in some other federal grant and contracting agencies.

There seems to be little or no understanding that a focus on behavior change can yield outcomes of both scientific and applied significance (Bronfenbrenner, 1979). The two are seen as not mixing. This book makes the case that they can and should be mixed.

BEHAVIORAL SYSTEMS FRAMEWORK

What are the assumptions, guidelines, and directions of the behavioral systems framework? In some ways, it is first easier to say what it is not. Frequently, when I have told other professionals in consumer behavior, marketing, or communication that I have a behavioral systems approach, their response has been, "So, you're interested in using behavior modification with consumers (or through the media)." This is partly true, but it is missing the main point. The framework here does have a strong tradition of application and experimentation with behavior change, i.e., there is a behavioral technology. For example, behavioral modeling and contingency contracting are two widely used behavioral technologies. But, the individual procedures are merely derivatives of an overall approach.

A behavioral systems framework has these two basic assumptions stated a number of years ago by Bandura (1977a):

1. Behavior and environment are best studied as reciprocal systems. That is, person-centered variables must always be studied within an environmental context.

2. The reciprocity notion means that influence is bidirectional. The environment shapes, maintains, and constrains behavior. However, people are not passive in this process. They are architects of their environments, although their architectural plans are influenced by the prevailing environment, and the environment that is constructed, in turn, influences their behavior.

Two important guidelines are:

1. The principles are derived from scientific knowledge in such fields as learning, social psychology, cognitive processes, and more recently from diverse fields such as environmental psychology, systems, and ecological psychology, marketing, and behavioral economics.

2. Hence, the framework is not static, but is dynamic and evolving. For example, it is only recently that behavioral scientists have seen marketing as an appropriate "umbrella" for their work.

These guidelines are important. However, a number of important concepts are maintained from learning theory, and it can be said that notions about learning are the kernel of the approach. For example, if a question is raised concerning response to similar informational stimuli by consumers, principles of stimulus discrimination and generalization can be used. Or, if an interactive videodisc system is designed to teach social skills, the principles of modeling, shaping and successive approximation, feedback and reinforcement can be used. However, input on designing a communication also may be derived from social psychology. A classic example is the use of one-sided versus two-sided communications (Hovland, Lumsdaine, & Sheffield, 1949).

Social learning theory forms much of the psychological basis of a behavioral systems approach. It is becoming a sort of meta-paradigm in the behavioral sciences as social learning theory synthesizes knowledge from diverse fields, integrates cognitive and behavioral perspectives, and also retains learning concepts as a central core (Bandura, 1977a, 1977b).

Less developed is the system dimension in behavioral systems. Efforts to emphasize a behavioral systems perspective are not new (e.g., Morris, Higgins, & Bickel, 1982; Willems, 1974; Winett & Winkler, 1972), but have not been completely articulated and consistently applied. Perhaps, this is because a systems perspective often is just a perspective and not a set of very specific principles, such as reinforcement. Here, these system notions are emphasized: context, interdependency, and multilevel analysis. By *context,* it is meant that careful attention is given to such issues as the channels and modalities in which messages are delivered; physical, economic, and psychological constraints and barriers to behavior change, as well as cultural and situational facilitators of change. For example, the effectiveness of the same information strategy can greatly vary dependent on context. A meta-analysis of different energy conservation studies using frequent feedback on energy use, showed results as diverse as no reduction in energy use to 25% reduction in energy use. Analyses showed that consumer responsiveness to the same procedure was highly related to economic factors, i.e., the percent of their family budget that had to be allotted to home energy use (Winkler & Winett, 1982).

By *interdependency,* it is meant that there is a recognition that many behaviors are linked to one another and that change in one behavior affects other behaviors. Thus, a successful health campaign that persuades people to spend more time exercising, may have some unintended marital effects, for example, new acquaintances are made and less time may be available for the spouse. Or, thinking more positively, if some behaviors are interdependent physiologically, psychologically, or socially, change in one behavior (e.g., exercise) may facilitate change in other behaviors (e.g., smoking, dietary habits). Interdependencies, or linkages, of behaviors are critical from basic science and applied perspectives. In chapter 6, we see that how some information is perceived and processed appears to influence immune system responses and, potentially, disease and health status. The knowledge of which health behaviors are most strongly linked to other health behaviors should influence the design and promotion of health programs.

It is also recognized that interventions at one level are likely to have effects at other levels and such multilevel analyses seem critical to formulate interventions and to understand the impact of various innovations and programs. For example, only focusing on participant interactions or knowledge gains through teleconferencing may well miss the point that a larger and more important impact may be seen on transportation, restaurant, and hotel use. Likewise, only studying the effects of TV violence on children and demanding the removal of such violence from television without recommending equally attractive replacement programming ignores the major purpose of American television, that is, to deliver an audience to a sponsor (Rubenstein, 1983).

As a psychologist, most of my expertise is at the behavioral level. Some of my musings and conjectures about changes or impacts at higher levels may be seen as just that—unsophisticated ramblings. It is clear to me that such multilevel analyses are absolutely essential but their best articulation awaits more multi-disciplinary enterprises.

A new element in the mix of psychology, communication, and economic concepts and principles is an overarching "social marketing" framework (Kotler & Zaltman, 1971; Solomon, 1982). This is particularly appropriate because a behavioral systems approach emphasizes cognitive and behavior change. Social marketing calls attention to how a program should be packaged (the product), priced (monetary and social psychological costs), distributed (promotion system and place of delivery), and positioned (differentiated from their similar products), with regard to specific target audience segments. The "4P's" are seen as interactive. Social marketing is a framework for developing data and prototype programs to answer critical questions prior to implementation. Such data are gathered from considerable formative research using diverse strategies (Rice & Paisley, 1981).

Social marketing can be considered an information strategy in its own right, and indeed, is treated as such in chapter 4. Here, it is considered a necessary facet of any innovation or change effort.

Thus, a behavioral systems framework is a mix of some well-defined principles (e.g., social learning), a perspective (systems), and now couched within an overarching social marketing framework. Other aspects of this framework are noted in the following discussion of different communication models. The framework is then used in subsequent chapters, with a final explication in the last chapter. Table 1.1 is used to summarize the framework's main points. Again, the reader is forewarned that a major goal is to push this framework by demonstrating its utility to diverse issues in information and behavior.

TABLE 1.1
Behavioral Systems Framework*

Functions:	Analysis, planning, intervention, evaluation
Concepts:	Social learning as most basic
	Inputs from social psychology, communications, economics
Analysis:	Behavior in context
	Interdependencies of behaviors
	Multilevel
Focus:	Behavior change in (real) settings
Frames:	Social marketing (4P's)
	Other formative research
Method:	Experimental field study (preferred)
	Other methods to prepare for above
Applications:	Diverse content
	Basic and applied research
	Programs
	Policies
Status:	Evolving

*A framework is a structure and position as differentiated from a developed theory.

COMMUNICATION MODELS

In their short, but highly graphic and comprehensive book, McQuail and Windahl (1981) overviewed the development and evolution of models in communication. A model is "a consciously simplified description in graphic form of a piece of reality. A model seeks to show the main elements of any structure or process and the relationship between these elements" (p. 2). Thus, a model functions to: (a) organize and relate elements and systems, to provide information in a simplified way, information that would otherwise be complicated and ambiguous; the model, thus has a heuristic function because it can guide you to key points or elements; and (b) provide predictions about the course or outcomes of, in this case, information flows (these points are adapted from Deutsch, 1966). Models can also be depicted as structural and functional. A structural model seeks to only depict the organization of the components of a system. Functional models describe systems based on energy, forces, and directionality, and are concerned with the influence that one part of a model has on another. Communication models primarily are functional because communication is a dynamic process and often is focused on elements of change (McQuail & Windahl, 1981).

According to McQuail and Windahl (1981):

> in most general terms, communication implies a sender, a channel, a message, a receiver, a relationship between sender and receiver, an effect, a context in which communication occurs and a range of things to which messages refer. Sometimes, but not always, there is an intention, or purpose to 'communicate' or to 'receive'; communication can be any or all of the following: an action on others, an interaction with others and a reaction to others. . . . Sometimes the originators of models point to two additional processes, that of 'encoding' (at the sender end of the model) and that of 'decoding' (at the receiver end). Encoding means that the message is translated into a language or code suitable for the means of transmission and the intended receivers. Decoding referes to the re-translation of the message in order to extract meaning. (pp. 3–4)

McQuail and Windahl add that in many contemporary models there is the concept of feedback. That is, rather than simply a linear view of reality and the communication process, feedback means that each element of the model potentially can interact with any other element to modify the process.

The purpose here is to examine the evolution of models and offer one overall model that captures some of the main points of prior models and also to focus on behavioral outcomes.

Perhaps most models today are simply refinements or reactions to Laswell's (1948) original model. That is:

"who" "says what" "in which channel" "to whom" "with what effect"
communicator-→message ---------→medium ---------→receiver ---------→effect

Note that this is clearly a linear, persuasion model, and indeed, one impetus for this model was the need to analyze the effects of political propaganda in World War II. It can be made more contemporary by indicating the potential for feedback between steps (e.g., DeFleur, 1966); by differentiating steps such as Shannon and Weaver's (1949) early focus on the message, and by more focus on the cognitive processes involved by the receiver in perceiving, comprehending, and using (decoding processes) the message (e.g., Bettman, 1979).

COMMUNICATION EFFECTS

There is a certain irony and inconsistency involved in the history of communication models and the effectiveness of communications. The history shows periods where media were seen as very influential; other periods where media was depicted as noninfluential, and periods where both positions were held! The first developments, with the use of radio in the 1920s and 1930s, depicted the media as extremely powerful, as in Laswell's (1948) model. The audience was seen as a passive, mass aggregate set of "atomized" individuals, acting alone and with few personal and social constraints, who could potentially react predictably to any input. As McQuail and Windahl (1981) wrote, "The image was of a hyperdermic needle used to represent this approach. Media content was seen as injected in the veins of the audience that was supposed to act in foreseeable ways" (p. 41).

This was an extreme position that has to be understood within the context and needs of the time. Then, the goals were the development of a technology of message production and large-scale distribution that would influence many people; no account was made of intervening social or individual processes that could mediate exposure, reception, perception, and use of messages.

Reactions to this model were predictable. However, two points will be noted at the outset: (a) this extreme, linear S-R model has still been associated with modern behavioral and social learning theory, which is, at most, only partially justified (Thomas, 1982); (b) attempts to modify and change the focus of communication models have turned attention away from instances where aspects of the linear model are reasonable and where a clear focus on target behavior change is warranted. It also has created an interesting anamoly in the field.

Most contemporary communication efforts are at most seen as weakly influencing behavior because so many variables intercede in the process; yet, one of the greatest concerns (and largest literatures, e.g., Liebert, Sprafkin, & Davidson, 1982), is how much the media, particularly television, seems to influence children, as in frequent portrayals of violence leading to the increased likelihood of more aggressive behavior in viewers (chapter 2). How can the field support both weak and strong effects views? One answer to this anomaly is presented later when the comprehensive McGuire (1981) model used in this book is addressed.

Prior to that discussion, it is important to note some of the major modifications of the original Laswell model:

1. A greater differentiation of the message, i.e., signal (Shannon & Weaver, 1949).

2. Addition of a feedback function between elements (DeFleur, 1966).

3. More focus on the main actors, i.e., communicator, receiver (Osgood & Schramm, 1954).

4. Attempts to make the model more dynamic, i.e., to show changes in communication over time (Dance, 1967).

5. An emphasis on the perception of communications (Gerbner, 1956).

6. Placement of communication processes within social psychology studies of attitudes and behavior (e.g., Heider, 1946; Newcomb, 1953).

7. An explication of the role played by primary group (e.g., family) membership and norms and values in modifying and constraining responses to communication (Riley & Riley, 1959).

8. A greater differentiation of the message, medium, and audience characteristics (Maletzke, 1963).

9. The notion that media effects must be seen as a two-step process wherein mass media flows to "opinion leaders," who, in turn, influence less active people. Communication does not occur in a vacuum but is one input into complex relationships, with the communication competing with other sources of ideas and knowledge (Katz & Lazarfeld, 1955).

10. Much greater elaboration of the two-step model in approaches to the diffusion of innovation (chapter 3), a field largely first developed in rural sociology and separate from mainstream communication (Rogers & Shoemaker, 1971).

11. Further elaboration of the diffusion model by the development of a systems perspective and social network methodology (Rogers & Kincaid, 1981).

12. A differentiation of short-term (individual) and long-term effects of communication, e.g., how the entirety of television affects norms, values, cultural images and the stock of knowledge (DeFleur, 1966; and see below).

13. And, following this model, a view of communication and media having strong effects by setting the agenda on issues for the society (McCombs & Shaw, 1972).

14. Various models meshing psychological and communication principles to explain the effects of television (particularly violence) on behavior (aggressive behavior; Comstock, Chaffee, Katzman, McCombs, & Roberts, 1978).

15. A continued focus on issues in television's effects, but from an information processing and affective approach (Singer, 1980).

16. A renewed focus on the receiver ("audience-centered") in terms of what people do with information, i.e., for gratification and need fulfillment (Katz, Blumer, & Gurevitch, 1974).

17. Attempts to link information search models (e.g., from economics) with communication models (Donohew & Tipton, 1973).

18. Other integrations of this theme emphasizing information processing as the core of communication (e.g., Bettman, 1979).

19. And, finally, the continuation of an early theme with positions emphasizing the need to understand communication, media systems, and potential effects from the perspective of the role of the economic system in controlling what is portrayed and conveyed in the media (Comstock, 1980; DeFleur, 1966; Galbraith, 1973; Lazarsfeld & Merton, 1971).

McGuire's Model

Table 1.2 depicts McGuire's (1981) comprehensive model for communication and information technology. With some additional emphases, this model captures most of the changes and refinements that have taken place during the last 40 years. For example, in order to properly assess outcomes, it is necessary to address issues of saliency, risk, and involvement for the receiver (Engel & Blackwell, 1982). It is important to differentiate interpersonal and/or noninterpersonal message sources. Outcomes can be more focused on immediate indi-

TABLE 1.2
A Basic Communication/Information Technology Model
(From McGuire, 1981)

Dependent Variables	Independent Communication Variables				
	Source	Message	Channel	Receiver	Destination
Exposure	+	+	+	+	−
Attending	+	+	+	+	−
Liking	+	+	+	+	−
Comprehending	+	+	+	+	−
Skills	−	−	−	−	−
Yielding (attitude change)	+	+	+	+	−
Memory	+	+	+	+	−
Information search & retrieval	+	+	+	+	−
Decision	+	+	+	+	−
Initiate behavior	−	−	−	−	−
Reinforced behavior	−	−	−	−	−
Maintenance	−	−	−	−	−

+ *Much* research & consideration   − *Minimal* research and consideration

vidual changes, and societal impacts (e.g., on setting agendas) or on longer term outcomes (i.e., maintenance of behavior change; new societal norms).

There are a number of other points that the model addresses. The dependent variables denote a process of change, a causal chain, a hierarchy of effects (exposure, attention, interest, etc.) that can be investigated. However, the process need not be seen as strictly linear; Some steps may be skipped or steps may feedback to each other. For some applications where target behaviors are relatively simple, equally simple demonstrations (modeling) may suffice for behavior change. Where a flow-through process is needed, a major danger is not realistically assessing the probability of successful outcomes. For example, in a 4-step model where each step is (optimistically) assigned a probability of .50, the final probability of success is .06!

However, as discussed previously (see Fig. 1.3), it should not be assumed that change on one dependent measure predicts change on another measure with any high degree of probability (McGuire, 1981). Social psychology literature, at most, supports a weak connection between many of these variables. Variables influencing cognitive change may only partially overlap with those influencing behavior change, as controlling factors (such as situational constraints) may be quite different. This is a very critical point that is highly consistent with a behavioral systems framework. For example, knowledge of economic and nutritional food purchases may be influenced by the frequency and format of special TV spots. Enactment of new purchase behaviors may be more influenced by time constraints to optimal shopping, store design, and cultural patterns. The often observed lack of linkage between cognitive and behavior variables makes study of only one or the other inadequate.

McGuire's model tends to focus more on behavior than most other models, and is therefore very compatible with this book's framework. The independent variable, destination, is used to indicate that careful attention must be paid to the target behavior. For example, is the objective of a communication short- or long-term change, an increase or decrease in a behavior, a change in simple or complex behaviors, a preventive or treatment step? On the dependent variable side, attention is addressed to initial behavior change, reinforcement of initial change, and to some extent, maintenance of behavior change. Importantly, it is clear that there can be different processes and steps that pertain to the range of dependent variables (Prochaska & DiClemente, 1983), processes that are finally receiving much applied attention.

Partly based on the hundreds of references of this book and some other overviews, the interior of the model is filled in to indicate where there is vast research in such areas as effects of communication, consumer behavior, and information processing. Once the focus is on actual behavior, there is limited research to guide us. The reasons for this have been discussed previously in this chapter: (a) a more cognitive orientation suggests work be directed toward attention, memory, and attitudes; (b) even if a strictly linear perspective is not assumed, there still is some assumption that more cognitive variables will relate to behavior, so measurement of the cognitive variables may be seen as sufficient. Here, a third reason is introduced. As the "hypodermic needle" models were found inadequate, they were replaced by models with many intervening processes between communicator and receiver. The general result of these approaches was that processes were expected to be complex and the outcomes were expected to be weak. We must not expect much from any communication efforts, therefore we must measure information and attitudes. Elsewhere, the author (Ester & Winett, 1982) has noted that this belief may illustrate a marvelous self-fulfilling prophecy: do not expect much, so do not try that hard to develop good communication programs. And, not surprisingly, the poor results obtained support and reinforce this position, fulfilling the prophecy.

EFFECTIVENESS OF COMMUNICATIONS

In this section, more contemporary thought on the power of communications and specific types of information formats is presented. To highlight the main points here, it is argued that specific types of communications can be reasonably effective (i.e., information, attitude, and behavior change) when careful attention is given to receiver characteristics, message content and quality, delivery channel, type of change needed and constraints to change, and extent of exposure to information. For the most part, change is within the accepted mores and norms of society. This has been called *first-order change*. *Second-order change* entails change of systems or "the rules of the game" (Rappaport, 1977). Thus, communication and information technologies are most successful in promoting individual changes that are socially acceptable, or no more then at the edge of social acceptability.

This conclusion can be seen as reasonable and optimistic. For example, if the case can be made that the media can be effectively used to promote preventive health practices, then this can be seen as good. It is a reformist perspective congruent, in part, with this book's neoliberal approach. It is also an approach that is now politically favorable as social engineering and regulatory approaches have, in the past decade, become less preferred, and much maligned. However, some sections in this book address the issues of counter-norm messages and more equal access to the media, issues that return the focus to social engineering and regulation. These are contemporary concerns that mirror those in Lazarsfeld and Merton's (1971) classic article: "the very conditions which make for the maximum effectiveness of the mass media of communications operate toward the maintenance of the ongoing social and cultural structure rather than toward its change" (p. 578).

Here we return to a central question: Why does the idea continue that media and information sources cannot change behavior? And what elements are needed for effective communications? Perhaps the contemporary trend, the belief in communications' efficacy, can be traced to Mendelsohn's (1973) often quoted article. Mendelsohn did not endorse the simplistic hypodermic needle model, but noted that when this approach failed, the patients (viewers) were blamed. That is, the patients were disinterested and apathetic. This diverted attention away from examining the actual communication approach. Mendelsohn made the case that communication campaigns generally were not based on social science research, did not involve research in the process of change, and therefore, both the substance of the campaigns and their evaluations were often of poor quality. Campaigns, Mendelsohn noted, can succeed if middle range, and reasonable goals are picked (because the public is faced with many sources of information and has many other concerns), and if a social marketing approach is adopted. At its core, a social marketing approach emphasizes audience segmentation based on understanding that audience's demographics, styles, beliefs, information sources, and viewing habits, and designing a program, based on this knowledge, for the specific audience (see chapter 4). That is, specific communications are developed for specific audiences. Mendelsohn (1973) concluded that, "very little of our mass communications research has really tested the effectiveness of the application of empirically grounded mass communications principles simply because most communications practitioners do not consciously utilize these principles" (p. 51).

Many of the points noted by Mendelsohn in this chapter have been discussed at length by McLeod and Reeves (1981). To answer questions about the effects of media, they indicated that five general points need to be addressed:

1. The number of types of potential effects
2. The complexity of the media stimuli
3. The specific problems in documenting effects
4. The varying strategies of making inferences from evidence
5. The peculiar history and current structure of the communication research field

Some of these points are elaborated here. With regard to types of effects, they noted that it is rare to be able to demonstrate a one-to-one correspondence between media content and behavior change (although, this is shown later in chapter 2). It is also rare that every receiver will be affected in the same way by the same communication. Undoubtedly, mediating and intervening variables and conditional factors influence the impact of communications. These variables can include viewer characteristics, viewer cognitive sets, or for example, parental behaviors that may moderate the effects of their child's TV viewing (Singer &

Singer, 1983). McLeod and Reeves advocated a research and development approach that focused more on the specific content of particular campaigns, programs, and other information sources and the receiver's reactions to that specific content. They also called for a clearer delineation of intervening and mediating variables and conditional factors, with more attention paid to immediate and long-term behavior change, and of indirect effects. A good example of indirect effects involves TV. This medium has not only influenced specific beliefs and practices related to content, but, viewing has greatly changed how people use their time compared to an era when TV did not exist (Robinson, 1977).

McLeod and Reeves also noted the different ways people have interpreted the same data. Seemingly, some researchers have gone out of their way to show no effects. Field studies on persuasion often used media and measures (attitudes) that were extremely gross. For example, general health orientation and values may not be influenced by health TV programs, but very specific beliefs and behaviors may be affected (see chapter 2). Where there was limited evidence of effect, it was interpreted as no effect, or such evidence was seen as the media only being capable of supporting prevailing values, attitudes, and behaviors (i.e., the self-fulfilling prophecy).

An excellent example of these points is shown in chapter 2 on prosocial TV. There, the evaluations of the Public Broadcasting System's (PBS) health series "Feeling Good" is interpreted quite positively. In the past, the series was often described as another media failure! McLeod and Reeves (1981) reached a conclusion quite similar to this author's conclusion when he reviewed early (1940s, 1950s) communication studies and papers and their subsequent contemporary interpretation:

> It is interesting that much of the evidence cited was obtained before the advent of television . . . and that secondary citation of the original evidence has tended to move toward more limited inconsequential or no effects at all. (p. 262)

> Polemical writing about the effects of mass media was frequent in the post World War I era when massive propaganda impact was attributed to the persuasive content of the media. The mass model of society prevailed in these writings and the dominant influence mechanism was thought to be simple learning through repetitive messages . . . . It was in reaction to this view that the so-called "limited effects" model of media influence developed largely through the voting and functional media use studies at Columbia University in the 1940's . . . . This view became the dominant one in reviews of the field in various social science texts despite the lack of methodological sophistication in its original evidence and a dearth of fresh evidence from the post television era. (p. 263)

If it is even slightly believed that "the medium is the message," then it does not make much sense to entirely transpose the evidence from one set of communication channels and one era to another. For example, print and audio media

(1940s) appear to be not as effective as video media for some purposes, most specifically, for behavior change. Some of the author's research on changing home energy conservation practices provides very clear support for this conclusion (Winett & Kagel, 1984).

McLeod and Reeves believe that the results of the limited effects model has been to discourage communication research. Whereas no single model at this time has emerged as dominant, it is apparent that much greater attention will be given to models that include the specification of conditions under which media exposure will produce effects on certain audience members.

A final problem addressed by McLeod and Reeves also related to the peculiar history of communication. The field has been very applied and problem-centered and not discipline-centered. Whereas the application approach has often been admirable and had some benefits (e.g., the great interest in health communications), it has also had its costs. Only recently has communication become a separate discipline, not just a subfield of psychology, sociology, or political science, and started to develop its own conceptual positions from which applied communication can be derived. Still, there is no broad agreement on concepts or methodologies. One problem is that its concepts and methodologies are at various levels (e.g., individual, mass individual, institutional) of phenomena. Whereas multilevel analyses is important in the behavioral systems framework, it is readily admitted that the task of integrating knowledge, data, and methods from different disciplines is a very difficult one. Multilevel analysis, if done correctly, probably requires a multidisciplinary team.

In addition to the problem of multilevel analysis, two different (although not necessarily antagonistic) research traditions prevail. A "media-centric" approach is concerned with the structure and content of media and often involves monitoring media content, for example, some of the independent variables. The "effects-centric" position shows more concern for the dependent variables. The dependent variables are likely to be studied carefully with less care taken with the specification of stimuli and the social context. Obviously, both positions need to be integrated, which is the position of this book, and clearly a direction of the field (e.g., Wright & Huston, 1983).

The conclusions of this section bring us back to McGuire's model in Table 1.2. Note that this model in many ways is a synthesis of the media-centric (independent variables) and effects-centric (dependent variables) positions. Effective communication and information technologies must pay extreme attention to the stimulus, its framing, presentation format, amount of content, and channels of delivery. This position has been stated concisely before by Gross (1971):

> An effective, persuasive communication is one which is thought to emanate from
> an expert and trustworthy source which is able to capture and hold the receiver's
> attention while it conveys an easily comprehensible message and which offers the
> receiver clear and realistic channels of action in which to express his (sic) agree-

ment. Not one of these aspects can be overlooked except of the peril of the entire enterprise. (p. 621)

The conceptual basis for effective message content and presentation format appears to be a combination of social learning and communication principles. And, aside from content and format, the dose and duration of the communication must be considered (Lau, Kane, Berry, Ware, & Roy, 1980), that is, how much and how long. When these variables are minimal, as they are likely to be in many prosocial campaigns, then the focus on media content and context must be even sharper.

However, that is still not enough! Extreme attention must be directed to the receiver. The perspective and tools of social marketing must be used to develop specific messages, information sources, programs, and campaigns for specific audiences. Extreme attention must be directed to the processes of change from exposure to decoding, to comprehension, to information and attitude change, choice decision, and to the many steps involved in initial and long-term behavior change.

An overall behavioral systems framework also alerts us to understand and incorporate into our interventions and evaluations factors at the same level of the target behaviors that may facilitate or constrain behavior change. Change in these factors must be examined as well, and where possible, systems higher or lower than the target behavior should be incorporated into these processes (Winkler & Winett, 1982). For example, an effective approach to weight control must address issues in basal metabolism, caloric intake and expenditure, specific diet plans, complimentary activities (exercise), as well as other individual factors, family and other sources of support, and community structures and resources that may help or impede the process.

CONCLUSIONS

At the beginning of this section, an anamoly was presented. The behavioral sciences have been legitimately decrying the content and format (e.g., fast pacing) of TV programs and commercials and the effects of this content and format on attitudes and behavior. The assumption is that the effects are real and relatively powerful (Rubinstein, 1983; see Freedman, 1984). At the same time, the position of weak-effects for media presentations and communication campaigns has been held. It seems difficult to have it both ways. The anamoly was solved when it was realized that campaigns and information presentations often are not optimally devised, not well focused with respect to audience segment and target behaviors, and of low dose and duration. Many TV programs and commercials, for everything wrong with them, do illustrate the power of visual media when emphasis is placed on content, simple and vivid delivery, audience segmentation, and enormous dosage and duration. When more positively directed campaigns and programs mirror the technical (but, not content) aspects of commercial television and related media, then even attempts with fairly minimal dosage and duration may further dispel the weak effects model by demonstrating reasonable behavioral impact (Winett, Leckliter, Chinn, & Stahl, 1984). Whereas some readers may feel that many of these points are obvious and common sense, there are some good illustrations in the literature of the failure that awaits the media innovator who does not seriously consider points made in this chapter. The

TABLE 1.3
Elements and Variables Related to Ineffective and Effective
Information Campaigns

	Ineffective	*Effective*
Message (format & content)	Poor quality decreases attention	High quality to enhance attention (e.g., comparable to commercial ad)
	Overemphasize quantity vs. quality	High quality may overcome some problems in limited exposure
	Vague or overly long messages; drab, e.g., "talking head."	Highly specific messages; vivid, e.g., behavioral modeling
Channel	Limited exposure (e.g., late night PSA's)	Targeted exposure
	Inappropriate media (e.g., detailed print for behavior change)	Appropriate media (e.g., TV for behavior change)
Source	Not well attended to	Trustworthy, expert or competent; may be also dynamic and attractive
Receiver	Little formative research to understand audience characteristics	Much formative research to target message to audience
Destination	Difficult or complex behaviors resistant to change	Simple behaviors, or behaviors in a sequence, changeable and where long-term change can be supported by the environment
Conceptualization	Inappropriate causal chain (e.g., early events as predictors of later ones)	More appropriate causal chain and emphasize behavior change
	Little analysis of competing information and environmental constraints	Analysis of competing information and environmental constraints used to design messages
Goals	Unrealistic, i.e., expect too much change	Realistic, specific, limited

classic example is the well-known project by Robertson et al. (1974) that tried to increase a simple behavior, that of seat belt use.

Robertson et al. followed a very rigorous experimental design in their influential field study that revolved around an intensive and long series of TV spots (high dose and duration). However, several critical mistakes seemed to be made as far as message development. The messages were actually never pilot-tested for effects on behavior. Instead a panel of ad experts rated them as excellent. The messages themselves were based on a negative (loss), fear arousal model shown in the spots as in disfigurement from accidents where people did not wear seat belts. In light of recent findings of studies using fear arousal in health promotion efforts (Leventhal, Safer, & Panagis, 1983), their failure to find any increase in seat belt use was not surprising. Their general conclusion concerning the ineffectiveness of TV for behavior change needs to be modified to "some types of messages are ineffective."

In contrast to Robertson et al., the "Feeling-Good" TV series, broadcasted on PBS in the mid-1970s, followed a careful sequence of planning, targeting, pilot-testing, refinement, redevelopment, and distribution of messages and programs. The programs tended to be upbeat (positive) and to discuss, and at times to model appropriate information and behavior (gain). Evaluations of this program showed some evidence for change in simple health behaviors (e.g., seeking more information, checking blood pressure; Mielke & Swinehart, 1976a). These results generally supported the overall perspective and framework of this book and are discussed in detail in chapter 2.

Table 1.3, which is based on the prior sections, and one of Atkins' (1981) reviews, delineates elements and variables identified with ineffective and effective information campaigns. Most of these findings appear consistent with a behavioral systems framework.

PLAN OF THE BOOK

The basic plan of this book is to apply the behavioral systems framework coupled with McGuire's model and a knowledge base derived from Atkins and others to a number of different concerns in communication, information technology, and behavior change. In some instances, such as the effects of television, there is a wealth of studies and reviews. No attempt is made in those areas to do a comprehensive review. Rather, the topic is selectively approached from a particular perspective that represents aspects of the book's framework. For example, the chapter on television generally focuses on the positive use of television, and strategies to reduce the impact of network television. The chapter on information and consumer behavior addresses economic, legal, and psychological aspects of information remedies, and uses the behavioral system's framework to propose a design for effective information remedies. The chapter on diffusion does not review the thousands of studies on this topic, but rather critically evaluates the conceptual and methodological underpinnings of the research and applications. The chapter on health develops a systems and public health approach to health behavior and then shows the preventive potential of new information flows in various aspects of the health care and consumer systems. The chapter on new media is concerned with trying to understand the design, application, evaluation and impacts of new media from a behavior systems framework coupled with a task × audience × cost framework.

In some areas, such as the effects of new media, data are scarce, whereas conjecture and hyperbole abound. An attempt in those areas is made to critically examine new systems from the consistent framework of the book, provide plans for experimental evaluation, as well as address the issue of access to new media. However, parts of those chapters are admittedly speculative. In other areas such as health and consumer behavior, a firmer base is available for some very specific policy recommendations.

Some of these policy recommendations are very explicit, for example, "here are the elements of effective information remedies in the market place." Some of these points are more conceptual, for example, "a behavioral systems framework is useful for planning new information technologies and predicting multi-level effects." The goal is to make the concepts and principles in this book serviceable to public policy questions. At the same time, by demonstrating the applicability of this framework, there is the demand that, wherever possible, public policy design and evaluation follow science.

Finally, it should be possible to read the chapters in any order. This is because the framework remains the same throughout and the chapters are not so much cumulative, but rather more cross-referenced.

2

Prosocial Television: Effective Elements, Barriers to Broadcasting

A considerable and long-standing body of research has focused on the issue of the effects of violent television content on aggressive and other antisocial behavior of children (Liebert, Sprafkin, & Davidson, 1982). This focus is well warranted as television programs remain laden with violent content, and the effects on viewers also remain debated in scientific, commercial, and political arenas (e.g., contrast Milavsky, Kessler, Stipp, & Rubens, 1982, with Rubinstein, 1983). At the same time, the overriding attention to this issue has probably constrained study and implementation of television for prosocial purposes (Pearl, Bouthilet, & Lazar, 1982; Rushton, 1982). If concerns about the powerful negative effects of television are justified, it is because the medium has the capability of shaping beliefs, attitudes, and behaviors. Clearly, the medium is not just capable of shaping negative values and behaviors, but rather many diverse values and behaviors can be developed and maintained. It does not make sense to insist that television as a medium is a powerful negative force, and then also to conclude that its ability to influence prosocial behavior is limited!

This chapter examines the potential of prosocial television, commercial and noncommercial programs that simply depict or try to promote socially valued behaviors, by reviewing a number of noteworthy projects that developed positive programming. These projects are also closely studied from the perspective of the behavioral systems framework, McGuire's (1981) model, and the delineation of effective and ineffective elements in media approaches shown in Table 1.3 of the introductory chapter. At the same time, demonstrations of effective programming still leave unanswered the questions of changing current television fare and wider program distribution. The concluding sections of this chapter address those issues. However, prior to the review of positive television efforts, it is necessary to address the issue of the negative depiction of the medium itself by some behavioral scientists.

TELEVISION'S NEGATIVE DEPICTION AS A MEDIUM

Rather than depicting television as simply a different medium for conveying information and images than, for example, print in books, some behavioral scientists have apparently approached the study of this medium from a negative perspective. Singer and Singer (1983) are some of the better known critics of television as a medium. They at times have confused content and medium variables, a point that is extremely important in this chapter's analysis.

The Singers have adopted a relatively standard information processing model for their work that portrays people as active responders to environmental stimuli. They basically conclude that television: (a) undermines information processing because the rapid movement of television programming constantly diverts attention (i.e., an orienting reflex); (b) reduces short, and hence also, long-term memory, because of the rapid movement and use of too many stimuli (visual-images, print, and audio-voice and other sounds); and (c) reduces memory and comprehension because the pace of programs may preclude encoding strategies. The result is that contemporary television productions are seen as relatively incapable of transmitting complex messages and information, or information that will be long remembered and actively retrieved for some purpose.

The quick pacing of television was also criticized for leading to arousal and aggressive behavior in children. Television that is simple and passive was seen as replacing reading that they indicated required more planning, sustained attention, and therefore more comprehension, encoding, memory, and use of the content. Thus, television's fast-paced visual presentation holds moment-to-moment attention and is pleasurable, but at the expense of active involvement, reflection or critical evaluation, processing, and long-term memory.

At the extreme, the Singers' position can be construed as depicting television as the "boob-tube" or the "idiot-box" (Sprafkin, Swift, & Hess, 1982). The prior labels may be appropriate for much current television content, but not for the medium itself.

A POSITIVE DEPICTION OF TELEVISION: FORMAL FEATURES

Wright and Huston (1983) have taken a much more positive, and, indeed, refreshing approach to television. They have noted that television has demonstrated a great, but generally untapped ability to educate, socialize, and teach basic and symbolic communication skills in a very cost-effective way. Their approach that separates content and context is derived from McLuhan who alerts us to focus on how a medium's codes and formats influence thinking and communication.

Wright and Huston have studied the formal features of television that in some respects can be independent of content. These include visual features such as cuts, pans, dissolves, and special effects, and auditory features including music, sound effects, dialogue, and laugh tracks, and motor characteristics such as pacing, physical movement, and variation. The formal features of television, i.e., its syntax and grammar, can be used to present many types of messages, themes, or stories.

Wright and Huston's position is that it is exactly these formal features that can be used to enhance attention, comprehension, encoding, and memory—a position quite different from the Singers.

Wright and Huston indicated that many formal features are perceptually salient. They have qualities of intensity, contrast, change, novelty, incongruity, and surprise. These qualities often are used in entertainment programs. Reflection features such as long zoom lens scenes, singing, and moderate action, typical of some educational programs, may be well-suited for rehearsal, repetition, or elaboration on the content themes of such programs. They have done analyses of the formal features of children's programs from cartoons to "Sesame Street," and they are also critical of producers of children's programs, notably cartoons, that intensively use certain formal features including loud noises, rapid activity, many visual changes, and an emphasis on slapstick violence. However, their analyses have indicated that "Sesame Street" has not just mimiced these commercial programs, as some critics including the Singers have concluded. Rather, whereas some educational programs use many visual techniques, they tend not to be as rapidly paced or noisy as commercial programs, and do use more child-oriented language. The moderate pacing, and appropriate noise and language can promote reflection and rehearsal, and are not harmful.

Table 2.1 lists a number of common formal features and their purpose.

By separating content and form, Wright and Huston lead us to an extremely significant conclusion. For viewers (children and adults), the form (rapid race, movement, auditory and visual special effects) can hold attention. Violent or

TABLE 2.1
Common Formal Features and Their Purpose

Formal feature	*Purpose*
Instant replay; flashback skip forward	Organization between units; shifts in time
Dissolve	Change in place
Fade out	Mark subjective experience
Laugh track; serious music	Indicate type of experience
Rapid pace; special effects	Hold viewer attention

erotic content is not necessary for attention. Networks heads and television producers and writers claiming that changing current violent or excessively sexual content will result in reduced ratings, such as fewer viewers to see commercials, and hence, the demise of the networks, may be repeating an unsubstantiated refrain.

This statement is somewhat tempered by Johnston and Ettema (1986) who pointed out that formal features and content are not entirely independent. That is, certain formal features simply make more sense when used with certain content. However, this still does not mean that violent content is necessary to hold an audience.

But what of another claim? Is television viewing still harmful because it is essentially a very passive activity? Wright and Huston's research indicates that this claim is not true. As children get older, they learn more about television's formal features and how to use them. Formal features can be used as a guide to coordinate attention with program segments and highlight main points, and aid in encoding. Children are, therefore, seen as quite active information processors when they watch television, and "There is little evidence to support the view that children's attention is passively grabbed and held by audiovisual qualities of television programming" (Wright & Huston, 1983, p. 839). Television need not be a lazy, passive activity. Television viewing can demand attention for inferring motives and imagining scenes not shown in the program. These are some important cognitive activities that the Singers suggested were mostly the purview of reading! Considerably more research has been called for on how best to use certain formal features to increase attention and comprehension, processes that may be different, and call for different formal features and program formats for different aged viewers (Collins, 1982; Johnston & Ettema, 1986).

A final point concerns the arousal capacity of certain formal features, such as rapid pacing, to stimulate high levels of activity and aggression. Wright and Huston indicated that data are not conclusive on this score, and it may be true that a very high rate of certain formal features, in concert with conditional factors such as family modeling and reinforcement of aggressive behavior, may facilitate viewer aggressive behaviors. However, to fully address this issue requires studies that separate form and content.

Programs produced by the Children's Television Workshop ("Sesame Street," "Feeling Good," "3-2-1 Contact") have demonstrated the potential of TV programming for children's social, intellectual, and emotional development, but this potential has been barely tapped. The prior discussion was meant to dispel negative conceptions that some behavioral scientists have toward the medium itself, and at the same time, to identify formal features to be used in prosocial efforts. However, if the potential of prosocial programming for diverse audiences is to be realized, useful formal features must be combined with an approach to effective media that integrates the points made in Table 1.3 on effective media in the introductory chapter and a behavioral systems framework.

We begin the review of prosocial television efforts with the dilemma of the appropriate goals for these programs.

APPROPRIATE TARGETS AND GOALS

A major dilemma and conceptual and strategic decision is to pick appropriate targets and goals for prosocial TV programs. In particular, the problem is whether to attempt some broad change in beliefs and attitudes or a much narrower change in specific behavior. For example, in promoting more frugal use of natural resources, should the program designer develop images and messages that have the common theme of "living in harmony with finite resources" or rather aim to have viewers change one or two simple, but key, energy consumption practices in their home? The first approach is intuitively appealing on two fronts. First, it sounds like a noble cause and will probably attract attention. Second, the assumption is that the program will promote changes in some value and belief positions, and possibly attitudes, and, hence, have a broad and enduring effect on diverse behaviors.

In contrast, the second approach is clearly not grandiose. It offers no attempt to change broad values and beliefs and seems less likely to attract positive attention. It may be difficult to generate much enthusiam about the importance of thermostat changes in contrast to "taking a holistic view of resource use."

However, the convergence of perspectives and data in this book best supports the development of programs with narrow, but reachable behavior change goals. For example, McGuire's (1981) basic communication model does not necessarily conclude that there are close linkages between one set of early events (e.g., beliefs) and later events (e.g., long-term behavior change). A behavioral systems framework suggests that these are different processes that are often influenced by different factors. And, finally, elements of effective media (Table 1.3, p. 23) include very specific messages based on analyses of environmental barriers and with realistic, and often limited goals.

It is hoped that the dilemma is not so much as to decide where the evidence points, but rather to convince funding agencies and the public to support those (media) efforts with appropriate approaches and goals. This may be more difficult than it seems. Highly specific programs may not be very flashy and such programs may be more capable of offending certain publics because the message is very explicit (e.g., "Dial this number for abortion counseling" vs. "Isn't it about time you thought about family planning?") On the first point, prosocial program designers must learn how to make their programs entertaining and effective, for example, with appropriate formal features. And, perhaps, funding sources, legislatures, and the public can be educated to the programmatic (effectiveness), and democratic (diversity of information) benefits of specific messages.

PRESENTATION FORMAT

It has already been argued that prosocial efforts must effectively use formal features to enhance attention, comprehension, and memory. In addition, Lovelace and Huston (1982) have stressed that considerable research is needed to find optimal presentation formats for prosocial content. Such optimal formats may be even more critical if a program is to compete with commercial alternatives. In this case, the program must be entertaining to hold the audience; if it does not hold the audience, the program will not last on commercial television.

A program designed for PBS may have less concern with competing programs as PBS simply does not have a large audience. In this case, the program still needs to be enjoyable, but probably can focus more on the message. Programs may also be used in situations where there is a captive audience such as classrooms. Here the program may most explicitly focus on the message and key behaviors and also be supplemented by interpersonal activities (e.g., Evans et al., 1981). Thus, as a first step, prosocial programs must be clear on the delivery mode.

Table 2.2 describes three different presentation options, and their advantages and disadvantages, for prosocial programming derived from Lovelace and Huston (1982) that is based primarily on research with children.

Lovelace and Huston also addressed the critical problem of generalization and maintenance of behavior change. That is, specifically targeted behavior change strategies are, not surprisingly, most effective in changing specific behaviors in specific circumstances (Wilson & O'Leary, 1980). As different behaviors are needed in different settings across time, highly specific training will be less efficacious. For example, a television program can effectively teach a child of 11 to refuse cigarettes from teenagers at junior high school. However, the same response will probably not be effective when the child is a teenager and attending a party. If the television program is a singular intervention, then generalization and maintenance may be enhanced by showing multiple models in an appropriate range of situations showing diverse and appropriate responses. This approach will likely be effective with children and adults. In addition, using a person who is similar to the target audience but somewhat more competent, and showing the model being reinforced for the appropriate social behavior will respectively facilitate viewer identification with the model and actual performance (Wilson & O'Leary, 1980). Finally, a dramatic story, and where possible, post-viewing role play, may further enhance attention, memory, and behavior change.

Based on Table 2.2 and these additional comments, it is possible to describe the preferred format of a prosocial TV program with no interpersonal component:

1. Have one model or several models similar to the target audience, but a bit more competent, display prosocial behaviors.
2. Show multiple models in diverse settings display variations of the desired behavior.

TABLE 2.2
Presentation Formats for Prosocial Programs: Advantages and
Disadvantages*

Presentation Format	Advantages	Disadvantages
1. One model or several models only display prosocial behavior and no portrayals of antisocial or conflicting behaviors.	—Very clear —Most support from social learning theory —Can be very effective in classroom and therapy and easily supplement with interpersonal activities	—Not very dramatic —Few commercial programs in this format —May not hold attention —Most of research on captive audience and assessment in artificial settings —May have generalization problem when viewer encounters negative situations
2. One or more models exhibit prosocial behaviors while the same people or others display antisocial or inappropriate behaviors which *receive negative consequences.*	—Provides drama —Most similar to usual TV fare —"Sesame Street" and "Mr. Rogers" appear to successfully use	—Antisocial and inappropriate behaviors may be modeled —May need interpersonal supplement to sort out positive and negative behaviors
3. One or more models exhibit prosocial behaviors while the same people or others display antisocial or inappropriate behaviors, *but no final resolution presented.*	—Provides drama —May provoke post-viewing problem solving to solve conflict —May be effective when coupled with post-viewing interpersonal activities	—Antisocial and inappropriate behaviors may be modeled —Viewer may not generate post-viewing problem solving

*Based on Lovelace and Huston, 1982.

3. Show the models being reinforced for performing appropriate behaviors.
4. Accurately depict constraints and obstacles to performing prosocial behaviors.
5. Provide an interesting or dramatic story to maintain attention and increase comprehension and memory.

PROSOCIAL PROGRAMMING: BRIEF EXAMPLES

The purpose of this extended section is to review a number of well-known prosocial television efforts and to ferrett out their effective and ineffective elements. How well do effective programs fit within a behavioral systems perspective, and prior analyses of key media variables, formal features, and presentation formats? This section briefly reviews several of these efforts, and spends considerably more time on two of them, the "Feeling Good" series, and recent projects by the author. Two restrictions that were also used for this review were: (a) the TV program or spots could not be secondary to an interpersonal element, and (b) that the program could not simply be viewed by a few people in a special setting. Thus, some well-known health promotion efforts (see Chapters 4 and 6) that integrate media and interpersonal interventions are not included, although the Stanford preventive programs are reviewed in Chapter 4 and Chapter 6. Likewise, a number of excellent studies in the social learning tradition are also not included because the experimental program was viewed under circumstances that do not allow generality to a broadcast delivery mode. A final restriction is that one or a major goal of the program is behavior change, and not primarily information gain and education.

Freestyle. This was an ambitious program series developed by PBS in the late 1970s. "Freestyle" was funded by the National Institute of Education, and was developed in response to research indicating that boys and girls had rigid stereotypes of appropriate behavior (Johnston, 1982). Clearly, this was an important topic in the 1970s and the use of the programs was facilitated by Title IX regulations that required school districts to show efforts to remediate past sex discrimination. The goal of Freestyle, designed for children ages 9 to 12, was to alter the children's stereotypes and enhance the possibility of girls pursuing more traditionally masculine interests and, later, occupations.

The series, which included 13, one-half hour dramas, and took $3.7 million and 2.5 years to produce, could be used for home and school use, and data are available on comparative effectiveness. The program made its PBS debut in the fall of 1978, and at the same time, the programs, teachers' guides, and other print material were available.

The basic scenario and format of the programs entailed teenage actors choosing nonstereotypical activities and being rewarded for their choice. Thus, preoccupational activities (mechanics for girls), behavioral skills (assertiveness for girls) and nonsex-typed work and family roles were depicted. However, the characters usually had to overcome adversity to succeed and the programs were done in a dramatic fashion.

An ambitious, but misdirected, effort was made to evaluate the program. The evaluation included 7,000 children in seven cities who saw the programs under three conditions: classroom viewing with discussion, classroom viewing alone, and home viewing (with presumbably no discussion). From this book's perspective, an assessment of stereotyped and nonstereotyped behaviors prior to, during, and after the program sequence would have been the most straightforward evaluation consistent with the program goals. Long-term follow-up could focus on job choice, college major, and family status. Obviously, expecting the latter type of follow-up outcomes would be overly optimistic. Yet, if that was a stated, but unrealistic, goal of the program, some assessment of this outcome was needed, *or* a program should be developed for high school juniors and seniors not aged 9 to 12 years old.

Unfortunately, the evaluation primarily focused on attitudes toward those engaging in activities and occupations that are stereotyped as inappropriate (for example, policewoman), beliefs regarding the competence of boys and girls and men and women in nontraditional pursuits, and a viewer's interests in pursuing nonstereotypical activities. A pretest–posttest (4 months apart) design was used with adequate attention given to the representativeness of the sample children's background. A 9-month follow-up was done in one of the cities. The evaluation was also laudatory for not simply presenting significant findings, but for indicating the educational importance of a statistically significant change (see Johnston, 1982).

Generally, the detailed evaluation showed some expected changes on attitude and belief measures in the direction of the programs' content that tended to diminish over time. Not surprisingly, the more intensive format, classroom and discussion, provided better outcomes than classroom viewing alone. Assessment of the impact of home viewing was badly contaminated by the fact that only about a third of the experimental children watched *each* show, and only about a quarter viewed seven or more programs. The heaviest home viewers showed some modest changes, although less than the classroom viewing only condition. However, the program was not explicitly designed for home viewing and improved production qualities were noted as needed for attentive and repeated homeviewing.

"Freestyle" can be described as a good idea with poor execution. Some of the content and format such as behavioral modeling in a drama, seem consistent with the points for effective TV programming made earlier. The goals, however, appear too vague and poorly timed (e.g., occupational choices). An evaluation with, perhaps, only 100 children, not 7,000, where home viewing was better orchestrated, and with a focus on actual behaviors, could have told us much more about the impact of "Freestyle."

Television Spots and Seal-Belt Use. The study by Robertson, Kelley, O'Neill, Wixom, Eiswirth, and Haddon (1974) using television spots to increase the use of seat belts is extremely pivotal in any discussion of the potential of television for prosocial, behavior change. This is because: (a) The study was an excellently controlled field experiment; (b) The television spots received wide exposure, including during prime time, thus eliminating a common problem of other prosocial programs; (c) The target behavior was simple and easy to perform, and (d) The inability of the effort to show any evidence for increased seat belt use has been widely reported (seat-belt use remained only 9%) and generalized to mean that television is ineffective for behavior change. Indeed, the succinct summary of the article that appeared in the widely distributed *American*

Journal of Public Health said that "television campaigns do not have any effect on use of safety belts, thus supporting the argument that approaches directed toward changing behavior are inefficient and often ineffective. . . ." (Robertson et al., 1974, p. 1071). Thus, it is important to critically examine this study.

In this field experiment, messages were only shown on one cable of a dual cable system that had been purposely designed for marketing studies. Actual seat-belt use was observed unobtrusively in standard community settings 1 month prior to the study and for the 9 consecutive months of the spots. Recording license plates allowed matching of driver and vehicle to the appropriate cable outlet. Thus, the design and data system were excellent.

However, a critical problem appears to revolve around the message's theme and content. Through survey research, it was decided to emphasize in the message that use of safety belts will decrease the probability of disfigurement and disability. Other factors or themes such as adapting to seat belts and risk taking behavior were not pursued. The use of physician endorsements and a theme of family responsibility were also used. But, the major approach was based on fear tactics. Behavioral modeling and discussion was not used to demonstrate the ease and protection of seat belt use, for example, it's convenient, you get used to the belt; you will not be trapped in the car; but it is more dangerous to be thrown from a car. Thus, fear was seen as an antecedent and mediator of behavior change. As with other approaches that primarily focus on supposed antecedents (e.g., information gain) of behavior change in a hierarchy of effects model, and deemphasize direct behavioral change, this approach was also ineffective.

The following is one such spot as reported by Robertson et al. (1974):

A woman whose face cannot be seen is shown in front of a mirror applying makeup. A full face picture on her dressing table shows her as a beautiful woman. Her husband enters the scene and suggests that they go to a party. She asks him not to look at her without makeup as she turns to reveal a scarred face. An off-camera announcer describes a crash in which the wife was driving slowly and carefully. The announcer continues, as the picture on the table is showing, "Terry would still look like this if she had been wearing safety belts." Announcer: "Its much easier to wear safety belts than to hear your husband say . . ." Husband: "Honey, I love you anyway." (p. 1073)

The spots were written and produced in collaboration with an advertising agency and six spots were developed. They were strategically placed on or adjacent to an appropriate program. For example, the spot described previously was used with soap operas.

Despite the strategical and methodological care of the investigators, one crucial mistake was made. The only apparent pretesting and evaluation consisted of ratings by panels of "advertising experts." The fact that these spots were rated as excellent in no way means that they will actually be effective in yielding behavior change. The acid test is piloting with a representative sample and monitoring behavior change. This was not done.

Robertson et al. advocated more structural approaches to driver and highway safety, for example, passive restraint systems, and this type of approach (vs. changing behavior) is discussed in the health chapter. However, it must be restated that Robertson et al.'s conclusions about the ineffectiveness of television must be questioned. Clearly, not any type of message and format will promote behavior change, and recent evidence suggests that fear tactics are generally ineffective (Leventhal, Safer, & Panagis, 1983). A more warranted conclusion is that some types of messages are ineffective. Further, where there is little public interest or support for particular behavior changes, as was the case for seat-belt use when this study was done over 15 years ago, it is unlikely that any behavioral strategy will be effective. Not surprisingly, behavioral technology needs a supportive context (e.g., public interest, legal/regulatory levers, economic contingencies) to be effective (Winkler & Winett, 1982).

Over Easy. This program was developed in 1977 and was originally funded by the Department of Health, Education, and Welfare's Administration on Aging and the Corporation for Public Broadcasting. The program was aimed at a target audience of persons 55 years and older and had cognitive, affective, and behavioral objectives. The basic philosophy of the program involved seriously questioning the cultural preoccupation with being, looking, and acting young. The program developers also were convinced that the cultural stereotypes of aging and the preoccupation with youth were the causes of many problems faced by the elderly.

The specific goals of the program entailed reversing the negative images of aging (affective); informing viewers of specific services and self-help activities (cognitive); and having viewers initiate a number of these self-help behaviors. The program's format mixed information and entertainment. An older person hosted the program, serving as a positive role model, and providing information and entertainment through interviews with celebrities and experts. Self-help behaviors in a wide range of areas—medical, nutritional, legal, interpersonal, financial—were discussed and evaluated in the programs. In addition, the program tried to increase viewers use of existing private and public community and social services by emphasizing that viewers were entitled to use them.

This last behavioral objective is well worth describing in detail. At the end of many "Over Easy" programs, local information would be listed. Rather than simply advise viewers to contact local agencies, in some markets agency or community information and referral numbers were listed. Thus, the program attempted to embed itself in existing networks of related social programs and services, and the behavior requested of the viewer was simple and specific— such as "call this number." From the perspective of this book, this was an excellent approach. The behaviors requested could easily be done and in this way the program could serve as a connector between viewers and services.

Having received federal funding, congress mandated that ''Over Easy'' be evaluated. Five separate studies were done to look at diverse impacts and to provide information for future programs. These studies are outlined in Table 2.3.

Table 2.3 suggests that the program was successful in meeting its objectives, but that broader impact (more viewers) would require better scheduling of the program and more funds for promotion. However, with its viewers, the program mix of entertainment and information was effective in reaching cognitive (information), affective (e.g., recall of positive images of aging), and behavioral (information requests) objectives. The program also provided important guidelines for future preventive TV efforts: (a) Use an ''upbeat'' program to focus on preventive behaviors, and *not* have an individual crisis intervention approach; (b) Use a program to link viewers and existing services; do not create a new set of services (see McAlister, 1982, for a similar approach); (c) Focus on simple, reachable behaviors important to prevention and linking the individual with appropriate services and organizations. For ''Over Easy'', this entailed having viewers call community and service agencies.

Improving Social Behavior.   Sprafkin and Rubinstein (1982) reported on an experiment with 132 institutionalized, behaviorally disordered children (mean age = 14 years) that demonstrated the potential of prosocial, available, commercial programs. They reasoned that if prosocial television programs can positively influence normal children (Rushton, 1982), prosocial programs could also positively influence children with behavior disorders.

During an initial assessment, it was found that the usual television ''diet'' of these children consisted of many action and violent programs. The children apparently modeled many of these behaviors, making their behavioral problems worse. Their study compared the usual TV diet with commercial programs picked from an extensive videotape library following the criteria of prosocial programs containing at least 29 prosocial acts and less than 3 agressive acts per hour. These criteria were based on an extensive scoring system used in prior research. Examples of programs used included segments from the ''Brady Bunch'' (comedy), ''Room 222'' (drama), and ''Fat Albert and the Cosby Kids'' (cartoons). The themes of these programs included compromising when there is a conflict, considering others feelings, cooperating with teachers, and refraining from stealing and practical jokes. The control programs consisted of the 10 most watched programs during the initial assessment period.

In addition to the different television diets, half the children also received a 10-minute discussion period following exposure to the programs (i.e., a 2 × 2 design). The prosocial discussion highlighted those behaviors, whereas the discussion with the usual diet pointed out the inappropriate behaviors in the pro-

TABLE 2.3
Evaluations of the "Over Easy" Program*

Type	Purpose	Method	Impact
Viewership	Scheduling, size and demographics of audience.	Assess ratings, audience, competing programs.	Reaching by 1978, 2.5 million different households. Females 2 to 1; but only about 6% of adults and 7% of persons 55 and older had seen at least once; minimal funding for promotion and scheduling conflicts with news programs which attract older viewers
Awareness	Effectiveness of program promotion and public response.	National sample of 3,000, evaluation and recall.	Viewers liked and appreciated a different approach to aging; about 3/4 retained at least one positive pro-aging message and able to reproduce the message (i.e., day after recall)
Effects–individuals	Assess information gain, attitude change.	Special sample of 600; pre-post test.	Significant increase of information in such areas as medical needs and employee rights; can identify a specific way to use information.
Effects–institutions	Assess target groups use of services.	Surveyed 566 agency directors across the country.	Most basic support activity of the agencies was to promote watching program; 39% of directors documented an increase in service utilization since the start of the program, mostly in information and referral services, transportation, in-home services, and senior centers. Most frequent behavior

TABLE 2.3 (*Continued*)

Type	Purpose	Method	Impact
			were requests for information about a service.
Product quality	Assess product values and recommended improvement	Panel of producers	Programs judged as adequate but recommended improvements in set design, casting, and script development.

*From Keegan, 1982.

grams. The main part of the study was conducted over a 2-week period with 10, half-hour programs shown each weeknight.

Besides explicit criteria for prosocial programs, and an experimental design, this study also is noteworthy for conducting actual behavioral observations on the children's wards following a time-sampling system developed in other research. Interobserver reliability was somewhat low (about 70%), but acceptable. Observational categories for prosocial behaviors included altruism (acts of sharing, helping, or concern toward others); affection (displays of fondness, reassurance, or concern toward others), and appropriate interaction (conversing; asking permission). Aggressive behaviors included physical (acts to hurt others; kicking, hitting, biting); verbal (threats, teases, name calling); symbolic (displays of threatening gestures and acts), and object (damage to any part of ward environment or personal property). Other measures included attention during television viewing of the programs and comprehension of program content. Both attention (77%) and comprehension (61%) were reasonably high.

The results of the study showed that children viewing the prosocial programs showed an increase in altruism relative to their baseline mean, whereas the control children showed a decrease in altruism. For the prosocial viewers, those high in physical aggression showed the increases in altruism, whereas those low in aggression showed no change. Symbolic aggression also decreased for high aggressive, prosocial viewers.

The results for the additive discussion were not as clear-cut. For prosocial viewers, verbal and object aggression decreased if there was no discussion. However, control viewers showed a decrease in verbal aggression with the discussion, and an increase in verbal aggression without the discussion. Sprafkin and Rubinstein (1982) explained these results by noting that the prosocial discussion may have undermined the programs by being too moralistic, whereas the control discussion seemed effective in concretely giving pragmatic reasons to behave or not behave in certain ways. This point strongly indicates that an interpersonal supplement to a television (or other media) intervention must be well conceptualized, fit with the media, and also pretested.

Interestingly, the attention scores of the children to either set of programs was equally high. This somewhat detracts from the argument of others (Milavsky et al., 1982) that aggressive children are primarily attracted to violent, action programs, and other television fare will not be regularly watched by them.

This study serves as a good example of experimental research using behavioral measures advocated in this book. Its use of available, previously taped television programs has obvious cost savings and it appears possible that other selected, commercial programs would be suitable for interventions with additional, special populations. Although this study did define the criteria for prosocial and generally appeared to present multiple models performing positive and inappropriate behaviors (with negative consequences) in a dramatic format, it is likely that effects would have been more substantial if programs featuring prosocial content were especially designed in light of assessments of the children's behavioral excesses and deficits. This presents an important cost-effectiveness question, particularly if specially developed programs are useable with children in diverse settings who are behaviorally disordered.

PROSOCIAL TELEVISION: EXTENDED EXAMPLES

In this next section, two other prosocial television efforts are discussed in detail. "Feeling Good" illustrates potential health behavior outcomes of a television series, whereas the author's work in residential energy conservation shows some of the benefits of programs that are extremely tailored to a population and explicitly focus on only several key behaviors.

Feeling Good. This was an experimental series aired during prime time on 250 Public Broadcasting Service stations in 1974 and 1975. It first began with an hour-long weekly format covering many topics and then its format was changed to a half-hour focusing on one specific health topic. The programs were designed for adults, and the series differed in one major way from similar health promotion, media-based efforts (such as PSA's): The objective of the program was not just information gain, but also was motivational—to change health behaviors. This is no easy task even for seemingly simple behaviors. Adults may have correct health information, but may fail to act on it for any number of reasons: long-term habits; immediacy of reinforcers versus long delayed negative effects (e.g., smoking); monetary, psychological, and social costs of change; fear of outcome (e.g., breast self-examination); lack of social and environmental support, and counteracting forces (e.g., advertising of junk foods). The more typical belief in the communication literature is that television alone will be ineffective in changing health or other complex behaviors (e.g., Wallack, 1981).

The original notion of the series was to overcome these obstacles by programs that were carefully developed through formative research to specifically target young parents and low-income families, and which combined serious content and entertainment with a story line. The formative research efforts were substantial and were conducted over a 2-year period. These efforts included extensive interviews, pilot testing entailing actual observation of viewers, and development of community aspects of the program effort.

After six, 1-hour programs, it was apparent that audience share was declining and the mix of serious content and entertainment directed at a variety of health behaviors was not viable. This format was discontinued after 11 weeks, and was replaced with a half-hour format stressing more serious content, generally one health practice, and more emphasis on information and attitudes. This format change appears consistent with a more focused, behavior change effort. Clearly, in an experimental venture, such change is warranted and is not tantamount to failure as some have suggested (Wallack, 1981). However, a major problem was that a good deal of the summative evaluation was geared to the original format.

Despite these problems, the research plan was admirable. The basic idea was to gather different kinds of evidence from different kinds of evaluations conducted by different agencies, including a multi-city, large sample panel study of voluntary viewing; four national surveys to measure trends in awareness of the series, viewing, and health behaviors; a field experiment of viewers and nonviewers in one community, and national audience estimates for the series. An important community study using relatively nonreactive health indicators (for example, type and frequency of visits to health care centers) could not be mounted because of problems in assessing records. It was apparent in viewing these evaluation efforts (Mielke & Swinehart, 1976a, 1976b) that a myriad of problems existed in each evaluation study, e.g., reliance on self-report: confounding of monetary inducement to watch a program with outcome, failure to evaluate the effects of all programs, and sample selection problems. Yet, the sheer effort and the strategy of multiple evaluation methods remains laudatory even more than a decade later.

The evaluations of "Feeling Good" are highlighted here:

1. Between 1–2% of the (then) 68.5 million TV households in the U.S. on the average viewed each program, figures that are high for PBS programs.

2. About 5% of the adult U.S. population reported seeing at least one program during a 2-month period; however, it appeared that viewers tended to be young, well-educated and higher socioeconomic status (SES). The last two demographic characteristics are in line with typical PBS viewers, but not with the program's prime audience (lower SES). Lower SES households reported lower awareness of PBS and the "Feeling Good" programs.

3. The programs had a number of behavioral goals, and the convergence of data from the different studies was used to indicate "strong," "partial," or "no

evidence'' for these goals. Table 2.4 presents the outcomes of these evaluations as reported by Mielke and Swinehart (1976a, 1976b). Of course, what are strong or partial effects (e.g., small significant differences on self-report items) is open to debate. However, it is reasonably clear that the program had some success in changing simple, but important behaviors, such as seeking information, talking to another person, obtaining screening examinations, minimal dietary changes. More complex dietary exercise, and other involved or, perhaps, fear provoking behaviors, showed no change.

4. A major premise of the program was that correct health information was an important antecedent of health behavior change. The program's goals included providing correct information and Table 2.5 summarizes results on knowledge and opinions. Results here appear more diverse, but one important aspect is missing. It is unclear how change in information related to reported change in behavior. As noted in chapter 1, a linear hierarchy of effects model, although useful for planning and having realistic expectations of outcomes, may not represent the actual change process, which needs to be investigated during the formative research stage, and as a process and outcome of the program.

As previously noted, although some have considered ''Feeling Good'' a failure because of format changes, limited reach, and less than clear outcomes, it is viewed here as a success. Changing simple, but strategic health behaviors is a realistic goal for television programs. These additional and supporting points were emphasized by Mielke and Swinehart (1976a, 1976b):

1. The series was particularly effective in motivating viewers to seek additional information about health concerns and to encourage friends and relatives to take appropriate preventive health actions.

2. Approximately one million viewers watched each week despite a variety of topics, formats, and length of the program. The cost per viewer was minimal (about the same cost as a health pamphlet) and cost-effectiveness can be great if preventive health measures are taken that reduce later clinic and office visits, and most certainly, hospitalization.

3. The fact that there was a small, but receptive audience suggested experimentation with less expensive, perhaps, more local productions.

4. Even though the absolute number of viewers was low, it still was large enough to suggest that purposive programming for health and related topics is worthwhile.

5. Extensive formative research is necessary to carefully tailor a program to a target audience. Failure to do this will make programs appear irrelevant to the target audience. However, note that ''Feeling Good'' was generally not successful in reaching its lower SES target audience.

6. It is difficult to combine entertainment, information, and motivation into one program. These are usually seen as separate types of programs by viewers.

This point needs to be further considered in future programs. It may be possible to exclude involved drama or entertainment if information is highly salient and effective formative features are used.

7. There are many factors besides the program format and content that need to be considered for audience acceptance. These entail promotion, competitive programming, signal clarity, and so on.

8. The difficult goal of behavior change warrants extensive pilot testing and refinement of programs. However, such pilot tests should not just emphasize viewer liking or attitude change, but actual behavior change.

From this book's perspective, "Feeling Good" was a qualified success. In particular, its second, more focused format can serve as a model for other programs (and may be less expensive than drama and entertainment), and its delineation of simple behaviors, not global health messages, also represents appropriate program goals.

Conservation.   Studies by the author (Winett, Leckliter, Chinn, Stahl, & Love, 1985) on the use of special television programs to properly inform and motivate consumers to conserve energy in their homes exemplify many of the key points noted earlier. There are also a number of points concerning the development of those projects that are also noteworthy for highlighting other issues raised in this chapter.

1. The original impetus for developing television programs came from social learning theory (modeling), and not communications literature. That is, based on modeling principles, it seemed quite likely that the careful depiction of energy saving strategies and the benefits and outcomes of such strategies would influence viewers (consumers) energy use practices. The author also viewed, before the start of this series of projects, Richard Evans' (Evans et al., 1981) films that demonstrated to young adolescents via simple vignettes how to refuse cigarettes from peers and parents, and how to understand and resist advertising. The data from this work were reasonably positive and showed an innovative, preventive use of modeling. From a social learning perspective, the important point is that modeling programs should be effective, and social learning theory does not provide the relative pessimism of the communications literature (e.g., see Wallack, 1981).

2. The modeling programs were introduced into a chain of experimental research studies that followed a systematic replication approach. In this approach, each study builds on and replicates, refines, and extends procedures from prior studies. In the course of these studies, one procedure, frequent, written feedback on energy use, was shown to be a highly effective (reductions on energy use of 15% to 20%), but not a cost-beneficial strategy (Winett, Neale, Williams, Yokley, & Kauder, 1979). However, the results of the feedback studies were very useful in showing that residential energy use was quite "elas-

TABLE 2.4
Behavioral Effects

Topic	Strong Evidence	Partial Evidence	No Evidence
Heart disease	Seeking information about obtaining heart checkups		
Alcoholism		Examining drinking habits to detect a potential problem Seeking information about help for a drinking problem	
Mental health		Encouraging someone to seek professional help for an emotional problem	
Nutrition	Having more fresh fruit or fruit juice	Using a steamer to cook vegetables	Reducing consumption of foods high in saturated fat
Breast cancer	Encouraging someone to have a doctor examine her breasts Women performing breast self-examinations		Women asking a doctor or nurse to teach them how to do a breast self-examination
Accident prevention or control	Learning and posting the number of the local poison control center and other emergency numbers	Storing hazardous substances out of children's reach	
Doctor/patient communication		Writing down symptoms before visiting a doctor Asking a doctor to explain diagnosis, treatment, etc.	
Prenatal care		Encouraging someone to see a doctor early in pregnancy	
Exercise			Engaging in moderate physical activity daily
Vision	Having an eyesight examination	Taking a preschool child for a vision screening	
Dental care		Cutting down on sweet snacks for children	Making a trial use of disclosing tablets
Hypertension	Seeking information about obtaining a blood pressure check	Getting a blood pressure check	

TABLE 2.4 (*Continued*)

Topic	Strong Evidence	Partial Evidence	No Evidence
	Encouraging someone to have a blood pressure check		
Hearing		Seeking information on where to get children's hearing checked	Taking a preschool child for a hearing screening
Health insurance			Seeking information about costs and benefits of health insurance plans
Uterine cancer	Encouraging someone to have a Pap test		Women having a Pap test
			Seeking information on how to get a Pap test
Immunizations		Taking a preschool child for immunizations	
Health information seeking	Sending for health information offered on television		
Physical examinations		Obtaining a physical examination	Encouraging someone to have a physical examination

tic,'' helping the research team to understand and become expert in residential energy conservation, and providing a yardstick procedure for comparisons of the efficacy of any new procedure, such as video modeling. Extremely reliable and frequently collected (several times per week) energy data also allowed for constant monitoring of effectiveness over the months of each study.

3. Prior to a study involving cable TV, three studies done in a chain were used to develop the approach (Winett, Hatcher, Fort, Leckliter, Riley, & Love, 1982; Winett, Love, Chinn, Stahl, & Leckliter, 1983). These studies clearly demonstrated that: Modeling programs shown in small groups (8 to 10 people) effectively reduced viewer's home energy consumption; the specific content and use of modeling were the critical features of such programs; efficacy was not lost when programs were viewed alone at home (over project equipment, especially brought in for that purpose); social interaction was not a necessary factor for effectiveness.

4. A strategy had been developed based on social marketing principles to closely tailor the program's content, procedures, and scenes (locations) to those highly congruent with the target audiences. That is, the language, life style, mores, and scenes closely matched the target audience. However, rather than base such social marketing on surveys and the like (see chapter 4), the social

TABLE 2.5
Knowledge/Opinion Effects

Topic	Strong Evidence	Partial Evidence
Heart disease		Veal is better than other kinds of meat for persons with heart trouble.
Alcoholism	Parents who drink a lot more are likely to have children who drink a lot. Alcoholism is easier to treat in its early stages. People can be called alcoholic only if they drink so much that they can't work (disagree).	Teenagers with parents who drink a lot, or who don't drink at all, are more likely to drink.
Mental helath		A person seeking help from a psychologist or psychiatrist is basically a weak person (disagree).
Nutrition	Eating fruit helps clean the teeth. Butter contains more cholesterol than margarine. It is not good for health to eat the skin of chicken or turkey.	Eggs contain a lot of cholesterol. It takes less time to steam vegetables than to boil them. Steamed vegetables are better for you than boiled vegetables.
Breast cancer	Learning how to do a breast self-examination from television	A woman is still capable of having a normal sex life after breast removal. Women should examine their breasts for lumps every month. With early detection and treatment, the large majority of women recover from breast cancer. Only a minority of lumps discovered in the breast turn out to be cancerous.
Patients' rights		A patient has the right to refuse treatment.
Dental care		With proper care, teeth can normally be expected to last a lifetime.
Vision		People over 35 should have a glaucoma check every year. A person with diabetes in the family runs a greater risk of having glaucoma. A child's eyes should be checked before age 6 and can be done

TABLE 2.5 (*Continued*)

Topic	Strong Evidence	Partial Evidence
		before he/she learns the alphabet.
		A person can have glaucoma and not know it.
		Amblyopia is the condition of underuse of one eye.
		A child with amblyopia may see well with one eye and appear to have normal vision.
Stress		Taking tranquilizers is not a good way of dealing with stress.
		Stress can be helpful as well as harmful.
Hypertension	High blood pressure can be asymptomatic.	Blacks are particularly susceptible to high blood pressure.
Hearing		Parents can't always tell if their child has a hearing problem.
		Nearly one in five preschool children has less than normal hearing.
Allied health personnel	Much of the work a doctor does can be done by specially trained personnel who are not doctors.	
Uterine/Cervical Cancer		Cervical cancer has a cure rate of nearly 100% when caught early.
Colon/Rectum cancer		Most colon/rectum cancers can be diagnosed by a proctoscopic examination.
		Nearly 75% of all deaths from colon/rectum cancer could be prevented with early detection.

marketing (at least matching the program to the audience) was based on many years of working in the field with similar audience segments, and observing receptivity to the programs.

5. By working in the field for a number of years, the team was expert in energy conservation—what procedures worked and which did not, and which procedures were acceptable to the audience and which were not. The television medium was also a good match for the simple low-cost, no-cost energy conservation strategies (e.g., thermostat changes, use of small electric heaters; use of simple passive solar strategies, etc.) that were depicted in the program. The strategies were simple, but virtually guaranteed energy savings when adopted. In addition, because the strategies were so simple and required minimal cost or effort, there were few monetary or physical barriers to change. Finally, because

few steps were required and little skill was involved, a direct focus on long-term behavior change was taken (although this should be the goal for many programs).

As in most of the author's experiments in energy conservation, participants were recruited from one central area (neighborhood) that best represented the audience characteristics most appropriate for the program, in this case, middle-class homeowners. Using a door-to-door recruitment approach, between 50% and 75% of the households in an area have been enlisted into projects, thus, virtually eliminating the problem of volunteer bias that has plagued other media research.

During a baseline period of about a month, readings were taken three times per week on outdoor energy meters thus requiring no contact with participants. Some other measures (measures of perceived comfort; continuous measurement of temperature and humidity using special devices; clothing worn; knowledge of energy conservation, strategies used) that did require contact with participants and were pertinent to other aspects of the project (developing new comfort standards) were taken in 60% of contact participant households. Persons hired to collect these measures (forms) on a weekly basis were unaware of participants treatment condition.

After the baseline period, and just prior to the first airing of the program, households were randomly assigned to one of five conditions:

1. *No-contact control* ($n = 30$): Households were informed that they were in a control condition for an energy conservation study. Only outdoor energy meters continued to be read, and these households were not involved in other measures in the study. That is, contact ceased.

2. *Contact Control* ($n = 30$): This condition was the same as the prior condition except other measures that required contact were continued.

3. *No-Contact Media* ($n = 30$): This condition was the same as the no-contact control except that mail and phone prompts were used to inform participants about the time of the program.

4. *Contact Media* ($n = 30$): This condition was the same as no-contact media except the other measures requiring contact continued to be taken.

5. *Contact Media-Visit* ($n = 30$): This condition was the same as the contact media condition except that a few days after the program a home visit lasting about 30 minutes was conducted. The purpose of the visit was to further explain procedures, adopt them, if necessary, to the participant's situation, and develop more interest and commitment. This approach had been used before with some success (Winett, Love, & Kidd, 1982).

The television program "Summer Breeze" was about 20 minutes long and was shown on the public access station of the cable system at 7 p.m. on Monday, Tuesday, and Friday, and 9 p.m. on Thursday. This schedule provided excellent reach; 98% of the participant households viewed the program at least once.

Viewing was verified by a special insert at the end of the program that required participants to mark a form with an ''X'' if they had watched the program. The procedure and mark was noted only in the television program. Only 2% of the control households watched the program, meaning that the integrity of the experimental design was maintained (a problem in other research, for example, ''Feeling Good'').

The most significant features of the program were: (a) a theme song, ''Summer Breeze'' that was used for audience recognition (it was a popular song) to tie program parts together and to represent the main point of the program—that the use of natural ventilation and fans could replace much air conditioning; (b) a two-sided visual and auditory format was used in the beginning to counter beliefs that energy conservation was no longer important, and only resulted in discomfort; (c) characters and locations closely fit the audience; (d) fairly rapid pacing was used to hold attention; (e) voiceovers and captions were used to emphasize main points and strategies that were depicted (modeled) a minimal of three times, and summaries at different points were used.

The program had a story line based on modeling and diffusion principles, which provided some minimal drama and conflict. A young couple (early 30's) was dismayed at their high summer electric bill and was in a quandary about what to do. They recalled that their older neighbors who lived in a home similar to theirs had very low summer and winter bills. After a number of scenes with social situations (e.g., playing tennis), the younger couple asked the older couple to show them ways to save energy and money. The rest of the program revolved around the older couple demonstrating the simple strategies. The couple tried each strategy and were pleasantly surprised how easy the strategies were, how much money they saved on their next bill, and how they were able to maintain comfort. In a final scene, the younger couple suggested that the older couple could help them in the winter, which served as a lead-in for the second part of the study conducted 6 months later.

The results of the study showed that households viewing the program (regardless of contact or home visit) reduced their overall electricity use by about 11% (compared to control conditions) for a period of 2 months (end of the summer) after the program. The study's design strongly indicated that simply seeing the program *once* was the crucial factor.

Six months later a similar winter program was delivered over the cable access station following the No-Contact Media condition for all experimental households. For this program, the results showed about a 10% reduction in energy use (electricity or natural gas). Finally, with no program shown, the following summer outdoor meters were again read. There was still some evidence for savings (about 5.5%) 1 year later for experimental households.

Figure 2.1 shows the results of this project for the summer phases represented in electricity use (kWh) and savings. Note that the Contact and No-Contact conditions are depicted separately, but the pattern of energy use and savings is

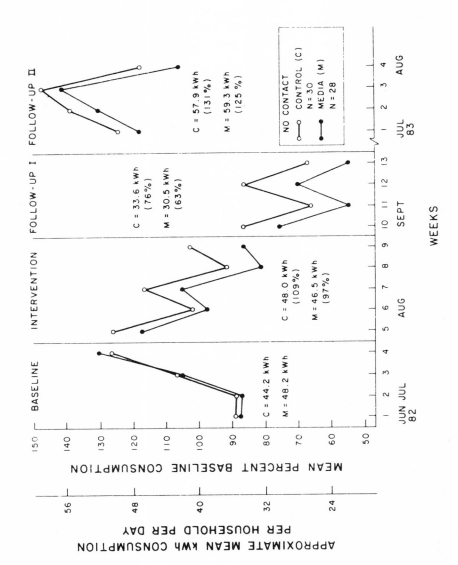

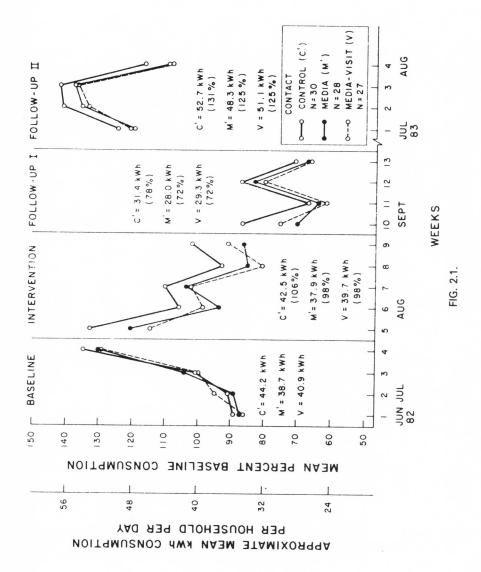

FIG. 2.1.

51

virtually the same between Contact and No-Contact media conditions. Finally, note that the savings began immediately after the program and were continuous from that point.

The results of this study were seen as quite positive. One program showing (very low dose and duration) was sufficient to produce change. The outcomes, 10%–11% reductions, are quite meaningful for energy conservation (on an aggregate level), and also represented savings of 20%–25% on the major targets for the program, cooling or heating. That is, it was possible using standard procedures to accurately assess the savings from reduced air conditioning and heating. Despite these changes, as in other studies of the author, there were no reported changes in comfort level, that remained quite acceptable. This is because the programs offered viewers a set of simple strategies that could offset reduced air conditioning or heating. Indeed, the hygrothermographs indicated for example, that in the summer the electrcity savings were achieved with a constant (baseline through intervention) temperature in the homes of about 77 degrees F.

In addition, given that the programs were shown at a time (1982–1983) when there was not great interest in energy conservation, and in an area where energy prices were quite low (Winkler & Winett, 1982), the results seem even more promising. This is because many external barriers (attitudes, beliefs, economics) to receptiveness and action had to be overcome.

To balance these positive optimistic results it may be noted that participants only tended to adopt the simplest no-cost strategies; more effortful or costly procedures (for example insulation of the hot water heater) tended not to be adopted. In addition, the simplicity of the procedures and lack of strong barriers to change (i.e., barriers existed to attempt change, but not to actual enactment of the behaviors) may not be general conditions for other problems (such as health).

Beyond these immediate issues, more general points were also raised by the study. Because the objective of this project was to conduct a well-controlled experiment and to continue the research on comfort and energy conservation strategies, the program was only shown to a small, preselected audience. The estimated cost of the summer program, which had over 20 locations and numerous short scenes, and hence required extensive editing, was $40,000 for a commercial production. The total savings of all 90 homes watching the program in 1982 amounted to somewhat less than $1,500 and about half that for 1983. This is hardly a benefit–cost (B/C) ratio to write home about (let alone put in a book). However, because the intervention lends itself to being able to be used in many locations (e.g., many southeastern small city, suburban, and rural areas) at only the additional cost of prompting viewers ($1 per home), the potential B/C ratio is excellent. For example, if 1 million homes viewed the program, then over the course of a summer $15 million for energy could be saved at an initial cost of slightly over $1 million, or a B/C ratio of about 15 to 1. Also, because energy use is much higher in the winter, a similar program can yield about the same percentage savings (on greater energy use) and the B/C ratio would then be 30 to 40 to 1.

Obviously, this B/C analysis does not take into account the complex political, economic, and social issues of the distribution of benefits and costs (Levin, 1983). In this example, initial costs would be incurred by government, utility companies would lose revenues and would probably face employment and other ramifications; but individual consumers would gain. Presumbably, some consumer savings would be put back into the economy in ways that are not very clear at this point. For example, the purpose of the program would be undermined if consumers used savings on home energy to drive more miles in personal cars! Quite obviously, these are complex B/C questions that are particularly germane as the technology for effective interventions becomes more developed and as such program find delivery modes to reach wide audiences.

PROSOCIAL TELEVISION: OPTIMISM AND PESSIMISM

This chapter must conclude on a mixed note. On the side of optimism, it appears that the qualities of effective, prosocial programming can be identified. A number of projects support the common effectiveness of several key strategies and elements including:

1. Considerable formative research about the target audience focusing on beliefs, attitudes, and behaviors pertinent to program objectives and considerable pilot testing of programs with representatives of the target audience and preferably a focus in pilot tests on behavioral measures (e.g., not just recall or recognition of a program message).

2. The strategic use of a range of formal features to maintain interest and attention and to underscore key points.

3. The development of some story line and drama in which multiple models in multiple settings depict the prescribed behaviors and are reinforced. If a story line and drama is not possible, direct information and modeling can be effective.

4. The depiction of relatively simple behaviors with few barriers to performance which nevertheless yield significant beneficial outcomes (e.g., thermostat changes) or represent important first steps in a chain of behaviors (e.g., phone a social service center).

5. The development of realistic, reachable goals based on the type of behavior change needed, barriers to change, program exposure, and effects that can be expected from simple behavior changes.

In the future, there needs to be more experimentation with prosocial television. Of particular interest are studies that further study the relationships of formal features to attention, comprehension, and behavior change. In addition, it is unclear how the same processes are affected by program length, number of program exposures and duration of exposure (e.g., massed vs. spaced viewing of a series). Research also can be directed to attempts to change seemingly more complex behaviors. For example, the author has started a study supported by the Natural Science Foundation that will try to use all the key points previously noted to create an optimal television program to promote less expensive, and more nutritional food shopping. The purposes of the study fit in with the role of the government developing "information remedies" for problems in the marketplace, e.g., ineffective information flow and consumer search. The study will also further investigate medium and other communication variables as well as the processes of cognitive, affective, and behavior change.

There is little doubt that there are a number of other investigators involved in prosocial television and viewer, interactive systems (Swift, 1982). However, as the benefit–cost analysis for the energy conservation television program so clearly showed, most prosocial television programs, particularly those with some story line and/or diverse locations, require a large audience to justify the production costs. Thus, the question is how can such programs gain access to a wide audience? The answer requires some brief discussion of the nature of television in this country, and it is here that the other side—pessimism—is presented.

American television remains a unique communication system compared to its counterparts in other Western countries because its primary goal is the profit motive, compared to broadcasting with the first objective of the public interest (Kellner, 1982). Other countries have centralized the production and distribution of television programming, but the *network* ownership of the hardware (cables, satellites, a microwave relay station); the control of software (i.e., paying studios to produce certain programs); the control of outlets (affiliates) by producing the software, with the entire enterprise revolving around advertising fees based on Nielsen and Arbitron ratings, is a profit-making marvel.

Network television reflects American capitalism in that it remains relatively free of government regulation or accountability, and that no other type of system has ever been considered, much less tried, in America (Kellner, 1982). As Kellner (1982) states, "Most radical theories of television have highlighted its dual functions of producing both profit and hegemonic ideology, seeing television as a business machine and an ideology machine within a monolithic capitalistic society" (p. 415).

Two other aspects of American television are criticized by Kellner and others (e.g., Galbraith, 1983). First, the myth continues that network television is good because it is essentially "free" entertainment dictated by public tastes and advertising support based on such tastes. Presumably, in a free-market, any idea, program, or product preferred by the public reaches ascendancy, i.e., a perfect counterpart to political democracy. However, American television is what it is today partly because the free-market system essentially does not exist in the realm of large corporations (Galbraith, 1983). Clearly, only a few select American corporations and multinationals can afford network television advertising. Thus, American television is dominated by the powerful for the benefit of the powerful.

The second criticism follows from this point and again involves the profit motive. As Kellner (1982) put it, one way to continually "keep the wheels greased" is by conveying the message in programs and commercials "that happiness and values are located in the private sphere, encouraging a privatized, consumer existence" (p. 419). Programs or spots instructing the public on how to consume less and be satisfied (e.g., the energy conservation programs), are counter to the norms of network television. They are unlikely to be widely broadcast.

Cable stations have been offered as one way to reduce the stranglehold of the networks. During the last 5 years, viewership of network fare during prime time has declined from about 78% to 70%, whereas viewership of alternatives (cable stations, pay TV, VCR's) has increased from about 22% to 30% (Newsweek, April 1985). However many cable stations are now owned by communication giants or the networks (Don LeDuc, personal communication, February, 1985). Thus, control remains in the hands of the few.

In the new media chapter, regulatory issues in communications are discussed at length. The point is made that during the last 50 years regulatory policy has focused on increasing outlets with the goal of creating diversity in programming. For the most part, it has not worked because of the centralization of control and programming by networks. Regulatory policy may have to focus more on programming content to create diversity. For example, networks may be required to present several hours per week of educational programming during prime time. In today's political climate, such regulations seem a fantasy. It may take years of disenchantment with typical network fare and some unusual coalitions of charismatic leaders, citizens, interest groups, politicians, and a friendly court to regulate network television (Pertschuk, 1982), or at least provide some vocal criticism (Rubinstein, 1982).

In the final chapter, the issue of access and diversity is discussed at length and particular strategies to gain access are outlined. At this point, four approaches for wider distribution of prosocial television are discussed:

1. *PSA's*—It may be possible to have impact with a series of short PSA's that also follow the important elements identified in this chapter. Likewise, much of the content of the prosocial programs described here can fit the PSA format (e.g., separate conservation practices; self-help behaviors for the elderly). However, in the absence of regulations requiring PSA's in specific times for specific audiences, PSA's now typically appear at times that an affiliate could not sell (for example, 2 AM). Solomon (1982) noted that PSA's may be fit better to the target audience through the development of personal relationships with affiliate staff.

2. *Narrowcasting*—It is possible to reach a select target audience by gaining access to local cable systems. This was the approach used in the energy conservation project described in this project (although regulatory policy is changing on local access; see chapter 5). However, if a program is aimed for a limited audience, its production qualities usually must be very inexpensive. The inexpensive format may not appeal to viewers. Most of the key format points needed for behavior change seem able to fit within inexpensive (e.g., studio) productions.

3. *Cassettes*—As VCR's make even further inroads in the home market, prosocial programs can be widely distributed on cassettes. Although the cost of cassettes should decrease via increased distribution, it is likely that the approach would make programs available to those who need them the least, for example, the wealthier elderly.

4. *Reciprocal Benefits*—There should be some programs beyond sheer entertainment that can be beneficial to the networks and viewers. Certainly health programs appear to be one candidate. Given the great interest in fitness, nutrition, and other personal health habits, it is possible that a revised "Feeling Good" program could find a wider audience. With more money for production and promotion and a better delineated behavioral technology, such a national program may be commercially and behaviorally effective.

POSTSCRIPT: INDIVIDUAL RESPONSIBILITY

This chapter has emphasized that there is nothing inherently bad about television and that its potential to be a positive social and educational force in our country is enormous, but it is relatively untapped. In the end, current television fare remains what it is because people will watch many network programs and commercials, seemingly never satiated, and not watch much of other programming such as that on PBS.

Clearly, for some segments, television serves a unique function. For the housebound elderly, it may be their only stimulation and companion. For the poor, it may be the only affordable and palatable entertainment. For other segments, it becomes more difficult to "blame the system".

Television's hold on individual behavior and time is well-demonstrated in studies of "how Americans use time" (Robinson, 1977). Generally, in these time-allocation studies, data is accumulated from representative cross-sections of people using time-activity logs. People are usually asked to record each activity engaged in, where, with whom, for how long, and to assign some affective value to the time and activity; measures are taken to assure reliability. Such data can be very revealing either for individuals studied over time (Winett & Neale, 1981) or large cross-sections of people.

Robinson (1977; Sahin & Robinson, 1982) has extensively used this method. Robinson noted that from 1965 to 1975 there was a decline in actual work time of about 4.8 hours per week for men and women in the labor force. For women in or out of the labor force, there was also a decline in "compulsive time" (e.g., child and home care) of about 5 hours. For men, there seemed to be an increase in free time of about 3 hours, and for women, about 4 hours per week. What was this new free time used for? For men and women working outside the home, about 3.5 hours per week more was devoted to television; for women not working outside the home, about 7 hours more per week was allocated to television. Sahin and Robinson (1982) critically commented on this situation:

> According to most models of "post-industrial" society or the "self-actualization era" into which the U.S. has presumably been moving . . . one would have expected the increased free time to be devoted to educational or organization activity, or increased physical fitness or training. Contrary to such characteristics, however, practically the entire increase in available free time . . . was directed toward the television set . . . the increased time devoted to television suggests the U.S. had entered a post *industrious* instead of a post-*industrial* age. (p. 487)

Sahin and Robinson also noted a leveling in differences in TV viewing by socioeconomic groups. The trend is for truly mass viewing with the exception of those with less than high school education who reported 40% greater viewing than other groups. Sahin and Robinson also reported that television time was relatively elastic; if something else needed to be done, television time was reduced. Further, television time was not rated as particularly enjoyable or necessary. But, once people were in their homes, without other pressing activities, "the set appears to have an irresistible hold on their time" (Sahin & Robinson, 1982, p. 489).

Sahin and Robinson (1982) further noted the great interest of TV program planners in time allocation data. Their purpose is by sequence and flow to control and maintain the audience:

> In planning the flow of viewing, discrete items are carefully interlinked so that they become inseparable parts of a large whole. Programming tactics such as "block programming," "blunting," "counter programming," and "long forms" are designed to carry the audience through the flow for as long as possible. This means closing off possible exits, whetting appetites for what is yet to come, and transforming television viewing into a *continuous* experience. . . In essence, the colonization of free time by television in the United States can be seen as another manifestation of the historical process in which free time has been turned into a commodity and re-expropriated by the forces in control of the realm necessity. For the great majority of people, free time has become time for television rather than "time for higher activity." (p. 490)

Although Sahin and Robinson's data and perspective puts us back to a system blame position, a number of points need to be made on balance. Several hours per day of TV viewing has become a norm, yet it is a private norm. Few, if any, other people outside of a home are overtly pressuring family members (although this may be less true for children) to watch hour after hour. In a very real sense, the individual has some responsibility in ending the mesmirization of television and choosing alternative activities such as conversation, reading, games, hobbies, fitness activities, and community service.

Clearly, the potential of television for educational and social ends is great. However, one goal of prosocial television efforts can be to create more discriminating viewers with more diverse interests. An unlikely goal of prosocial programs is the creation of a robot-like audience for four nightly hours of education and behavior change.

3 Diffusion from a Behavioral Systems Perspective

This chapter focuses on Rogers' (1983) diffusion of innovation model. Its special purpose is to show how the diffusion model of information exchange and innovation implementation can be subsumed under the behavioral system's approach. At the same time, integration of some diffusion concepts and methods with the behavioral systems paradigm can help to expand the behavioral approach.

This chapter also is different from the others in one major way. Rather than being a focused review of different sources, this chapter almost exclusively reviews and analyzes Rogers' model. This is because Rogers has, every 10 years or so, comprehensively reviewed the diffusion research in book form.

However, the review and analysis of Rogers' current model is pivotal. Rogers' recent effort is quite different than the earlier models (Rogers, 1962; Rogers & Shoemaker, 1971). The earlier efforts optimistically and boldly introduced this new paradigm. The 1983 book can be characterized by words such as "cautious" and "critical." The heady days of paradigm emergence appear replaced by the beginning of paradigm descendance. It is important to see why this seems to be the case. Thus, although the diffusion paradigm is still very influential, some of its major thrusts seem open to question and reinterpretation.

The stance of this chapter is only possible because of Rogers' integrity in critically analyzing his and other diffusion scholars efforts. It is unusual in our highly competitive research environment to cast doubt on our own work. It is hoped that Rogers' openness can serve as a model for other approaches at a crossroads.

POINTS OF CRITICISM

Before reviewing the diffusion model, it is, at the outset, instructive to delineate aspects of the approach that are now points of criticism. These points, particularly those germane to a behavioral systems framework, receive more analysis as the review of diffusion unfolds. The major points are:

1. Most diffusion research has been post-hoc. It needs to take a more active intervention stance. In this respect, diffusion and social marketing may become indistinguishable.

2. The basic methodology of post-hoc surveys of adopter's recall of innovation decisions needs to be replaced.

3. The emphasis of research needs to shift away from merely studying verbal reports of decisions to adopt an innovation, to long-term study of actual implementation.

4. The pro-innovation stance needs to be replaced by a more cautious approach that fully explores consequences of innovations, and at times, may emphasize non-innovation.

5. Much innovation is organizationally based and diffusion research needs to study processes of organizational innovation.

6. The linear, one-way influence model needs (and is) to be replaced by an interactive convergence model of information exchange. Information is seen as reducing uncertainty where choice exists among a set of alternatives.

7. The meaning of an innovation as perceived by potential adopters must be understood within a cultural context.

8. The model must reduce its static focus on person and organizational individual differences and increase the dynamic study of strategies and processes of change.

9. The effectiveness of highly centralized diffusion approaches need to be compared, where applicable, to more decentralized approaches.

10. The relationships of the interests, methods, and goals of diffusion to such fields as communications, consumer behavior, and social learning needs to be more fully developed.

WHAT IS DIFFUSION?

Diffusion is the process by which an innovation is communicated through certain channels over time among the members of a social system. It is a special type of communication in that the messages are concerned with new ideas. Communication is a process in which participants create and share information with one another in order to reach a mutual understanding. This definition implies that communication is a process of convergence (or divergence) as two or more individuals exchange information in order to move toward each other (or apart) in the meanings that they ascribe to certain events. (Rogers, 1983, p. 5)

One of the newer aspects of diffusion theory is conceptualizing and studying communication as a two-way process, rather than the more linear one-way models of persuasion (Rogers & Kincaid, 1981). One-way models fit more with highly centralized diffusion systems in which experts will create and provide new information to potential adopters. This approach was later modified (as was true in the more general communications model) to a "two-step" approach. In this model, mass media information could be conveyed to "opinion leaders," innovative people capable of informally influencing others. This is similar to a type of "trickle-down" approach.

However, these approaches were also seen as too simplistic. As the previous quote suggests, diffusion researchers recently started to study the interactions of a person with his or her social network as a way to understand why some people decide to adopt, and other reject, innovations (e.g., family planning; Rogers & Kincaid, 1981). The most succinct focus of diffusion is now on the processes of behavioral modeling by near-peers of innovations. One of the dangers of this new focus is downplaying, and even ignoring, instances where innovative behaviors appear more attributable to media than interpersonal processes.

The diffusion process can also be seen as a kind of social change. Alteration occurs in the structure and function of a social system when new ideas or products are invented, diffused, and are adopted or rejected. These actions lead to certain consequences and social change occurs. Thus, the analysis of the diffusion process can include these elements:

- The Innovation
- Communication Channels and Diffusion System
- The Decision Process and Adopters and Rejectors
- Consequences and the Spread of the Innovation Over Time
- Methods to Study These Processes

INNOVATIONS—INFORMATION

An innovation is an idea, practice, or object (product) that is perceived as new. This means that an innovation (e.g., nutritious diet) can be around for a long time, but what is critical is that it is new to some people. Recent and traditional study in diffusion research includes information aspects of innovations, characteristics of innovations, and "re-invention" of innovations.

Rogers discussed technological innovations that provide a means of action for achieving a desired outcome; prior to the innovation, uncertainty is seen as existing in affecting specific outcomes. Technology has two components. A hardware aspect embodies the technology in a material or physical way (e.g., computer circuitry). The software provides the information base for the tool (e.g., a computer program). Often innovations are almost entirely information and software. Examples here include new management techniques, a new philosophy of education, and diet and nutrition regimes.

The basic mechanism for seeking innovations entails identifying a problem, being uncertain how to solve it, and hence, being uncertain about new ideas or products apparently designed to solve the problem. Thus, according to Rogers (1983), the process is very similar to that described in chapter 7 for consumer information search: "the innovation decision process is essentially an information seeking and information processing activity in which the individual is motivated to reduce uncertainty about the advantages and disadvantages of the innovation" (p. 13).

In seeking information, an individual is likely to find out about software information (What are the elements of this diet?) and innovation evaluation information (Does this diet really work and what are its side effects?). The latter information will most often be sought from peers or local authorities.

A more recent addition to the paradigm is the notion of technology clusters. A *cluster* contains one or more distinguishable elements of technology that are perceived as being closely interrelated. Some change agencies may decide to promote a cluster or a package of innovations in the hope that innovations may be adopted more quickly this way. For example, in personal health change, it may be more effective to try at the same time to promote dietary, exercise, and stress management procedures. Obviously, this should be subject to empirical test. However, for some technology clusters, each innovation may be dependent on another one, or each may follow in a logical sequence. For example, acquiring a PC is a requisite for other home-based computer activities. Word processing capabilities then require a printer, and so on.

INNOVATIONS—CHARACTERISTICS

One tradition in diffusion research involves studying characteristics of innovations that may expedite or retard their diffusion. Rogers (1983) indicated that this type of study should be increased because the dominant research focus, i.e., person variable differences in adoption decision, has not been particularly productive:

> When one peruses the diffusion research literature, one may be impressed with how much effort has been expended in studying "people" differences in innovativeness . . . . and how little has been devoted to analyzing "innovation" differences.

The latter type of research can be of great value to change agents seeking to predict the reactions of their clients to an innovation, and perhaps to modify certain of these reactions by the way they name and position an innovation and relate the new idea to existing beliefs. (p. 210)

The prior quote should leave little doubt that diffusion and social marketing approaches are merging. Thus, more attention to the actual design and active diffusion of innovations is recommended. This objective fits nicely with the study of innovation characteristics. Rogers has tried to develop a set of trans-innovation characteristics as a means to standardize study. However, at this point, most of the research here is post-hoc and not prospective.

The five key characteristics that Rogers has identified are relative advantage, compatibility, complexity, trialability, and observability. Importantly, these are characteristics as perceived by the potential adopter.

Relative advantage is the degree that the innovation is perceived as better than the idea or product it supercedes. Typically, this has been thought of as economic advantage; however, many innovations have appeal on a status dimension (e.g., designer clothes). Also, the relative advantage of an innovation can change over time. For example, a pocket, four-function calculator bought in 1975 cost about $150. Today, a more complex calculator can be bought for less than $10, or even come as part of a $15 digital watch!

Relative advantage may be thought of as the rewards and punishments of an innovation. This is one reason (plus observability) why it is difficult to promote preventive innovations. The benefits are generally uncertain, and almost by definition, (may) occur sometime in the future. These problems with innovations may be overcome by offering incentives for adoption (and, perhaps, for continued implementation). The goal here is to get the initial 15% to 20% adoption rate quickly started. At that point, incentives may be discontinued as most diffusion curves (adoption over time) show rapid adoption after this point is reached. Incentives may also induce certain population segments, such as low income individuals to become early adopters, where this is not typically the case. Rogers recommended more empirical studies to aid policy on how incentives affect the rate of adoption, continuation, and consequences of innovations.

Compatibility is the consistency of the innovation with existing values, past experiences, and needs of potential adopters. Presumably, the more compatible an innovation is, the higher its rate of adoption, although Rogers noted that this characteristic may not be as important as relative advantage. Rogers recommended considerable positioning research to identify an ideal niche for an innovation to fill. It is important to find out from the perceptions of potential adopters how the innovation is similar to and different from existing ideas. The goal is to change the innovation's perceived characteristics to fit an ideal niche. "Positioning research puts the diffusion researcher into the role of designer (or at least co-designer) of innovations" (Rogers, 1983, p. 229).

Of critical importance is the innovation's name. Rogers noted that often this is given minimal thought. He cited examples in which lack of attention to the name and prevailing culture resulted in birth control devices in some countries to be given an obscene name, resulting in minimal adoption. Another more subtle example is from the author's work on energy conservation. Because of all the negative connotations of the term *energy conservation,* we replaced it with the term *energy efficiency* in many of our promotional materials and video programs.

The other characteristics, though important, may not be as critical as relative advantage and compatibility. *Complexity* means the perceived difficulty to understand or use an innovation and is negatively related to the rate of adoption. For example, personal computers (PC's) that appear to require extensive knowledge of computer languages should not have mass market appeal. *Trialability* means the ability to experience an innovation on a limited basis. Numerous free samples received in the mail are an example of attempts to exploit this dimension. *Observability* means the results are visible to the adopter and to others. This can be thought of as a feedback dimension. For example, newer exercise equipment (e.g., Life-Cycles) provide the user with continuous heart rate, caloric expenditure, and other performance-related information.

Rogers conjectures that these characteristics of innovations may account for a considerable amount of the variance explaining adoption. For some innovations the power of these design characteristics may be greater than how the innovation is communicated and promoted, and perhaps, of even more importance than personal and social system variables. This point emphasizes the need for considerable research on the design of innovations.

INNOVATIONS—REINVENTION

A new area in the study of innovations is the notion of reinvention. That is, people or organizations may modify an innovation to fit particular needs or circumstances. One reason this is a relatively new area is that much diffusion research only focused on the decision to adopt an innovation, not actual implementation. The research rarely indicated how the innovation was used and for how long.

With a new emphasis on implementation, it became apparent that many innovations were not being used in the way they had been designed. People had modified the innovation or put it to an unanticipated use. Rather than a failure of diffusion, this phenomenon suggests considerable success through an innovation's adaptability. Invaluable design information is lost when actual implementation is not tracked and instances of reinvention not fed back to the design process.

COMMUNICATION CHANNELS AND THE DIFFUSION SYSTEM

Communication channels are the means by which messages get from one individual to another. Most of Rogers' recent study has involved the nature of communication networks, and the place of an "adopter" or "rejecter" within that network. This is because Rogers holds to the idea that for most people mass media is used for information gathering, but actual adoption depends on information obtained through interpersonal channels. Rogers indicated that, except for the first adopters, most people do not use mass media information or scientific data (e.g., from *Consumer Reports*) to make a decision to adopt. They depend mostly on the subjective evaluations of people similar to themselves who have already adopted the innovation. "This dependence on the communication experience of near-peers suggests that the heart of the diffusion process is the modeling and imitation by potential adopters of their network partners who have adopted previously" (Rogers, 1983, p. 18). This is an important quote that indicates integrations of diffusion and social learning theory, a point that is addressed later in detail.

To return to the first point, ascertaining the major source of influence for adoption decisions requires more thorough review of communication channels. Rogers traced the history of the development of communication models (see chapter 1) from the "hypodermic needle" model to various 2-step flow models, of which diffusion theory is one example. The usual notion of 2-step models was that mass media informed certain innovators or "opinion leaders" who, in turn, influenced others through interpersonal means. However, Rogers noted that most 2-step models are simplistic. Some people are directly influenced by the mass media; for others, there may be a combination of media and interpersonal influences. The degree of influence also may depend on the source (and its credibility) and what part of the adoption decision process (e.g., knowledge or persuasion) is being addressed.

As important source variable that can be examined in mass media and interpersonal channels is the degree of homophily (similarity) or heterophily (difference) of the source with the potential receiver. For example, in TV commericals there are, at times, attempts to have characters and settings similar to the target population segment, presumably to enhance receiver identification and modeling. However, some commericals use celebrities for other purposes, i.e., association of a name and status with a product—and similar purposes to the prior example—to enhance modeling by high status individuals. Comparative evaluations of ads using similar versus high status models have rarely been done.

These ideas seem better developed for interpersonal communications. We are more likely to communicate with people similar to ourselves. However, this can be a barrier to diffusion in that similar people, interacting with the same or similar people, may have little new information to communicate. Hetrophilic communications may be crucial for diffusion to occur. For example, an ideal diffusion path may entail two somewhat similar individuals whose major communications occur with two different cliques in a larger network, are from different networks, or who act to span different cliques or networks.

Research interest has been growing in the nature of hetrophilic communications. Some of this interest was spurred by Granovetter's (1973) research on how individuals obtained jobs. He found that homophilic individuals, and/or those who frequently communicated together, often had the same job information. Functional job information often required stepping one or two communication links beyond the initial contact, e.g., ''I don't have any new information for you about jobs. But, I remember last night this guy at the gym said his friend is looking for sales people.'' Granovetter coined the classic term, *strength-of-weak ties* to describe the value of such information flows.

Considerable research has also focused on opinion leaders, people who can informally influence others' attitudes and behaviors. Initial research, predictably, focused on the characteristics of opinion leaders. They were shown to have more exposure to mass media and new ideas; to be more accessible to face-to-face contact with others to spread ideas; to have a higher SES than their followers, and when a social system favored innovation, they were more innovative (an opinion leader in a traditional or conservative system would *not* favor innovation).

The further study of opinion leaders received lasting impetus from the Coleman et al. (1966) study of the diffusion of a new drug. The attention to objective measures of adoption and use (through prescription records) and adopting and rejecting doctors' connectedness to their social (professional) system (e.g., percent of meetings attended at hospital staff meetings) yielded methodology and results that are exemplary models for research. Sadly, these procedures and data sources are still not that common in diffusion research. The network connectedness ''links,'' not individual variables, proved to be good predictors of adoption and use. ''It seemed that the 'between people' variables were more important than the 'within' people variables'' (Rogers, 1983, p. 291). The most connected individuals were early adopters and opinion leaders who influenced other doctors to use the new drug.

For Rogers, the Coleman et al. (1966) study and subsequent research means that because modeling by potential adopters of their near-peers who have already adopted is the core of diffusion, there is a need to study interpersonal networks. Such study (Rogers & Kincaid, 1981) includes the structure and stability of networks, the nature of links, cliques, and so on. These investigations have been aided by computer programs capable of integrating the elaborate data used for network analysis. Some of these network variables appear related to adoption and are discussed later.

TABLE 3.1
Similarities and Differences Between Social Learning and Diffusion

Similarities	*Differences*
1. Focus on behavior change	1. Diffusion measurement is aggregate
2. Interpersonal networks and links critical to behavior change	2. Social learning measurement is micro
3. Information exchange is essential to behavior change	3. Diffusion research is mostly field/survey
4. Re-invention, not mimicking, is process	4. Social learning research is mostly lab/experimental
5. Moving away from linear models	

If modeling is the core of diffusion, it can be argued that more must be known about message content, actual demonstration, and subsequent observer behavior. Such study could focus on other key elements of effective information as shown in Table 1.3 of the introductory chapter. Diffusion research generally has not followed these points, nor attempted to collect fine-grain behavioral data. The primary data used in the Rogers and Kincaid (1981) network analyses to explain adoption of family planning consisted of retrospective general accounts of interactions between study participants. Often such accounts are not very accurate (Rogers & Kincaid, 1981, pp. 96–122) and fail to tell us what actually occurred.

To Rogers' credit, he recognized this limitation of the diffusion research and called for integrations with social learning theory. He noted two overriding similarities between social learning and diffusion theory: (a) both theories look *outside* the individual at information on exchanges to explain behavior change; (b) modeling, a key element in behavior change, is not seen as imitation, but similar to re-invention; modeling is a product of interpersonal networks and mass media (particularly visual media).

Table 3.1 summarizes these, and other, similarities and differences.

An integration of these approaches has much to offer. Diffusion research can become more experimental and fine-grain. Social learning can gain a more social system and time dimension perspective, and perhaps, focus on more varied issues and behaviors than has been true in the past. These points are further elaborated on later.

CHANGE AGENTS

A discussion of communication channels and diffusion systems would be incomplete without some review of the literature on change agents. As opposed to an opinion leader, whose influence may be more informal, a change agent (teacher, salespeople, consultant, extension agent) tries to directly influence people in the desired direction of the change agency. In the traditional extension model, change agencies are composed of scientific, technical, and administrative experts. What is needed is a way to link up to the client system (farmers, regular teachers, certain population segments) to convey information about innovations and receive feedback about the use of the innovation.

This process may require a sequence of change agent roles including: (a) developing a need for change in the client system; (b) establishing an information exchange relationship; (c) diagnosing problems; (d) creating intentions to change; (e) translating intentions into action; (f) stabilizing adoption and preventing discontinuances; and (g) achieving a terminal relationship so that clients can repeat this process for another innovation on their own.

One major problem for change agents involves the homophilic–hetrophilic dimension. As change agents receive more technical training, and perhaps, identify more with professionals in the change agency, the social and economic differences between the change agents and the client system increases. Increased hetrophily decreases the probability of effective information exchange. Two strategies have emerged in light of this problem: paraprofessionals and use of opinion leaders. As in other fields (e.g., Durlack, 1979), there is increased use of paraprofessional aids and paraprofessionals doing most of the face-to-face contact and intervention. A legendary example of the extensive use of paraprofessionals is China's "barefoot doctors." Individuals receive limited training on basic health care and medicine for periods as short as 6 months. The goal, which apparently has been achieved, is to provide enough technical ability to impact health but without many professional trappings that could distance the barefoot doctors from their patients. "One of the most important lessons learned from the barefoot doctors in China is the great importance of change agent-client homophily in contributing to the safety (trustworthy) credibility with which clients perceive the change agent" (Rogers, 1983, p. 328).

A second strategy to reduce hetrophily is for change agents to work through opinion leaders. For example, a change agent may persuade one influential family to adopt new health methods and to then persuade their peers to use the same methods. Although this is a highly recommended approach, it has two pitfalls. Change agents may overuse opinion leaders as far as promoting one or more innovations too extensively. For example, when the author worked with a group of teachers in a service/research capacity, he overused one influential teacher by having her show and recommend too many innovative approaches at one time. A second problem is that by working closely with the change agent, the opinion leader may become too much like the change agent, thus, increasing distance between the opinion leader and the client system. This also happened with the same teacher. She quickly became enamored with our elaborate data collection system and the research process. Neither interest was prominent for the other teachers, and thus, our opinion leader further removed herself from her peer group.

A final strategy to circumvent these problems that is being investigated is more decentralized approaches to diffusion. Such approaches may be optimal for less technical innovations and may not require a hierarchical diffusion organization. However, if there is one overriding conclusion from the discussion of communication channels, it is this: Diffusion theory has provided a broad overlay of the process. It is time to perform more fine-grain studies to more fully understand critical behavior change mechanisms.

INNOVATION DECISION PROCESS

Rogers' schema for the innovation diffusion process follows a typical ''hierarchy of effects'' model. Many of the problems of that model previously discussed are only briefly noted here. The decision process is broken in a 5-part sequence: knowledge, persuasion, decision, implementation, and confirmation. Over time, a series of actions and choices are made about whether to incorporate the innovation into ongoing practices. It is the perceived newness of the innovation and uncertainty about its characteristics and performance that makes this a special decision process.

Rogers pointed out problems or special concerns at each point in the process. In the knowledge stage, there is the problem of selective exposure. That is, people generally will only expose themselves to information consistent with their attitudes, beliefs, and needs. This point suggests gearing information content and style to particular population segments. It also suggests that for many innovations, the innovator must first create the need for the innovation so that information is salient.

Rogers also indicated a knowledge sequence. The first information might note what the innovation is, how it works, and how it is used. Later, people may have some interest in the innovation's underlying mechanisms. However, Rogers noted that many change agents may spend too much time on information exchange that may be more easily done by mass media.

The persuasion stage in this model focuses on attitude formation and change. However, this may not be a simple linear process. The attitudes that are formed may or may not be the same as the source's. Selective exposure to information, evaluative information from peers, and the perceived attributes of the innovation are critical and may lead to nonintended attitudes. Rogers is well aware that attitudes can be discrepant with adoption behaviors. For example, a number of family planning campaigns have led to favorable attitudes toward contraceptives, but for a variety of reasons, limited actual use. Rogers noted that there is often a need for cues-to-action to propel a person from attitude to behavior change.

Examples for contraceptives are incentives for use, or news of pregnancy, abortion, or birth complications.

In the decision stage, the innovation is adopted or rejected. The decision may be greatly influenced by the behavior of peers and free-trial opportunities. It is probably here that diffusion research truly breaks down. Much of the research has ended at the decision process sequence with a verbal report about the decision to adopt or reject. Further, given the pro-innovation bias of much diffusion research, it is not surprising that there are few studies of the rejection process.

Rogers (1983) is quick to admit this deficiency in the model and research: "It is often one thing for the individual to decide to adopt a new idea, and quite a different thing to put the innovation into use" (p. 174). The innovation may not be available or be used correctly. Thus, Rogers urged more attention and research to the implementation stage. For example, it is here that change agents may best use face-to-face contact for technical assistance. It is also important in research studies to carefully monitor implementation behavior and thoroughly understand the process of reinvention.

Consistent with the emphasis on studying actual behavior, Rogers noted another critical research area where there are few studies. Tracking must continue past the early implementation stage to the confirmation stage. This is particularly true because there is ready evidence for discontinuance of an innovation after initial implemention (e.g., diet and exercise habits). Two types of discontinuance were identified: *replacement* and *disenchantment*. The latter term suggests virtually total discontinuation of interest in a set of practices. Again, the pro-innovation bias may, in part, explain the limited focus on discontinuance.

Another new concern that also demonstrates movement away from the pro-innovation bias is the start of the study of forced discontinuance of former innovations. For example, pesticides and other chemicals were heavily promoted in the 1950s and 1960s as a way for farmers to increase productivity. Some of these pesticides are now banned, or are being replaced, as a result of their environmental impacts. Key questions are what effects does forced discontinuation have on the credibility of the diffusion agency, faith in research and science, and adoption of other innovations?

Rogers (1983) noted that the diffusion model has changed so that consequences of innovations are seriously addressed: "Every innovation produces social and economic reactions that run through the social structure of the client system" (Rogers, 1983, p. 372). He further stated:

Innovativeness, the main dependent variable in past research, now becomes only a predictor of a more ultimate dependent variable, consequences of innovation. This new model seeks to explain consequences, a research goal that is closer to the objectives of most change agencies. They usually want to bring about desirable consequences among their clients, not simply the adoption of innovations per se. (p. 375)

Recall that most diffusion research ended with the "decision to adopt" variable so that actual implementation and consequences were never observed. Rogers is now searching for a classification system for individual and system consequences including desirable and undesirable effects, anticipated and unanticipated (not intended or first recognized) effects, and direct and indirect effects. An example for the last category is the automobile. Direct effects included convenient, rapid, personal transportation; indirect (and undesirable and unanticipated) effects included deterioration of inner cities, the rapid growth of suburbs, increased congestion, and air pollution (Brown, Flavin, & Norman, 1979). One reason that nonplanned and often negative consequences result from an innovation is that although innovators can often anticipate the form and function of an innovation, the meaning of an innovation within a culture is usually not anticipated. For example, it is doubtful that the original inventors of cars foresaw that each car would be seen as a reflection of the owner's image and persona.

Of prime interest to Rogers is another system level variable—how innovations promote increased or decreased equality. It may be the case that technical innovations can lead to more inequality. For example, this is one of the many issues in the rapid proliferation of computers (see chapter 5). Those who are less educated and poorer now will be left further behind if they remain computer illiterate. To avoid increased inequality, Rogers recommended a segmentation strategy so that messages and programs may be directed more to those less likely to respond to innovations. He also suggested that change agents attend more to "late adopters" and "laggards," rather than an easier audience such as "early adopters."

In order to properly study consequences, Rogers (1983) states: "a long-range research approach must be taken in which consequences are analyzed as they unfold over time. Otherwise, the consequences of an innovation can be neither properly assessed nor predicted" (p. 372).

Innovation Decisions in Organizations

Another new emphasis in diffusion theory, and particularly in studying the decision phase, is the realization that many innovations that are adopted are done so within organizational settings. Much prior diffusion research focused on individual decisions for individual adoption. In organizations, adoption decisions are more likely to be collective or authoritative. In order to understand innovation in organizations, researchers studied "innovative" and "non-innovative" organizations, much as they had studied person differences in innovation. The results here seem to be equally non-illuminating. Research focusing on some aspects of organizational structure, distribution of power, formalization within the organization, rules, roles, ranks, and the division of labor does show some promise.

However, Rogers once again urged movement away from a static, cross-sectional research model, toward the dynamic study of the change process in organizations. He presented a two-phase innovation model for organizations. The initiation stage includes agenda setting (what's important) and matching, i.e., fitting an innovation to organizational problems. The implementation stage includes redefining and restructuring, i.e., modifying the innovation and/or the organizational structure, clarifying (which is a continuation of this process) and routinizing. As of now, though, there are few organizational studies following this model.

These points in the decision process indicate that diffusion theory and research is headed in directions consistent with this book, such as more focus on the processes of long-term behavior change. In turn, diffusion theory can provide more psychologically-based frameworks with a greater focus on social systems and environmental impact.

TIME DIMENSION

The time dimension is the prominent aspect of diffusion and this dimension has been noted in the discussion of communication channels, the decision process, and consequences. Other types of diffusion research related to time include extensive study of categories of people (innovators, early adopters, etc.) as to when they adopt an innovation, and studies of the spread of diffusion, generally through retrospective reports of the date of adoption. It is ironical that research largely interested in time has primarily used time-bound research methods, such as surveys conducted at one point in time! Rogers is well-aware of this inconsistency and has included in his book considerable criticisms of prevailing research methods in diffusion. It is to this subject that we now turn.

RESEARCH METHODS

One of the ironic pitfalls of contemporary diffusion research is traceable to its own highly auspicious beginnings and diffusion. Ryan and Gross (1943) studied the diffusion of hybrid corn. This innovation spread rapidly and was highly beneficial to individual farmers and the country (it raised productivity by about 20%). The early study examined individual variables related to innovativeness, attributers of the innovation, and role of different communication channels, and the rate of adoption. The effects were so positive that the evaluation of long-term consequences was not done. The study relatively and rapidly diffused and many subsequent researchers did *not* model the study—they mimicked it. States Rogers (1983):

> the Ryan and Gross hybrid corn study also established a prototypical methodology for going about a diffusion investigation: one-shot survey interviews with the

adopters of an innovation who were asked to recall their behavior and decisions regarding the innovation. Thus, the typical research design for studying diffusion was established in 1941. It has lived on with only rare and minor modifications to the present day. The alternative methodological paths that were not taken by diffusion scholars represent a shortcoming in the field today. (p. 56)

Throughout his book, Rogers suggested that diffusion researchers turn to field experiments or longitudinal panel studies. Endemic to this methodology is a more active stance than simply retrospective accounts of the diffusion process. It is likely that much could be expeditiously learned by field experiments that evaluate contrasting diffusion processes. Models for such research are available in psychology, public health, and marketing (Fairweather & Tornatzky, 1977).

Such studies, though, must move away from the reliance on self-report, another major deficiency of diffusion research. For example, in Rogers and Kincaid (1981), there is a section that details the reliability and validity of retrospective self-reports. The kindest synopsis is that often such self-reports are not very reliable (people say different things at different times or places) or valid (do not accurately reflect reality). In most research paradigms, once basic data is of questionable reliability and validity, what follows is presented in a highly guarded way, or dismissed. However, in Rogers and Kincaid, even after this was pointed out, we are still presented with an elaborate study using computer network analysis, primarily based on such data. Is this a classic case of GIGO?

It is clear that retrospective self-reports have to be replaced by ongoing reports and preferably ongoing observations of the use of innovations and unobstrusive measures. Rogers (1983) readily admits these problems:

> One weakness of diffusion research is its dependence upon recall data from respondents as to their date of adoption of a new idea. . . . This hindsight ability is clearly not completely accurate. . . . Diffusion research designs consist mainly of correlational analyses of cross-sectional data gathered in one-shot surveys of respondents . . . a methodology that amounts to making the diffusion process "timeless". . . . Survey research is intellectually destructive of the "process" aspect of the diffusion of innovations. If data about a diffusion process are only gathered at one point in time, the investigator can only measure time through respondents' recall, and that is a rather weak reed on which to base the measurement of such an important variable as time. (p. 113)

These points call for more linkages between diffusion researchers and those researchers with a behavioral system's approach. However, aside from methodological traditions that may be in need of an overhaul, there are certain long-term biases in diffusion research that need to be addressed. One is the pro-innovation bias that is now being tackled by some diffusion researchers who emphasize caution in adoption of technology, or even nonadoption (e.g., where technology can dismantle traditional societies), and the careful study of consequences. However, another bias in the research concerns the acceptance of the prevailing communication's paradigm that mass media primarily produces only some information change and that interpersonal communication networks are the essential focus for most information, attitude, and behavior change.

It has been argued here that visual media, in particular (chapter 2), can be reasonably effective for behavior change. Next, a case is made where media seems (at the least) partially responsible for behavior change, yet diffusion researchers interpret the basis of change much more along the lines of interpersonal networks.

DEFUSING THE CURRENT DIFFUSION PARADIGM

It is the contention here that diffusion scholars are beginning to err by over-emphasizing complexity, systems models, and interpersonal processes. This is not said to promote a return to simplistic mechanistic positions, but rather to make the point that aspects of some phenomena may be approached from a more linear perspective. In the example that comes directly from Rogers and Kincaid (1981, chapter 6), a case will be made that mass media exposure, particularly exposure to television, appeared to explain far more variance for information, attitude, and behavior change than interpersonal networks. Indeed, it appeared that the data supported the well-known 2-step communication behavior change models.

The data for Rogers' investigation was derived from a study of the adoption of family planning innovations in Korea during the late 1960s and early 1970s. The main vehicle of this government supported effort was Mothers Clubs that were organized in many villages so as to use existing networks of interpersonal communication and local leadership. Mothers Clubs could also distribute oral contraceptives, and each township was provided with a field worker responsible for about 50 to 60 villages.

The Mothers Clubs were small, limited to about 12 women, and the initial membership tended to be better educated and a bit older than the typical mother of child-bearing age. The role of the Mothers Club included information giving, encouragement, support and reinforcement, distribution of oral contraceptives, recruitment of new members, and involvement in community development activities. Rogers and Kincaid (1981) reported:

> The basic idea of Mothers' Clubs was to facilitate interpersonal communication about family planning at the village level and to legitimize the practice of family planning among village women. In short, the promotion of Mothers' Clubs was an intervention in the communication structure of Korean Villages. (p. 261)

The Mothers' Clubs were apparently successful and were given credit for the adoption of family planning and the reduction of fertility. However, it was not clear *how* these clubs were successful. What was the relationship of the clubs to family planning communication networks in the village? What were the relationships between structural aspects of the villager, the clubs, communication networks and information, attitude, and behavior change? What kind of network variables were most important?

The overall study was based on interviews with over 1,000 women from 24 villages that were representative of the many villages (about 23,000) in Korea involved in this program. Rogers and Kincaid's major approach in their study was to use retrospective accounts of verbal interactions about family planning so as to recreate communication networks and primarily relate village-level, mass media, club, and network variables to information, attitude, and behavior (self-report) indices of family planning. The approach is regression, and as with any correlational technique, tells us something about relationships but not causality.

Problems began for this author when Rogers sought to give the reader a more in-depth and first cut of the data by providing detail from two villages. At the outset, Rogers indicated that the two villages were extremely different across geographic, economic, and cultural dimensions. For example, one village (*A*) could be described as more urban-oriented, more prosperous and less traditional than the other (*B*). These differences alone should make any comparisons about the effectiveness of Mothers Clubs attributable to other variables highly questionable. This problem is confounded by an exemplar table used to illustrate further differences in the two villages and is shown in Table 3.2 in modified form.

Village *A* was the more urban, prosperous, and less traditional village and had about double the reported rate of adoption of family planning. Some differences between the Mothers Clubs are also noted in the table. Note, however, two other striking differences between the villages: TV ownership (23% vs. 3%) and exposure to family planning through TV (96% vs. 10%). Indeed, in their description of Village *A*, Rogers and Kincaid (1981) noted that its prosperity ''is evident to a visitor by the numerous television antennas sprouting over village rooftops'' (p. 263–264). Note also that ownership of radios and exposure to family planning through other media is about the same in the two villages. However, it appears for the subsequent analyses of the data for the 24 villages (of which the comparison of Village *A* and *B* is illustrative), exposure to family planning via TV was combined with exposure through other media to yield one variable, mass media exposure. If, in fact, data from Village *A* and *B* are illustrative, then *not* using TV exposure alone as a predictor variable seems to be a mistake.

Even with use of the one variable, mass media exposure, media seems more influential for information, attitude, and behavior change than network variables. In the subsequent analyses of the data from the 24 villages, the following types of variables were used: village (e.g., mass media family planning exposure, economic level); club (e.g., membership rate, activities); club leader (e.g., training, influence); communication network (e.g., connectedness, overlap between com-

TABLE 3.2
Exemplar Table Illustrating Differences Between Two Villages*

Variables	Village A	Village B
Contraception		
Percentage of married women of reproductive age that have adopted family planning	57	26
Mass Media Ownership		
Percentage owning a radio	85	97
Percentage owning a TV	23	3
Mass Media Exposure To Family Planning (percentage)		
Through radio	87	90
Through newspapers	31	18
Through magazines	36	23
Through posters	69	54
(Mean exposure)	56	46
Through television	96	10
Mothers Club		
Date founded	1968	1971
Funds in club's credit union	$300	$175
Club leader received official training	yes	no
Attendance of field workers at meetings	Regular	1–2 times per year

*Adapted from Rogers and Kincaid (1981) Table 6-1, p. 263.

munication and family planning networks); family planning (e.g., average knowledge, adoption rate).

A first analysis was presented that showed the intercorrelation of network variables. Next, the relationships between network variables and knowledge/attitudes and adoption was depicted. Here, key variables appeared to explain 24% of the variance for knowledge/attitudes (network overlap and leader's expertise) and 52% of the variance for adoption (overlap and leader's network connectedness).

In a third analysis, village variables and selected communication network variables, also measured at the village level (the prior analysis used network variables at the leader and club level), were examined as predictors of knowledge/attitudes and adoption rate. A partial list of these results is shown in Table 3.3.

Table 3.3 suggests that although some network and other village variables are related to knowledge/attitudes and adoption, media exposure seems more important.

Rogers' next analyses focused on club variables and club leader variables. For club variables, club members network homophily (extent club members interact with other club members and nonmembers interact with other nonmembers) correlated .35 with knowledge/attitudes and explained 12% of the variance.

TABLE 3.3
Village Characteristics and Their Relationship to Knowledge/Attitude
and Adoption*

Variables	Knowledge/Attitude		Adoption Rate	
	r	R^{2a}	r	R^{2a}
Mass media exposure	.66	44	.51	26
Network overlap	.19	2	.51	16
Connectedness	.38	0.2	.40	12
Economic level	.53	16	.09	0.6
Advice index [+]	.30	10	.25	—

*Adapted from Rogers and Kincaid (1981) Table 6-5, p. 275
[a]Percent increase in variance explained
[+] Percent positive advice exchanged across network links

Field worker visits to the club ($r = .48$) and club membership rate ($r = .09$) together explained about 39% of the variance for adoption. For club leader variables, the leader's family planning credibility was highly related ($r = .59$) to knowledge/attitudes and explained about 35% of the variance. Leader's family planning network connectedness ($r = .50$), training ($r = .41$), and prestige ($r = .44$) together explained 57% of the variance for adoption.

In a final analysis, all the network and non-network variables were entered into a stepwise regression analysis to determine which independent variables were most important in explaining the two dependent variables. Table 3.4 shows the results of that analysis.

TABLE 3.4
Relationship of Key Independent Variables to Family Planning*

Independent Variables	Type	Knowledge/ Attitude		Adoption	
		r	R^2	r	R^2
Mass media exposure	Village	.66	44	.51	26
Economic situation	Village	.53	9	—	—
Leader's family planning network connectedness	Network	X	X	.50	23
Network overlap	Network	X	X	.51	17
Family planning network connectedness	Network	.23	8	—	—
Field worker visits	Club	X	X	.48	9
Leader's family planning credibility	Leader	.59	8	X	X

*Adapted from Rogers and Kincaid (1981), Table 6-8, p. 280
[X] Only data for four best predictors were given

The results of this analysis fit within Rogers' prior 2-step model of adoption of innovations (Rogers & Shoemaker, 1971). That is, mass media seems particularly important for knowledge and attitude change and in concert with change agent behavior (field worker visits) and interpersonal processes, these information and persuasion sources influence behavior change. There does not appear to be anything unusual in these data, although it would appear fruitful to examine the effects of TV exposure alone. What is useful in the analyses is a more definitive approach to examining interpersonal processes, something not done before in prior research. Of course, such a fine-grain approach to media exposure might also be illuminating.

It is argued here that Rogers and Kincaid took the results shown in Table 3.4 and overemphasized the importance of network variables. After reviewing the results shown in that table, they indicated that the connectedness of the village family planning communication network was highly related to the club variables of membership rate and educational diversity. Higher club membership and more similar educational levels were predictive of connectedness.

Rogers and Kincaid (1981) stated that:

> the organization of village women in Mothers Clubs has an important impact on the communication structure of the village. The connectedness of the family planning network, network overlap, the amount of positive family planning advice, the homophily of network links, and the leader's opinion leadership are all affected by Mothers Club variables. These five network variables, in turn, are substantially related to the rate of adoption of family planning innovations. The structure of the village communication network intervenes between the Mothers Club variables and the rate of adoption of family planning innovations. The most important effects of the Mothers Club on family planning adoption are indirect, operating through their direct effects on village communication networks. . . . the Mothers' Club program has achieved one of its primary objectives (by) the utilization of interpersonal communication networks in villages to promote family planning. *Thus, the formation of groups within systems is an effective intervention in changing the communication structure of the systems.* (p. 281)

Rogers and Kincaid diagrammed (p. 281) their main conclusions as:

Mothers' Club ⟶ Communication ⟶ Adoption of family
activities   network structure   planning innovations

The use of arrows, *implying* causality (and linearity), seems to be a tenuous step to take with correlational data. However, this diagram does not appear to best represent the data as presented here. A better diagram appears to be the following:

Mass media ⟷ Mothers' Club ⟷ Communication ⟷ Adoption of family
activities   network structure   planning innovations

This diagram shows mass media as a "potential trigger" for the other levels of behavior change. However, any level of activity can influence another level (e.g., village communication network influencing adoption). The two-way arrows also show better reciprocal influence than the one-way arrows. For example, word of adoption of family planning can spread back to the Mothers Club, in turn influencing their mass media exposure. Thus, in this schema, arrows represent relationships and influence, but not linear causality.

Again, it might be stated that fine-grain analyses of interpersonal communication are laudatory. However, such efforts may best be done without ignoring what appear to be other, perhaps, antecedent events and interactions. Finally, it is also apparent that if the researcher decides to pursue such fine-grain analyses, then the data on which the analyses are based must be more detailed and of known reliability and validity.

INTEGRATIONS OF DIFFUSION AND BEHAVIORAL SYSTEMS APPROACHES

Throughout this chapter, it has been noted that there appears to be a number of areas for fruitful integrations between diffusion and behavioral systems approaches. Because to this point, the chapter has focused more on the deficiencies of diffusion theory and research, it appears more appropriate to focus here on what behavioral systems can gain from diffusion research.

Except for the focus on new ideas, products, or techniques, diffusion theory and research appears subsumable under other broader fields. Social marketing (chapter 4) and consumer behavior (chapter 7), fields that are also closely related, can fit this purpose. Indeed, texts in either field often have a chapter or section on diffusion (e.g., Engel & Blackwell, 1982). Another possibility is for diffusion research to be a somewhat special study in the larger field of communications. The Rogers and Kincaid book is clearly trying to do this by offering a new paradigm for communcation research. Basically, they advocate a systems perspective and an actual focus on communication processes, e.g., the study of networks.

Diffusion research can profit by closer association with these fields. For example, from the study of consumer behavior come more inputs concerning information processing. Social marketing has most of the same interests as diffusion research. These similarities are becoming more and more apparent. Examples here include the awareness by diffusion researchers of the need to consider design and positioning issues. Indeed, diffusion and social marketing are becoming interchangable fields, but with one important exception. Diffusion researchers are becoming more concerned with value and negative side effects of innovations whereas social marketers have not shed their promotion bias. Finally, the overall communications field has much to offer to diffusion efforts. For example, Rogers' review of media effects in his two recent books (Rogers, 1983;

Rogers & Kincaid, 1981) does not incorporate some of the perspectives and data from prosocial television and the advent of new media. Fine-grain analyses of media are needed to complement the fine-grain analyses of interpersonal processes.

The overall behavioral systems approach also has much to gain from diffusion. Note that behavioral systems is a general framework whereas diffusion started as a specific area of study. Diffusion researchers borrowed ideas and methods from a number of fields (but, mostly sociology), and now are developing a more coherent approach. Thus, one (diffusion) started from a more specific focus and is now becoming more general, whereas the other (behavioral systems) is a general framework that needs more specific development of a number of its elements.

Table 3.5 summarizes some of the major commonalities and differences between diffusion and behavioral systems. The reader may also want to review Table 3.1 which noted some of the same points in comparing diffusion and social learning models. Because much has already been said about what diffusion concepts and research can gain from social learning and behavioral systems, the discussion here is what can behavioral systems gain from diffusion?

Diffusion research is beginning to articulate critical network and other social, physical, and economic variables that influence human behavior. It is beginning to accomplish this in a fine-grain manner that is highly compatible with and needed for a behavioral systems approach. With some exceptions (e.g., Wahler & Fox, 1981), this step has not been done by us. Multilevel influences are often noted without actually defining, and then researching what they are and how they function. This part of our approach remains vague and unsophisticated. We have, for the most part, been thinking about and examining static structures and systems and not functional relationships of dynamic system-level processes. Perhaps this point best reflects, at this time, that behavioral systems is actually a contextual framework.

Some other points are less technical and more value-laden. Rogers traced a number of innovations that have had decidely negative and largely unanticipated side effects. The study of innovation consequences will probably become a major research area. This work has given diffusion researchers serious pause about spreading every new wonder and modern technology. It has given diffusion researchers more respect for understanding culture and fully assessing a range of impacts within a culture before promoting an innovation. Diffusion researchers also have come to understand that the idea of ready "technical fixes" to complex problems is decidely an American approach that is now subject to serious debate (see discussion of these points in chapter 5 on New Media).

Only recently have psychologists, particularly of a behavioral persuasion, begun to voice some of the same issues and concerns. Willems' (1974) landmark paper describing integrations of ecological and behavioral approaches started to spur more system-like thinking and consideration of "side effects" (e.g.,

TABLE 3.5
Commonalities and Differences Between Diffusion and Behavioral
Systems Paradigm

Dimension	Diffusion	Behavioral Systems
1. Level of analysis	Multilevel and starting analyses of networks	Multilevel but more on individual variables
2. Social, economic change	Exclusively proinnovation, until recently	Exclusively reformist until recently
3. Roots	Rural sociology, sociology	Psychology
4. Focus	Innovations as perceived by potential adopters	Any behavior change
5. System aspect	Emerging notion of person-network interactions	Mostly, contextual
6. Stance	Post hoc, passive, until recently	Active intervention, but now more assessment
7. Hierarchy of effects	Focus more on information and attitude change	Focus more on behavior change
8. Methods	Post hoc surveys, correlation studies; few experiments	Field experiments, few surveys and correlation studies
9. Data	Mostly aggregate rates of decision to adopt but starting network analyses	Fine-grain analysis of some processes and responses
10. Social marketing	Becoming synonymous with social marketing	Social marketing as a framework
11. Consequences	Forced recently to study unanticipated outcomes	Forced recently to study unanticipated outcomes

Rogers-Warren & Warren, 1977). With some exceptions (e.g., Wahler & Graves, 1983), these points, central to the ecological viewpoint, remain only minor considerations in behavioral research. For example, although publication in some areas such as reduction of health risk behaviors requires demonstration of long-term outcome, there is no similar requirement to assess various side effects as may be done with more medical interventions.

Closely related to this issue is the failure to come to grips with the fact that many behavioral interventions have been done without knowledge of the complexity of problems (Willems, 1974), i.e., without system assessments, and have yielded no positive effects, or worse, negative effects. It is only recently that psychologists have begun to publicly trace how uniquely American behavioral psychology is (Sarason, 1981; Wolfolk & Richardson, 1984). In not discerning the linkages with prevailing American culture, psychologists have not understood the roots of their scientific and "fix-it" mentality. Some issues may best be left unexplored for a time, and some problems not intervened with until more is understood (Sarason, 1981). Perhaps this is an un-American position but one that can become prominent as the side effects of modern technology, such as toxic wastes, become more and more salient.

Thus, it is undoubtedly true that adoption of the behavioral systems framework can make diffusion research more active. more sophisticated, and more appreciative of psychological processes such as modeling. A behavioral systems framework can start more true system conceptualization and investigation by incorporating some of the concepts and methods from diffusion research. The study of networks within the behavioral systems approach is one example that has started to develop (Wahler & Graves, 1983). Perhaps a larger contribution from diffusion research is the lesson learned from not respecting culture and the ecology, and from innovation leading to destruction. The need is for caution and analysis to proceed prudent action.

4

Social Marketing: Ethics, Concepts, Methods, Strategies, and Applications

Social marketing has two special places in the study of information, behavior, and systems of influence. First, social marketing can be conceptualized as a set of flexible, information feedback strategies for solving problems (Novelli, 1984). Second, social marketing is becoming accepted as an essential, overarching framework for virtually any endeavor entailing change in human behavior. Thus, the delineation of this framework and its processes, methods, strategies, and applications is very central to the purposes of this book.

This chapter is more comprehensive than the prior chapter on diffusion. However, there is no attempt to review every recent article or book; rather, the chapter revolves around a few well-known sources. In addition to the attention to methods, strategies, and applications, considerable time is spent discussing problems and issues and the future directions of social marketing. Also a personal introduction focusing on the author's exposure, shunning, reexposure, and embrace of social marketing is of interest to behavioral scientists not that familiar with social marketing.

PERSONAL EXPERIENCES

The author's experiences with social marketing can be construed as a process in the adoption of an innovation, but a process that followed a somewhat irregular, although perhaps, typical course. This course can be described as a felt need, exposure, rejection, refelt need, reexposure, trial, initial adoption, and final adoption.

After a decade of doing many school, organizational, and community-based, behavioral intervention projects, it was apparent that some of these projects were very successful, whereas others were failures. This categorization does not necessarily directly correspond to the strength of the intervention, i.e., amount of behavior change. Some projects that resulted in reasonable change were poorly received by project participants and required enormous effort by the author and project staff to be successful. Success that requires a tremendous degree of effort, probably never to be duplicated by anyone else, at the least, requires examination on the scientific grounds of external validity.

Other projects seemed to require some "hit or miss" tactics until a viable approach was found. For example, as a graduate student, I remember that great effort was expended on securing radio spots announcing the start-up of my smoking cessation projects. Only a few people responded to these ads. Detailed credible, newspaper stories quickly resulted in many people inquiring about the project. Other approaches to participant recruitment were developed based on these experiences, and they often were very successful. Sometimes recruitment involved door-to-door personal contact, and other times they entailed meetings at work sites on work time. Although methods of recruitment were being developed, the techniques were almost too empirical and not tied to any larger framework (Winett, Neale, & Williams, 1979).

Other projects and services were simply offered to the public in what can be called a *seller* or *product mentality*. That is, the program was such a wonderful idea that it should create its own demand. The best way to summarize the results of some of these offerings is: "What if you gave a party, and nobody came?" Literally, some programs, and workshops for example, designed for 40 people were attended by 4 people.

At this point, a colleague, Dr. M. J. Sirgy from the Department of Marketing, attempted to introduce the author and other psychologists to social marketing. Even though Dr. Sirgy was himself a psychologist and "not really a business type," this initial exposure was not successful. The reasons for rejecting social marketing at this point were its associations with foreign fields such as business and wholesale manipulation (of course, similar and worse things had been ascribed to behavior modification). The entire approach and its values appeared to be in a different realm.

I believe this has been a common response of other behavioral scientists. For example, Rothman, Teresa, Kay, and Morningstar (1983) have noted that social marketing and diffusion research are virtually one and the same (a point made in the prior chapter), yet perceived value differences have kept these fields quite separate:

> While the fields have been separate, almost airtight in their compartmentalization, their objectives and many of their methods overlap. . . . Both are concerned with the dissemination and utilization of innovations—new products, techniques, ideas, programs. The difference is that the diffusion people approach their subject from a humanistic or nonprofit point of view, while the social marketing writers draw

upon a body of literature that originally had overriding profit-making motivations. The differences have made close similarities appear to be distant incompatibilities . . . the techniques and methods evolved in the marketing field can be applied, as well, to social causes, social movements and philanthropic organizations. At that point diffusion and social marketing as areas of study meld. (p. 10)

Perhaps social marketers, convinced of the utility and efficacy of their approach, need to concentrate on how to market social marketing. One suggestion is to initially call it something else. These points, though, are getting ahead of the story.

After the rejection of social marketing, several projects were completed that did use some marketing concepts and provided the feedback and motivation for reexposure, adaption, and adoption. One energy conservation project for a variety of logistical and research needs was done with an audience that was known to be less than optimal (Winett, Love, Stahl, Chinn, & Leckliter, 1983). Prior (and subsequent) projects generally had focused on middle-class conventional families; often the families owned their homes. These families had fairly predictable schedules and their income level assured enough ability to finance a comfortable home, but with little "disposable" income. Their motivation to save energy was high (Winkler & Winett, 1982). Most of these projects went smoothly and there was good responsiveness (reduction in energy use; Geller, Winett, & Everett, 1982). For the next project we needed many people who lived in close proximity to each other, and in all-electric homes (higher cost), so we settled for persons with lower middle incomes, but who were mostly single and lived in townhouses and apartments that were rented. Despite not having large incomes, the singles' status seemed to result in much disposable income and an "unpredictable" schedule.

This study had a host of problems from the day of its inception. Participants were difficult to reach, difficult to contact later, and difficult to persuade to go to meetings. This was true even though meetings were held at the apartment complexes, often in places no more than 75 yards from their homes, and at (what we thought were) convenient times. We showed some energy reductions in this project, but the effort required to achieve it made the approach and outcome questionable for future application.

In the next energy conservation project (Winett, Leckliter, Chinn, Stahl, & Love, 1985), middle-class homeowners were targeted. We attempted to carefully depict their lifestyles in our TV programs that were shown over cable TV. No attendance at meetings was required. With some attention to segmentation, place, price, and promotion variables (although they were not fully conceptualized this way), this project went very well from recruitment through a 1-year follow-up.

Other projects at this time also helped propel me to reexamine and adapt social marketing strategies. A TV series we developed in collaboration with PBS on problems in current changes in social–sexual roles (e.g., problems of dual-earner families), was a startling, and not forgettable failure (Winett, Frederiksen, & Riley, 1981). The production qualities of the programs were poor; its goals were unclear (i.e., information, attitude, or behavior change), and it targeted the wrong audience. The program was geared to single and married people in their late 20's or early 30's. We later found out that the bulk of PBS viewers were considerably older.

After this episode and a few unsuccessful attempts to attract people to workshops on sex roles, a new project was designed by Dr. Abby C. King. She focused her project exclusively on the job and family stress of working women. She did a considerable amount of formative research, i.e., surveys, interviews, focus groups, and pilot-testing so as to tailor her program to the needs of her audience. For example, major training was done in time management. The program was also delivered at times and places endorsed in the formative research by the potential target audience.

The response to all phases of this project was excellent. Rather than just supporting the efficacy of the psychological procedures, we felt that the study showed even more clearly the appropriateness of social marketing strategies (King, Winett, & Lovett, 1983). Subsequent projects followed some of these same tactics (e.g., Israel, Hendricks, Winett, & Frederiksen, 1983).

At this point we were at the adaption stage because we were using only a few aspects of social marketing without full appreciation of the conceptual and methodological framework. This stage is reminiscent to me of mental health, health, or business practitioners who borrow a behavior modification technique or two, but continue other procedures as before. This can really be a poor adaption process because often a procedure only makes complete sense within a conceptual and methodological system. It is a prostitution of the overall system to use one technique in isolation, and at times, the worst example of eclecticism.

Perhaps this is too strong a position, typical of a recent convert. To see more clearly if this is the case, it is necessary to describe fully social marketing, it's processes, applications, strengths and weaknesses.

WHAT IS SOCIAL MARKETING?

This section and the ones that follow rely chiefly on two main writers in the field, Kotler (Fox & Kotler, 1980, Kotler, 1975, 1982; Kotler & Zaltman, 1971) and Fine (1981). Their approaches are quite similar, but are presented separately.

Kotler (1975) is well aware that *marketing,* which is the management of exchange relationships with markets and publics, cannot just have its concepts and methods transferred to the nonprofit and idea sector:

> the transposition of a conceptual system from one domain (the profit sector) to
> another (the nonprofit sector) poses a number of challenges that call for new

creative conceptualization. The concepts of product, price, promotion, and distribution, which are employed by profit-sector marketers, have to be redefined for maximum relevance to organizations. The concepts of markets and exchange processes must be generalized. The concept of profit maximization must be translated into benefit-cost maximization so that marketing models can be applied fruitfully in the nonprofit sector. (p. II)

Kotler's primary focus is nonprofit organizations that typically in the past have not seen the explicit need for marketing. In fact, such organizations usually eschewed the whole notion of marketing. However, any organization frequently seeks to change the amount or type of exchanges with specific "publics." For example, nonprofit organizations may seek funds for specific purposes; they may want to sway congressional votes on certain issues (e.g., environmental protection), or have certain audiences become more favorable to new ideas (e.g., epilepsy is controllable by drugs). In each example, the organization is trying to modify its exchange relations with others, and in each example, the organization is facing a marketing problem.

Any organization, according to Kotler, has three basic tasks: (a) to attract sufficient resources; (b) to convert those resources into products, services, or ideas, and (c) to distribute these outputs to various consuming publics. For example, a political action, environmental group must develop appropriate positions to attract contributions from like-minded, concerned citizens; these contributions can be used to train and finance lobbyists and to run ads in various media. The lobbyists can influence congressional votes and the ads spread the organization's ideas and attract more contributions. Obviously, a feedback and spiraling process is involved. Successful lobbying efforts that receive media attention may result in more contributions and more political influence.

Note that this is not a coercion process, but rather a "free-market" approach. That is, the organization relies mainly on the exchange value of its offerings to elicit the cooperation of different parties. Kotler and Zaltman (1971) state that at its best (and most optimistic) "this marketing philosophy restores consumer sovereignty in the determination of society's product mix and the use of national resources" (p. 5).

Exchange is the sine qua non of marketing. According to Kotler (1975), marketing is:

the analysis, planning, implementation, and control of carefully formulated programs designed to bring about voluntary exchanges of values with target markets for the purpose of achieving the organizational objectives. It relies heavily on designing the organization's offering in terms of the target market needs and desires, and on using effective pricing, communication, and distribution to inform, motivate, and service the markets. (p. 5)

Marketing then, is a managerial process. It entails analysis, planning, implementation, and control, and manifests itself in specifically developed programs.

Marketing seeks the voluntary exchange of things of value (money, time, attention). In order to optimize the marketing process and achieve organizational objectives, highly specific programs must be developed for specific market segments.

Marketing need not involve a tangible product. It can be done for more public interest outcomes, yet the process must be highly specific. The organization's objectives must be designed to fit the target market's needs and desires and not the seller's personal interests and tastes. This point emphasizes that marketing is a democratic technology in that the organization's objectives and offerings must fit the customers.

Modern marketing does not only involve one tool, such as advertising. In fact, marketing is often confused with the singular tool of advertising (promotion). Marketing uses and blends a set of tools called the marketing mix that includes the product design, and pricing, communication, and distribution variables. In a real sense, a marketing framework takes on the attributes of a multi-level, interactive systems approach (Novelli, 1984).

What then is *social marketing?* This term was originally defined by Kotler and Zaltman (1971) to mean "the design, implementation, and control of programs calculated to influence the acceptability of social ideas and involving considerations of product planning, pricing, communications and marketing research" (p. 5). The use of the word "influence" is important. It suggests that social marketing is just one set of forces that may be set in motion to modify beliefs, attitudes, and behaviors. It also implies much less (sinister) power than words such as "manipulate" and "control." These points are outlined further when the effectiveness of social marketing is examined later on in this chapter.

MARKETING'S OBJECTIVES

When marketing is done correctly, it allows organizations to be more effective in two ways: (a) the target audience is more satisfied with the offerings; (b) improved marketing efficiency results in better use of organizational resources. Before explaining specific strategies to achieve such outcomes, a general approach to meeting objectives is described.

Marketing is primarily interested in the relations between the organization and its various markets and publics. A *public* is a distinct group of people or organizations that has an actual or potential interest and/or impact on an organization. What does the organization and its publics exchange and what does each party gain from the transaction? This first analysis can be very revealing to any organization. It may often point to the involvement with multiple and diverse publics. For example, universities are concerned with government and alumni that support them financially; other government agencies that regulate them; faculty and staff that service them; students who partly pay the bills by consuming their offerings, and groups and private citizens concerned with educational and other community impacts.

Whereas not all potential publics are equally involved or influential with a given organization, they are interrelated and affect one another. An organization that ignores particular publics or does not construe interrelationships between them, risks an early demise.

A market is a potential arena for the trading of resources. It also means a distinct group of people and/or organizations who have resources that they conceivably may exchange for certain benefits. As Kotler (1975) stated:

> Once the organization starts thinking in terms of trading values with (a) public, it is viewing that public as a market. It is engaged in trying to determine the best marketing approach to that public. (p. 22)

Kotler is, however, careful in delimiting the role and power of marketing. Although it is true that all organizations face marketing problems, Kotler is not saying that the only function, "the essence" of organizations, even business ones, is marketing. Rather, Kotler is arguing for the use of marketing as a conceptual system that can provide insights and strategies for problems faced by all organizations.

FINE'S APPROACH

Fine (1981) has attempted to restrict his scope to "idea" or "concept" marketing. Social marketing, Fine noted, has come to mean too many things. In particular, he is concerned with social issues and causes and with ideas unrelated to specific products (e.g., good nutrition, and not a particular low-calorie food). Consistent with Kotler, Fine feels that "the dissemination of ideas is a marketing process" (p. 1) and that the marketing of ideas is highly consistent with democratic principles, i.e., allow many ideas to viably compete.

Fine indicated that micro- and macro-processes are at work in the dissemination of ideas. At both levels, ideas represent a way to deal with a problem. Ideas may originally be of individual interest, but as they become adopted by groups, they become issues and causes. A chain of events in this process includes identifying a problem, reasoning about it, formulating an idea, culminating in a belief, leading to social issues and causes, social action and social change. Current examples of ideas and social causes include a Nuclear Freeze, HMO's, Physical Fitness, and the Information Society.

The dissemination of these ideas and causes is a marketing process which entails the "planning and movement of a product offering from the supplier . . . to those who are to use it" (Fine, 1981, p. 18). Marketing includes all aspects of the four P's, and its central philosophy is that the consumer's interest is the major point from which the process evolves, i.e., a consumer orientation.

Fine (1981) differentiated between "pull" and "push" marketing:

> Idea marketing . . . can be either consumer or producer oriented. Marketers, having ascertained consumer's felt needs and wants, disseminate ideas in such a manner that those ideas become available for adoption by interested individuals. This is called "pull" marketing because it is based on the premise that informed consumers seek out or pull at the product offering on their own initiative. Producer-oriented idea marketers engage in the opposite or "push" marketing which is alternatively termed "high pressure" or simply "persuasion." (p. 20)

Fine noted that every discipline has its own unique way of solving problems. Marketers attempt to solve problems by matching products with people's wants and needs that are identified through market research. However, marketer's approaches are different from economists in that they recognize that rationality and utility maximization do not necessarily underlie satisfying wants and needs. Rather, many factors besides reason influence wants and needs and utility is not usually satisfied, but merely "satisficed", i.e., good enough under the circumstances.

Although Fine noted these differences from a strict economic position, he still attempted to explain the marketing of ideas within utility theory. For example, he discussed how ideas can be seen as substituting for tangible products. Fine developed a typology for marketing (profit, nonprofit) and products (tangible, abstract). However, social marketers, he noted, really do not just tap consumer beliefs, wants, and needs, and fit ideas around their market research findings. On the contrary, social marketers most often are trying to persuade people to do controversial things, or engage in behaviors (e.g., exercise, nutritious eating) for which they have shown little interest or inclination in the past. This point is critical for questioning marketers' assertion that they are just satisfying needs as they exist. It suggests that if this is not the case then some ethical and empirical basis for social marketing activity is needed.

Perhaps this is particularly the case, because as Fine pointed out, social marketing occurs virtually everywhere and all the time but under different labels. It is basically an exchange transaction that refers to many activities. For example, time spent watching TV is exchanged for time that could have been given to another activity. Time spent watching entertainment on TV is exchanged for time when the viewer can be influenced by commercials. Lobbying, advocacy, and fund raising are all exchange transactions. However, many nonprofit and public organizations, do not construe their tasks in marketing terms and, hence, approach their tasks haphazardly. According to the results of a survey study done by Fine, (1981):

> Concept producers seem close to the realization that marketing philosophies and methodologies are applicable to the social products they sponsor. Some have

known it for years. But to most others, it is a revelation, and one may expect that those newly initiated will embark upon exciting ventures. (p. 44)

SUMMARY

Both Kotler and Fine feel that many of the operations of nonprofit and public organizations can be construed within a marketing framework. Both see idea marketing as quite compatible with democratic principles, as far as placing many ideas before the public in a viable way. Both recognize, however, that the mere transposition of commercial marketing plans to the noncommercial sector is probably not appropriate. There is also the recognition that social marketing, in particular, does not just involve assessment of consumer wants and needs and product design to meet these wants and needs. These important points are discussed more fully later in this chapter. At this juncture, we discuss the methods and strategies of social marketing.

OVERALL STRATEGIES

Product

Fine's description of the four P's in social marketing is first reviewed. Later, Kotler's work is used to describe more specifically the methods used in marketing research and how all the methods of marketing are orchestrated.

Fine started his discussion with product strategies. Product management includes packaging, positioning, product life cycle, product mix and forms, product differentiation, and new product development. These aspects of product management were generally not considered that important in the promotion of concepts. Fine indicated that this was wrong, particularly when the definition of *product* is expanded to mean anything that can be exchanged for some scarce resource, and anything that can satisfy some human need or want.

According to Fine (1981), the most important concept relevant to product strategies is market segmentation:

> Market segmentation is the partitioning of a market of consumers according to some criterion in order that marketing planning may be custom-tailored to suit the unique needs of each segment. By catering to differing characteristics possessed by several submarkets, it is hoped that deeper overall penetration of the target population will be accomplished. A prerequisite for a segmentation study is the selection of a criterion most likely to account for differential response to the four controllable marketing factors, and on the basis of that criterion, partitioning the market that is, forming submarkets such that each submarket is different in some way from the others. Ideally, the difference between these groups should be indicative of the unique manner by which each group responds to differences in product offerings and/or to differences in the promotion strategy planned by the marketer. (p. 63)

The critical questions are how many segments should there be and what are the criteria used for segmentation? The optimal number of segments is a compromise between the largest number accounting for group differences and the smallest number containing a worthwhile number of target individuals. Clusters of segments can often be combined to form a smaller number of manageable segments. The main criterion for segmentation is the selection of variables most relevant to the focus/product of the social marketing effort. For example, in the previously mentioned energy conservation project using cable TV, our target audience was segmented by income (middle), energy use level (medium to high), home ownership (versus rental), and location. Other projects had focused on all-electric consumers because the higher cost was associated with interest and responsiveness. Thus, several variables were used to define a small, but distinct segment whose characteristics were highly relevant to the project.

Although the present example represents a segmentation strategy based on logic and past field tests, some segmentation practices remain an art form, whereas other efforts attempt to rely on surveys and other instruments to measure consumer response on variables that may be relevant for segmentation. Effective segmentation should, however, follow these guidelines (from Fine):

1. Criterion must be appropriate for the particular product.

2. Individuals in different segments will most likely respond differentially to one or more marketing policy instruments.

3. Relatively homogeneous behavior must exist within a segment.

4. The number of segments formed is such that it is economically feasible to reach the most important target groups.

5. Segments must be sufficiently large to warrant an individualized approach.

6. By segmenting the market, one of the four P's is modified to fit the segment.

Other major product strategies are branding, packaging, and positioning. The major purpose of branding is to create an easy-to-recall label or product name, associated with quality and/or economy, so as to facilitate repeat purchases. In some extraordinary cases, the brand name can come to mean the product class (for example, Coke, Nautilus machines). Commercial producers spend considerable time and effort to name their products; less care has been taken in the idea sector, a point made in the diffusion chapter.

Packaging attempts to link various products and/or ideas together. For example, promotion of exercise may be appropriately packaged with nutrition and stress management advice. The general notion is that the package may be more easily promoted and adopted than a single component promoted separately.

Positioning is both a product and consumer related concept. It means creating a unique niche for a product so as to have differential advantage in the market. Positioning is based on the product's attributes and consumers' (segmentation) characteristics. The challenge is to put these two sets of variables together. If a mismatch occurs, the product must be redesigned or offered to a different segment.

Product position according to Fine (1981) entails:

1. Determining the competing brands, products, and other alternatives vying for the consumer.

2. Determining the most important criteria by which consumers choose products.

3. Determining where the products and its competition fit on these dimensions.

4. Plotting the position deemed as most desirable.

5. Examining the relative positions of the product, competing products, and consumers' ideal product.

6. Framing, from the resulting picture, strategic plans for other marketing variables (promotion, price, distribution).

Product differentiation entails the real or perceived attributes of the product. These attributes can be changed for better positioning. For example, there may be a large interest in marital therapy, but the perception of such therapy may be one of emotional upheaval and catharsis, and not more rationale problem solving. The first perception may curtail procurement of the service, and promotion of the second perception may enhance procurement.

Product form means the characteristics of exactly what is delivered. The ideal approach is to make the form uniquely suited to each segment. Usually in health and mental health, the form of the product is taken for granted, i.e., one-to-one or group procedures. Yet, the same product often can be delivered in workshops, TV programs, and other forms that may better suit the purposes of the intervention (i.e., a population effect) and the target audience (McAlister, Pekka, Saeanen, Tuomilehto, & Koskela, 1982).

Social marketers must also be aware that ideas and concepts have a lifecycle similar to tangible products. The social marketer must determine the optimal marketing mix at a particular point in the lifecycle. As information about a product and actual adoption spreads, it may be necessary to rename, redesign, or differentially price or promote a product. For example, as negative and often wrong information was spread about energy conservation, we renamed our approach "energy efficiency" and sought to deliver information in an upbeat, entertaining way. The social marketer needs to be aware of prevailing trends, and based on these trends and product penetration, be prepared for revitalization of the product and what Fine called product "encores."

The product mix refers to the assortment of products. Is the mix too wide, narrow, or just right? Nonprofit firms must carefully consider their product mix.

For example, a mental health center may realistically not be capable of offering all manner of therapies and community consultation and education. On the other hand, offering only one-to-one outpatient therapy may be far too narrow.

Although the discussion here suggests that there can be a wide range in product design and offerings in the nonprofit and idea sector, this can be misleading. Government, for example, may regulate service offerings or only provide reimbursement for certain services. Also, the social marketer is often trying to promote complex behavior change. It may be difficult to develop catchy, simple names, phrases, or concepts. Again, these points serve as reminders that the transposition of marketing from the commercial to nonprofit and idea sectors is quite challenging.

Price

Several years ago, not only were our wonderful programs poorly attended, but they were poorly attended despite being offered at a very low price, or even for free. Obviously, we were not considering other dimensions of price or what economists call "opportunity costs." Adoption of almost any idea or attendance at virtually any program entails time, effort, and various psychological costs. In essence, the consumer surrenders resources of one kind or another for adherence and participation.

The task of the social marketer is to try to delineate these various costs and attempt to develop an ideal price positioning stance based on this analysis. For some products, a higher monetary cost may be preferred if it reduces time and effort costs. As an example, in designing a program to promote better nutrition at lower cost, the author set up an approach that only sought to moderately lower costs so that consumers could save time and effort by shopping in only one supermarket.

Promotion and Place

Most of Fine's discussion of promotion revolved around communication strategies. Fine briefly took the reader through the history of communication models, i.e., hypodermic, 2-step, and multistage. He also offered his own "hierarchy of effects" model, which is less comprehensive than McGuire's model.

Fine's major contributions for consideration of promotion strategies are twofold. He emphasized that much of what we know about communication comes from promotion of commercial products or the diffusion literature, also generally concerned with a tangible product, (for example, a birth control device). How well similar approaches work with idea or behavior change promotion is less clear. In his analysis, however, Fine did not note the prosocial media literature (chapter 2) that provides a growing research base to address this issue.

Fine also emphasized that social marketers must analyze and plan for the interface of impersonal communication with personal group processes. In this regard, his position is similar to Rogers' (1983) described in chapter 3.

The place variable is also one variable that is typically ignored by health, mental health, and other nonprofit programmers. In our own case, it took several failures and a few successes for us to realize that offering the same product, with the same promotion, but at a different time and place, could greatly alter interest and responsiveness.

Fine (1981) noted that:

An important objective of the channel is that the product offering be made available at a time and place convenient to consumers. In fact, the distribution process is referred to as the 'place' component of the marketing mix. Place is a measure of whether, and to what extent, the product will be accessible to the customer when purchase is to be affected. With any product offering, no matter how well designed, attractively priced, or elaborately promoted, the strategies and tactics leading up to the point of purchase are to no avail if the product is inaccessible to the consumer at the crucial point in time and at the proper place to suit target consumers' needs and wants. (p. 105)

The place variable has much to do with price, time, and effort. Marketing distribution channels also must be carefully examined to understand what institutions and roles are involved and how activities will be carried out. Some guidelines provided by Fine for analyzing channels included:

1. Involving only those institutions and organizations making a meaningful contribution to the dissemination process.

2. Arranging for accessible outlets which permit translation of motivation to action (from Kotler & Zaltman, 1971). For example, an effective channel will provide information *and* skills training about new behavioral practices.

3. Deciding on the number, size, and location of appropriate outlets.

4. Delineating roles and behaviors within such settings.

5. Providing proper incentives for those involved at the distribution settings to properly perform their functions.

One need only compare the care taken by commercial franchises relative to these guidelines to nonprofits in order to understand that the place variable is often poorly considered (if, at all) in the nonprofit sector. Again, Fine pointed out that processes may be more difficult in the noncommercial sector. Yet, in order to be successful, the social marketer must fully address the intermediaries in the dissemination of concepts—i.e., mass media, opinion leaders, community-based organizations, and pressure and advocacy groups—and understand how target consumers relate to these intermediaries.

ORGANIZATIONAL AND RESEARCH METHODS FOR
THE MARKETING MIX

Kotler (1975, 1982) provided more detail than Fine on how social marketing is to be done within organizational settings. If social marketing is to be successful, it calls for a new orientation for organizations. The fully responsive organization is one that conducts formal audits at regular intervals of its present and potential consumers with regard to needs, perceptions, preferences, and satisfaction with current products. It also actively encourages information input from its constituent publics, and constantly adjusts its offering based on this information and other input from the organization.

The basic notion is to serve consumers and to provide to them what they want. However, Kotler is well aware that simply serving short-run wants can have deleterious long-run effects, for example, witness the effects of cigarettes, junk food, and large cars. In light of these concerns, Kotler (1975) has modified one definition of social marketing:

> The societal marketing concept is a consumer's needs orientation backed by integrated marketing aimed at generating consumer satisfaction *and long-run consumer welfare* as the key to satisfying organizational goals. (47)

The major premises that should underlie the philosophy and operations of an organization seriously involved in social marketing are:

1. The main purpose of the organization is to create satisfied and healthy consumers and contribute to the quality of life.

2. The organization must search for products that combine high appeal and benefit to the consumer. Information needs to be provided to the consumer on the proper use of the product so as to maximize consumer benefits.

3. Consumers are discerning and intelligent, and prefer organizations that treat them humanely, show social responsibility, and are concerned about their immediate satisfaction and long-run welfare.

Further, consumers will spread the word about good and poor organizations, and (at least in the 1960s and 1970s) are represented by advocates and agencies who are capable of providing negative attention and other countermeasures for poorly performing organizations.

Thus, according to Kotler (1975):

> . . . the modern organization exists to serve its markets. It receives its validation from the marketplace. . . . It is production for the sake of consumption, not consumption for the sake of production. The marketing concept is a philosophy about the relations and organization should have with its markets and publics. It is

essentially antibureaucratic, anti-production-oriented, and anti-sales-oriented. It calls for a highly responsive organization . . . the organization seeks to sense, serve, and satisfy its markets and publics, and through this makes its contribution to increasing the well-being of society. (p. 48)

Marketing Tools

The primary tool is the marketing audit. The audit is a complete study of the marketing efforts of an organization including its objectives, programs, implementation strategies, and its organization and control; plus factors external to the organization. The objective of the audit is to evaluate what is being done and to make recommendations for future actions. The parts of the audit should include:

Marketing Environment: Markets, customers, competitors, and the macroenvironment (i.e., consumer demographics, state of the economy, technology development, government policies and regulations, and cultural changes).
Marketing System: (within the organization) Objectives, programs, implementation strategies, internal organization, role relationships.
Marketing Activity: Products, pricing, distribution, personal contacts, advertising, publicity, sales promotion.

As a result of such regular audits, the organization can fulfill its major market managing task which is "regulating the level, timing, and character of demand in one or more markets of the organization" (Kotler, 1975, p. 80).

Market Structure Analysis

Two specific aspects of the audit center on market structure analysis and consumer analysis. Kotler's market structure analysis is similar to Fine's points, i.e., market definition (actual and potential members), market segmentation, market positioning, and market orchestration. *Orchestration* means harmonizing the marketing program so as to address different segments.

Kotler noted an array of potential segmentation variables, but emphasized the importance of basing segmentation on psychographic variables and the consumer's state of readiness. The organization that does segment potential and actual consumers must decide between a concentrated marketing approach (focus on one segment) and a differentiated marketing approach (design separate products and marketing programs for two or more segments). What is done here depends on the resources of the organization and the competition it faces. Many organizations start out with nondifferentiated or concentrated marketing; if they are successful, they may evolve into differentiated marketing.

Kotler stressed that any marketing decision must be made with full consideration of all major markets and publics. An organization must position itself with knowledge of multiple markets and know that "any position it takes with respect to one market will require compatible and viable positioning with respect to other publics" (Kotler, 1975, p. 114). The marketer's task then is to orchestrate the optimal placement in different segments and publics by determining how much the organization wants to, and will gain from, involvement in each segment.

Consumer Analysis

The market-oriented organization makes consumer research and analysis its highest priority. However, a major criticism of social marketing is that the models and methods of conducting consumer research are based on limited concepts and techniques.

Kotler (1975) states that the basic models of consumer behavior, which spawn the research, follow a fairly simplistic, linear, hierarchy of effects paradigm revolving around needs, preferences, information processing, and choice behavior:

> The consumer starts with strong needs in his system, and certain ones are aroused by cues and become directed toward offerings. He may then search for additional information which is selectively perceived and distorted. The consumer buys and then experiences post-purchase feelings. The various (consumer) models develop some version of this "buying decision process" to help the marketer correctly interpret consumers' wants and influence their choices. (p. 124)

There are serious questions concerning models used in social marketing. Can the same model work in different situations? Can a model developed in the commercial sector for frequent purchases be transposed to the nonprofit and idea sector characterized by more infrequent or singular purchases? What is the viability of studying needs, preferences, and attitudes as antecedents of choice behavior? To answer the first two questions, one general approach (for example, behavioral systems), may be applied to many situations and in many types of behaviors. As shown in the introductory and consumer behavior chapters, it is a broad multi-level approach, but yet one that conducts fine-grain analysis at different levels. In addition, the marketing *framework* is quite useful for social and behavioral applications. Thus, the quarrel is not with the overall social marketing framework (product, price, promotion, and place variables), but rather with the conceptualization and methods internal to the framework.

The measurement of needs must be prominent in current consumer research models because it is at the heart of the marketing enterprise. However, there are many problems associated with its measurement. Not the least of the problems is its definition. Is it a want or desire; or is it best represented by consumer demand, i.e., actual behavior? Methods to measure needs have included more direct instruments such as surveys, questionnaires, and face-to-face interviews. Very specific questions that relate to the issues and purposes at hand are more effective than more general, amorphous items. Simulation techniques that involve putting persons through an experience with a real or hypothetical product in order to observe and analyze reactions have been used. An array of projective techniques to discover the consumer's underlying dynamics also have been used, and were particularly popular under the rubric of motivational research. Partly predicated on Freudian theory, and based on notions of unconscious motivations, such techniques as word association tests, sentence completion, picture completion, and role playing were (and evidently continue to be) popular in some quarters. However, such techniques are based on now questionable theory and their predictive validity approaches zero (Wilson & O'Leary, 1980).

Research on a product's or organization's image has been quite extensive. "An image is the sum of beliefs, ideas, and impressions that a person has of an object" (Kotler, 1975, p. 31). The purposes of image assessments are (a) to see how an organization is perceived in relation to other competitive organizations, (b) its perception by different market segments and publics, and (c) for monitoring changes in image over time. Methods to assess images include unstructured interviews, object sorting, and multidimensional scaling. These methods do not prespecify images for the respondent. Judgment methods, including item lists and semantic differentials, specify the image attributes in advance and have the respondent rank, rate, or react to the product (or organization) on these attributes.

Image testing has some value in at least conveying general impressions of a product or organization. It is particularly important to go beyond the mere collection of image impression data to an understanding of the factors causing the present image and factors likely to produce image change.

There is much interest in images and their modification because many organizations feel that there is a close connection between their image and the behavior of people toward their organization. However, as other discussions in this book have indicated, the relationship between image and behavior may not be as linear as many believe. Images are only one aspect of attitudes, and certainly only one element in behavior (Kotler, 1975). Long-term habits and routines, and situational factors may have more to do with behavior than image. For example, my image of one chain supermarket may, at best, be mixed. However, its large produce section, close proximity, and convenient hours may be the major determinants of my shopping in that store. That is, different variables may influence images, beliefs, attitudes, and behaviors. This point reemphasizes the utility of a behavioral systems perspective for consumer behavior.

Preference, "the relative valuation a person places over a set of comparable objects when contemplating their value" (Kotler, 1975, p. 142), is another variable studied in consumer research. The goal here is to ascertain preferences between products and offerings to distinguish the preferences of different groups, understand market resistance to a product, and how people's preferences change over time. Kotler described preferences as a variable midway between attitude and behavioral intention. The measurement of preferences may be worthwhile because it may be a better predictor of behavior. Preference measurement has followed several relatively sophisticated models that primarily differ as to the weight given comparisons on one certain attribute or a set of attributes.

Organizations of all sorts have become concerned with measuring consumer satisfaction because this may affect repeat sales and word-of-mouth dissemination about the organization and its offerings. In the past, satisfaction was measured indirectly from measures of sales, enrollment, attendance, and so on. However, satisfaction needs to be measured frequently, and preferably before dissatisfaction affects market performance. Methods to assess more directly satisfaction include simply monitoring unsolicited consumer responses (with resulting problems in representativeness), reported satisfaction on surveys and the like, actual observation (with problems in sampling, and observer bias and presence), and measures of derived dissatisfaction, i.e., the difference between ideal and actual state of the product.

In reality, organizations may not be able to maximize satisfaction. It may be too costly to do so, or may not be possible to maximize satisfaction simultaneously for different segments and publics. Rather, some optimal level may be achieved.

The orientation of this book and the author's experiences put little faith in intensive measurement of need, preference, image, and satisfaction. At some extreme, such indices are useful. If a representative sample from significant markets and publics tells you that your organization is awful and your offerings are worse, your survival demands attention and change. For less incisive responses, the results of using need, preference and other similar inventories for planning programs, at best, has been slightly useful, and at worst, frequently misleading. For example, many times potential clients have highly endorsed needing and wanting (willingness to enroll) a particular service delivered in a certain way, at specific, price, times, and place—when completing a survey. The actual offering just as often has led to virtually no response.

When it is considered that answering a survey and enrolling in a workshop for $40 are two very different responses and response modes influenced by different variables, the lack of consistency between them is not surprising even if the survey explicitly describes the service. We have had much better success, as far as gaining useful information, by conducting small, but well-run pilot studies, i.e., assessing actual behavior in the actual setting. For example, in one project, the use of a Health Risk Appraisal to assess current health behaviors and methods of behavior change was highly endorsed by the patients from one physician's practice (Israel, Hendricks, Winett, & Fredericksen, 1983). However, a series of pilot studies indicated that attention to the form, its completion, and the taking of health literature keyed to the form, had much more to do with the design and placement of a prompt sign and the physician's behavior than patients' needs, preferences, or (best) intentions. In fact, in one pilot, no one took the health literature; a change in the sign's locations; and the physician's response led to a majority taking relevant literature. That is, setting variables greatly influenced patients' initial responses and, as was found, their subsequent responses to the health literature they received.

If setting variables are critical, and if there is doubt about the predictive efficacy of self-report measures, then there is no substitute for pilot studies, or in the current parlance, market testing. Thus, here is another example where the internal workings in the social marketing framework can find behavioral systems concepts and methods to be useful and compatible.

MARKETING MIX STRATEGIES

The way in which an organization orchestrates its product, price, promotion, and place strategies makes up its marketing mix. The product is the most important element and the foundation for all other elements. Products are anything that can be offered to a market for attention, acquisition, or consumption, i.e., physical objects, services, persons, places, organizations, or ideas. It seems particularly important for nonprofit organizations and idea disseminators to differentiate (where possible) the actual product or service and its qualities (styling, name, packaging), the core product (the benefit offered or sought and how that benefit is packaged), and the augmented product (total costs and benefits of the product). The notion here is that many nonprofit concerns may give little thought to these product aspects and certainly do not try to enhance them.

Consistent with Fine, Kotler placed considerable emphasis on product qualities similar to those described by Rogers (1983, e.g., trialability, simplicity; chapter 3) as factors that are related to adoption. Serious consideration must also be given to the product line's width, depth, and diversity (e.g., a family planning agency may not only give out birth control devices, but the agency may also provide counseling, abortion referals, etc.). Elements of the product line must also be planned with respect to a market growth strategy that includes an analysis of market penetration of the present products, market development (growth through new markets by new or improved products), and diversification (i.e., growth through entering new markets with new products). All these points entail attention to, and operationalization of, the product lifecycle concept described previously.

Whereas Fine's discussion was particularly instructive with regard to non-monetary costs of adopting a product or idea, Kotler was more informative as far as different price strategies that can be used in the commercial sector. Pricing can have the objectives of profit maximization, cost recovery, market incentivization (often entailing using a low price to achieve rapid penetration), and market disencentivization (pricing plans to discourage certain behaviors and/or segments). In practice, pricing can be cost-oriented, demand-oriented, competition-oriented, or be discriminatory, for example, differential rates for types of customers (the elderly), product version, place of product (type of seat at a cultural event), and time of product (time-of-day utility rates).

Although all types of pricing and actual policies can be ennumerated, it is very difficult to predict response to price changes, i.e., price elasticity of demand. Attitude surveys and econometric methods (e.g., examining demand in different times or areas with different prices) have been used, but again there seems to be little real substitute for an actual market test (Winett, Kagel, Battalio, & Winkler, 1978). However, a problem with market tests and demonstrations is determining whether short-run responsiveness will be predictive of long-run responsiveness. Because of the uncertainty in predicting response to price changes, Kotler urged that we must attempt to examine convergent evidence through multiple methods.

Kotler's discussion of distribution (place) decisions was similar to Fine's. Place variables are mainly concerned with how products are made available, the dissemination methods or delivery system. Decisions include the level and quality of customer service, the number and location of branches, and the use and motivation of middle-persons, and intermediaries. Often some of these decisions are compromises. For example, it may be necessary to reduce quality and service to customers in order to meet budget limitations. Distribution also entails that considerable attention be given to ways to maximize motivation and proper performance of middle-persons and other intermediaries. In this regard, some of the behavioral literature on training should be very useful (e.g., Bernstein, 1982).

Promotion, according to Kotler, involves the effective use of five major persuasive communication instruments: advertising, publicity, personal contact, incentives, and atmospherics. Major decisions are the reach of communications, the degree of exposure, and the costs for reach and exposure. The effectiveness of ads and other communications is a critical consideration. The reader may be surprised that ad testing is at best poor science. It is also an area where a behavioral systems perspective can be helpful to nonprofit organizations and idea disseminaters (see chapter 7).

Some ways that ads are typically tested prior to release include direct rating (a panel rates an ad on a number of dimensions); portfolio tests (respondents receive a groups of ads and later are asked questions to see what stood out), and various laboratory tests (e.g., physiological responses to measure attention and arousal). Two ways that ads are tested after release are recall tests (of the ad's appearance and content) and recognition test (identifying an ad from a group of ads).

Obviously, according to Kotler (1975), none of these methods assess actual response to the ad:

> It must be stressed that all these efforts rate the communication effectiveness of the ad and not necessarily its impact on attitude or behavior. The latter are much harder to measure. Most advertisers appear satisfied in knowing that their ad has been seen and comprehended and appear unwilling to spend additional funds to determine the ad's sales effectiveness. (p. 210)

Nonprofit organizations and others involved in social marketing usually will not have sufficient funds to achieve the saturation level and exposure of, say, lite beer ads. Often the goal of social marketing efforts is behavior change, not just information change and brand switching. Therefore, it is a mistake for social marketers to solely adopt the testing methods of commercial advertisers, for example, recall and recognition tests. Careful pilot testing must be done in order to assess ads' actual effects on attitudes, intention, and behavior, and decisions must be made about the use of various media, i.e., effectiveness, reach, cost, given the limited resources of most nonprofit organizations.

Kotler also provided a behavioral analysis of important variables for promotional methods through personal contact where the goal is to evoke appropriate behaviors from both field staff and potential clients. Incentives must often be used. When this is done, the objectives of the exchange must be specified; who (sales people or consumers), and exactly what, the incentives are for (e.g., coming to site, or trial, or actual purchase), and the form, amount, and timing of incentives must be specified. Here then, is another example where the internal workings of social marketing can be well derived from behavioral systems analyses.

Atmospherics is a term used for environmental design. That is, buying and consuming environments must be designed in a way to produce reliable and specific cognitive, affective, and behavioral effects on the target market. In chapter 7 on consumer behavior, the design of supermarkets is discussed. It is apparent that they were purposefully designed to promote impulse buying. It seems apparent that stores could be designed to decrease impulse buying and promote economic, nutritional purchases. Whereas few nonprofit firms will have this degree of control in the community at large, attempts must be made to at least maximize design under their own roofs.

Thus, effective social marketing entails the orchestration of all marketing variables. Every nonprofit firm must have a full marketing department and have all aspects of the organization reflect the marketing philosophy and strategies. The marketing department in collaboration with other departments must develop a sophisticated data base and information system on the macro-environment (economic indicators, technology changes, new lobbying efforts, cultural changes) and the task environment (buyers, channels, competition, suppliers). The eventual goal of such systems is to have the ability to constantly monitor the market and performance indicators to be able to make cost–benefit and cost-effectiveness analyses that point to change in one or more marketing variables.

STRATEGIES AND APPLICATIONS

The framework of social marketing is not difficult to understand and appears to lend itself, if not perfectly, at least reasonably well, to social causes and positive behavior change. There is not much doubt that aspects of the framework have and are being used for a range of social purposes. Questions are how effective are the strategies that are used and how effective is the overall social marketing approach? What has social marketing accomplished?

Fox and Kotler (1980) noted that it is difficult to answer questions about accomplishments. There are not very many experiments in social marketing. For example, there appear to be no real experiments where all the tools of social marketing were tried in one setting, and few or none in another setting, to promote the same product. More easily done are experiments where only one marketing variable is systematically altered. For example, aspects of the product or its distribution could be varied. However, experiments such as these appear not to have been done either. Further, where social marketing merely mimics some commercial marketing tactics, there is little reason to look for effectiveness, e.g., designing and disseminating ads based on recall and recognition data. More than likely, there will be no effects on behavior.

Fox and Kotler used cross-cultural data to suggest the effectiveness of social marketing. For example, countries (such as Sri Lanka, and Mexico) that have followed the basic tenets of social marketing in their campaigns have shown decreased birth rates. The well-known Stanford Heart Disease Prevention Projects (Solomon, 1984) have also used social marketing, as has the National High Blood Pressure Educational Program (Ward, 1984). However, much of the blood pressure program was developed prior to the appearance of a text on social marketing. Thus, although some aspects of social marketing were used, that program does not represent the most coherent, contemporary example of social marketing. The Stanford Projects are probably the best example.

The Stanford community preventive health project's social marketing efforts were considerable and sustained. For example, a good deal of pretesting (formative research) of health messages was done. Different messages were designed for different segments. Messages were pilot-tested and evaluated for-behavior change, with information fed back to the design process. Extensive baseline data on multiple types and levels of measures was available for assessing program impacts and then modifying program components. A reasonable hierarchy of effects model was constructed for all target areas. Its major purpose was to describe the chain necessary for behavior change, to ascertain where on that chain target audiences were located, to plan messages and other interventions based on this analysis, and to delineate reasonable yearly goals by working backwards from the end desired objective to the present state of affairs.

The product of the project, basically information and programs, was based on extensive formative research on what form and content were appropriate for different citizen and health professional audiences. Processes involved in using a program were also extensively studied. There were many distribution channels for the information and programs so that there were multiple opportunities, places, and forms for achieving self-directed behavior change. Formative research was done to ascertain the best distribution channel for a given message, about a specific risk factor, for a specific audience. Extensive study was also made of the social and psychological costs for adoption of health behavior changes for different segments, with programs design based on these costs. Finally, considerable formative research was done to ascertain which promotional channel (e.g., newspaper, direct mail, TV) was most appropriate for a given task and segment.

Thus the Stanford Heart Disease Prevention Projects used a systematic array of social marketing strategies. Solomon noted that he believed that the key aspects of this process were the problem analysis and strategy design; the media selection, message and community program design; extensive evaluation research for feedback purposes, and the picking of reasonable goals.

The Stanford projects sets the stage for discussion of issues, problems, and the future of social marketing. For example, although this project is serving as a prototype for others, it must always be kept in mind that outcomes to date of this and similar projects (e.g., McAlister, Pekka, Saeanen, Tuomilehto, & Koskela, 1982) have been very modest. What is clearly needed is the integration of the science of marketing with the emergent approach of the study of the processes of maintenance of behavior change.

PROBLEMS AND ISSUES

Thus far, when describing some of the limitations and problems of social marketing, this chapter has focused primarily on deficiencies in program and message construction and evaluation. A behavioral approach has frequently been advocated in light of these deficiencies. In these sections, more general problems and issues are addressed.

Kotler (1975) has emphasized this point:

> Although social marketing attempts to harness the insights of behavioral science and exchange theory to the task of social persuasion, its power to bring about actual

change, or bring it about in a reasonable amount of time, is highly limited. The greater the target group's investment in a value or behavioral pattern, the more resistant it is to change. Social marketing works best where the type of change counts for least. (p. 283)

Kotler and Fine also stressed that social marketers must understand and accept some basic differences between commercial and social marketing. These points are summarized in Table 4.1.

There have also been a number of different kinds of criticisms of social marketing that also point to its limitations. All these criticisms have grains of truth in them and include:

1. Marketing is really only for business and not appropriate (ethically, methodologically) for social causes. Here, it is agreed that marketing cannot just be transposed from the commercial sector, but that it is highly appropriate to market social causes. There is agreement with Fine and Kotler that social marketing *is* consistent with democratic principles when it allows diverse ideas to be effectively presented to the public.

2. Marketing is just another term for "manipulation". In actuality, some say, it is worse than commercial marketing because the objective is not just brand

TABLE 4.1
Differences Between Commercial and Social Marketing*

Commercial	Social
Objectives	
Meet wants and needs of target markets.	Change attitudes and behaviors of target markets.
Make a profit by serving interests of the market or society.	Serve interest of the market or society without personal profit.
Market products and services through the medium of ideas.	Typically, market the ideas themselves rather than the products or services.
Process & Outcomes	
Generally use established mass media channels.	May use diverse channels (lobbying, newsletters, phone calls).
Adopt a particular product class or brand—typically, more specific effects.	Adopt an idea, position, or set of practices— may have profound and wide effects.
Reinforcement for product adoption and use often immediate and specific.	Reinforcement for adoption of ideas, position, or practices may be delayed and unclear.
Product adoption and use may be more individually based.	Product adoption and use may be subject to group influences.
Social and psychological costs for adoption and use may be minimal or not apparent.	Social and psychological costs for adoption and use may be high.

*Based on Kotler (1975) and Fine (1981).

switching, but rather the creation of new attitudes and behaviors. This point overlays with point one and the author is in essential agreement with Fox and Kotler (1980) who noted that:

> The word "manipulation" usually connotes hidden and unfair ends and/or means used in the influence process. We argue that if a cause is marketed openly with the purpose of influencing someone to change his or her behavior, then the process is not manipulative, any more than is the activity of a lawyer, religious leader, or politician trying to convince others. If the social marketer simply makes the strongest possible case in favor of a cause without distorting the facts, the approach is not manipulative. Social marketing, especially when used in countermarketing, can provide a voice for those with competing points of view. (p. 30)

3. Social marketing is self-serving rather than really being directed toward social goods. For example, some insurance companies promote health by offering discounts to fit, nonsmokers. In recent years, a number of reasonable TV ads have shown people exercising and receiving lower insurance rates. Obviously, healthier policy holders may eventually result in less outlays for insurance companies. It is, therefore, in their interest to promote health. Rather than seeing this type of situation as self-serving, the social marketer should try to find more instances of reciprocal reinforcement for organizations and the public. It is under this condition that social marketing efforts are likely to be initiated, sustained, and effective.

4. Social marketing can quickly gain the reputation of being unsuccessful if it is continually used to promote less popular ideas and attempt to change difficult behaviors. This is undoubtedly true. It will also be unfortunate if social marketing is seen as another quick technical fix and indiscriminately applied. However, by tackling important, but recalcitrant, quality-of-life problems, a vacuum will be filled, and the reputation of marketing may be enhanced.

Another series of criticisms has to do with specific difficulties or hurdles faced by social marketers that, thus, also limit effectiveness (Bloom & Novelli, 1981). These hurdles include:

1. Less salient and useful consumer/market data than for the commercial sector. Often social marketers must create their own database and cannot simply rely on commercial or other secondary sources.

2. Difficulties in effectively targeting specific segments. Segmentation strategies may seem unfair or discriminatory and federal and state mandates may require servicing certain segments. For example, while poor people should be helped wth retrofitting (physically making homes energy efficient), and, in some instances receive utility subsidies, much more attention should be given to middle-class and wealthier individuals in energy conservation programs. This is because poorer people generally use much less energy than other income seg-

ments. Focusing on wealthier segments would save much more energy (Geller, Winett, & Everett, 1982). When social marketing is exclusively used with segments less likely to show change, then social marketing techniques will, as noted, appear ineffective.

3. A pleasant product or alternative is not available. Often social marketers are trying to get people *not* to do something, or not to do something so much. For example, social marketers may work to persuade people to drink less alcoholic beverages and eat less calorie-rich food. But generally, the social marketer is not offering a new and exciting product.

4. Pricing strategies are often precluded. This point is generally true, but by carefully attending to social psychological and effort costs, the social marketer can reduce the costs of different offerings.

5. Distribution channels often cannot be controlled. For example, the social marketer may not be able to specify exactly how nutritious food displays are to be placed in every supermarket. More often than not, the social marketer simply will not have adequate funds for extensive TV ads. In light of these points, social marketers must focus considerable energy on the behavior of intermediaries, and carefully assess the impact of messages on actual behavior and not count on repeated exposure for effectiveness (Winett, Leckliter, Chinn, & Stahl, 1984).

6. The difficulty of developing, pretesting, and widely distributing messages. This is a hurdle that presents problems, particularly when the social marketing is given an inappropriate time frame and budget. It must be emphasized to potential sponsors that pilot-testing is integral to the success of the entire process. Without pilot-tests, too often efforts are merely shots in the dark.

7. The poor management and direction of some nonprofit and cause organizations. Again, the social marketer must emphasize how different organizational functions need to address, if not revolve around, marketing concepts and strategies. A tattered and poorly organized marketing effort is more than worthless— it will waste resources and discourage others from adopting the marketing concept.

8. The difficulty in evaluating social marketing efforts. As a conceptual and technical system, social marketing has gotten ahead of itself. It has been pressed into service to tackle difficult problems (e.g., birth control) without a sound theoretical and empirical base. It is now time to conduct well-controlled studies with, perhaps, relatively circumscribed problems and to integrate findings from many studies.

All these limitations mean that social marketers will not be able to fully orchestrate marketing variables as is done in commercial marketing. Indeed, many efforts for social causes and health and safety have not understood that advertising is only one part of commercial marketing. Advertising can be effective because the other marketing variables are optimal. For example, a product is readily available at an affordable price. Campaigns that only focus on promotional activities (such as social advertising) are not true social marketing efforts and appear destined to fail to reach any behavior change goals.

FUTURE

The discussion of the future of social marketing can be examined in technical, conceptual, and ethical realms. Technical development is, perhaps, the easier issue to address. Throughout the chapter, the marriage of behavioral systems concepts, methods, and strategies with the social marketing framework has been stressed. This marriage seems a workable and ready match. It is likely that programs, for example, health promotion programs, already based on sound behavioral systems/social learning principles will greatly profit from a social marketing perspective. Solomon (1984) has noted that there will be probably five key areas where social marketing will greatly influence health promotion programs in the future:

1. Explicit, operational definitions of specific goals and objectives that can be evaluated will be used, not vague, broad ones.
2. Audience characteristics will be used as the "guiding lights" of programs, and the "sales mentality" will end.
3. Audience segmentation strategies will be increasingly used, ending approaches trying to be all things to all people.
4. Formative research will be used more and more for planning and monitoring program processes.
5. Cost-effectiveness will become more critical leading to an emphasis on collaboration with existing community and commercial concerns.

Social marketing, in order to survive and develop, must become more conceptual and experimental. For example, Fine (1981) has noted that most of what is known about consumer behavior is based on studies with specific products. The field applies this knowledge base with peril to the world of ideas and social, behavioral concerns. Fine called for a new field of study, social consumer behavior. Rothman, Teresa, Kay, and Morningstar (1983) also provided a good example of how, with relative ease, social marketing campaigns can be designed for experimental analysis. Their study of the effectiveness of different promotion strategies for the diffusion of a manual for modification of service operations directed at mental health workers is a model well worth emulation.

Both Fine and Kotler indicated that for many problems, social marketers may find more fruitful paths in trying to promote broader cultural and legal changes. For example, it appears very difficult to reduce the incidence of drunk driving when our culture and media still glorify drinking and where penalties for apprehension in some states are very minimal. Successful marketing for individual attitude and behavior change, may often first require effective marketing at the macro-level. It will not be surprising then to see more marketing efforts directed at key individuals, organizations, media, and bodies of law.

Whereas these last sections have emphasized its limitations, it should be clear that social marketing can be very powerful. This is, according to Fine (1981), because:

> social products enjoy a higher degree of independence than commercial goods and services (and) one may take the stance that social marketing is indeed the ultimate marketing. Moreover, the most potent products ever marketed were not goods or services but ideas such as those propounded by Marx, Freud, and Einstein. (p. 190)

Given this potential power, Fine and others (e.g., Laczniak, Lusch, & Murphy, 1979; Sirgy, Morris, & Samli, 1985) have urged that the ethical dilemmas posed by social marketing be treated in detail and with candor. Is idea dissemination justified by labelling them as *socially beneficial?* Who defines this term? What does it mean? What are its bases?

This book has admittedly not tackled these issues. A position is taken in a number of chapters that information is so asymmetric because of limited access that social marketing must be effectively used when any media access is gained by diverse political and social reformist groups. Regulatory reform is seen as critical for access to be opened (see chapter 5 on New Media). If and when such regulatory reform is achieved, the question of what is socially beneficial is sure to be critically pertinent.

5 New Media: Hyperbole Versus Reality

INTRODUCTION

With much fanfare and promise, we have entered the information age. As Dizard (1982) has noted:

> The U.S. is not stepping over some imaginary line in time from materialistic industrialism into a golden epoch of white-collar ease. Such boundary drawing is simplistic, given the still fragmentary evidence of the changes taking place and our own distorting proximity to them. Nevertheless, once we get past the exercise of labeling ages and epochs, we face the fact that the current shift appears increasingly to be a departure from the dynamics that drove our agricultural and industrial past. (pp. 182–183)

Although the quote from Dizard suggests that the transition may be more evolutionary than revolutionary, nevertheless it is apparent that the underlying dynamics of our society are different. One commonly used indicator of this change is that now approximately half the United States' gross national product (GNP) involves the creation, handling, and distribution of information (Rice, 1984c). It is evident that there have been "hardware" and "software" changes in our society, and these changes have been expressed in quotes much more hyperbolic than the one from Dizard. However, it is not clear what these developments portend (Caporeal, 1984).

Numerous writers have described scenarios for the future of the information age, but, perhaps an article by Picot, Klingenberg, and Dranzle (1982) still best summarizes the uncertainty. They presented three different scenarios focusing on technological replacements for verbal and written communication:

1. *Radical Change*—Inefficient and costly verbal and written communication is replaced by new electronic text media. This leads to new organizations and freedom. For example, people will be able to work at diverse locales and at diverse times.

2. *Modest Change*—Since interpersonal and nonverbal communicational are crucial to decision making, this form of communication is not replaced. New technology will only replace existing text communication (e.g., mail). They see the current euphoria about the new information technology as similar to the claims for management information systems in the 1960s and 1970s.

3. *Social and Economic Hazards*—They foresee a wide gap between information "haves" and "have-nots". The new information age will lead to isolation and alienation at work and difficulty in reaching decisions since there will be less and less social contact.

Not surprisingly, based on their study of teletext technology in West Germany, Picot et al., (safely) predicted the modest change scenario. For example, they foresaw telecommunications technology, in general, and new text-oriented media, in particular, taking over transfer of information tasks that involve simpler, coded content. The new technology may be able to do this cheaper. However, they noted that much work in organizations involves complicated content and/or social relations, for example, problem solving, innovation development, and a great deal of interpersonal trust. Sounding a theme that runs throughout this chapter, Picot et al. warned about the dangers of adoption of new technology without careful analyses of the ascribed tasks' content, interpersonal aspects, and decision processes. If such analyses are done, Picot et al. (1982) predicted "there will be an evolutionary rather than revolutionary impact on people's way of life" (p. 691).

This introduction sets the tone for the approach of this chapter on new media—questioning and restrained. The themes and anchors in this chapter common with the other chapters in this book include:

1. Attention to specific tasks and behaviors and resources matched to specific media. That is, given limited resources, what is the most appropriate media for the immediate task, and for promoting behavior change outside the media situation?;
2. Questions of effectiveness and application, using research data of acceptable standards to guide conclusions;
3. Questions concerning who controls the new media and for what ends.

This chapter is different from the other chapters in that it focuses on some very new innovations. New media-videotext, videodiscs, computer-mediated interaction, expert systems based on artificial intelligence—to name only four examples—have changed the communication modality and introduced more interactivity, feedback, speed, and timelessness in communications and information distribution and retrieval. However, given the newness, there is actually very little behavioral research available. Kiesler, Siegel, and McGuire (1984) who reported on their own seminal (but, almost singular) social psychological research on computer-mediated communication noted that:

> The (*research*) approach based on technical capability is a common and convenient means of analyzing new technologies. However, in real life, technological functions do not exist in isolation. Each technical component may be part of a larger context or may trigger certain social psychological processes. (p. 1124)

Caporeal's (1984) historical analysis of the introduction of computers mirrors Kiesler et al. Caporeal noted that most prophecies about the introduction of computers did not eventuate because they were made without consideration of cultural, social, and economic contexts.

Thus, a good deal of what is discussed in this chapter can be labeled *trends, frameworks, speculations,* and *issues.* Trends include how new media is being currently introduced and used at home, work, and other settings. One framework entails a task × media × resource model. Another involves tracing the development, diffusion, and specialization of what once were also new media, such as radio and TV, and past instances of one media replacing another. These frameworks are then used to understand new media in a way also consistent with a behavioral systems approach. In addition, different aspects (e.g., social learning principles, research methods) of the behavioral systems framework are used to assess current and future applications of new media. In a real sense, this chapter addresses this point: A behavioral perspective has been virtually nonexistent in the development and investigation of new media. Does this perspective have some unique conceptual and methodological contributions to make to this field? Although some of the applications of the perspective may be speculative, other applications are clearly extensions of current concepts and methods. Finally, issues discussed include access to information, the centralization and control of information, and potential social and economic effects of the new media.

This chapter is admittedly written from a skeptical standpoint, if only to balance relatively unsubstantiated, euphoric accounts of our entrance into the information age. New media have vast potential for good, but also for evil as this quote from Lovins and Lovins (1981) warns:

> If today we use our shiny new tools in ways that glorify their limitations—if we seek to get our news from machines rather than from people—then our tools may

enslave and befuddle us more than serve us. It would be all too easy to spread darkness with the speed of light. (p. 42)

SCHRAMM'S FRAMEWORK FOR USING MEDIA

Schramm's (1977) framework for media use, particularly for instruction and education, but also adaptable to other communication goals, is quite compatible with this book's approach. Schramm noted that instead of asking very grand and global questions (for example, Can new media enhance and expedite learning? What new media is best?), we should ask much smaller and sharper questions. Examples of these questions are: What new media should I select for this particular communication task? What new or old media are more cost-effective in this particular situation? What coding aspects of a particular medium are congruent with the task's learning objectives?

Schramm (1977) overviewed approximately 1,000 studies that typically compared media, programmed, or even computer-assisted instruction to traditional instruction. Although methodologically these studies were of varying quality, the overall review provided an important conclusion. Generally, there were no differences in learning outcomes between these special instruction methods and traditional lessons.

Much of that research had been with television, exemplifying a search for a new, powerful, super-medium. Schramm reported few useful questions that were asked in that research such as what media is to be used for what topics, and for what level students. Readers will recognize these questions as a treatment (form and content of media), abilities (characteristics of recipient or learner affecting response to treatment), and task model (Cronbach, 1975).

Schramm also quoted at length from Gagne (1965) concerning what media is best for instructional purposes; the quote has contemporary application and is quite sobering:

First, no single medium is likely to have properties that make it best for all purposes. . . . Most instructional functions can be performed by most media. . . . In general, media have not been found to be differentially effective for different people. It is an old idea that some people may be "visual-minded", and therefore learn more readily from visual presentations, while others may be "auditory-minded" and therefore learn more readily from auditory presentation. (pp. 363–364)

This quote should not be taken to mean that attempts to match media and learner characteristics are futile. Rather: (a) any new media that claims to be all things to all people must be seriously questioned, and (b) there is a need for more specifically focused research on media matches with learner characteristics because available research is not that helpful on that critical aspect.

Since research is generally not available to appropriately guide media selection, how is media and new communication technology often chosen in educational and business settings? It appears that such decisions are usually based on administrative and organizational requirements, cost, user preference, and availability, but not on evidence of instructional effectiveness (Campeau, 1974). To the list of factors affecting the decision process to purchase, can be added whatever is new and faddish. For example, many grade schools use personal computers (PC's) for teaching repetitious, rudimentary subjects to children, such as, times tables, that might be more optimally done, with more portability, and at a fraction of the cost, with an old standby—flash cards. Here, the question was never asked: "What specific capabilities does the PC have to do specific tasks with specific students that could not be done with present tools and media?"

Similarly, the author's university is quickly gearing up to give every faculty member their own PC. It is not clear exactly what tasks they will be used for, what personal and communication tasks will be replaced by the PC's, and what functions secretaries would then serve (see the following for further discussion). However, in defense of that university, the thousands of PC's will give the university some relatively exclusive stature, and there is not a great deal of research to guide a seemingly more cautious and rationale course (Rice, 1984c).

Thus, there is a need to specify the learning/communication tasks and develop taxonomies of task × media × learner interactions. Some taxonomies may need to be quite complex and carefully delineate the "events of instruction" (Gagne & Briggs, 1974). For example, an analysis could include methods to maintain attention, present learning objectives, review prerequisite skills, present stimulus materials, provide guides and heuristics for new learning, elicit specific performances, provide feedback, reassess modified performance, enhance retention, and train for transfer of the learning and training. Note the similarity of this approach to a hierarchy of effects model. Also note how complex this sequence is compared to such blanket statements as "interactive videodiscs are the media of choice for training personal interactions" (e.g., Broderick, 1982).

In addition to scientific concerns, Schramm introduced some very practical considerations. For example, can a particular medium be carried around; could it be used at home; can the user decide when to use it and control the flow of information; can the medium be used individually and/or in an interactive way? Seemingly, on most of these points flash cards are more adaptable than the PC for simple mathematics.

Schramm also provided a caveat about multimedia systems that is reminiscent of McLuhan. When different media are used (for example, a videodisc with computer-generated print assistance), there is a need to understand the use and combination of different coding systems. Combining different media is simply not additive as in putting together different levels of experience. It is really combining different kinds of experiences (Schramm, 1977, p. 91). When media are combined, it therefore needs to be known what the new experience is and how appropriate it is to the task and learner.

Cost must be a major consideration in which type of media to use. For example, a reasonably good quality videotape featuring different locations could cost from $2,000 to $5,000 a minute or from $40,000 to $100,000 for a 20-minute program (J. Moore, personal communication, May, 1985). A slide show that also could be broadcast with a simple voice-over costs about $1,000. The videotape may be more effective (e.g., for changing health practices), but is it cost-effective and cost-beneficial?

Schramm indicated that with any media system there are two important decisions related to economics:

1. How many users must the system serve? For example, radio and television are very responsive to the economics of scale.

2. What level of quality is needed for the communication/learning task? For example, a local studio production, ''talking-head'' videotape may cost only $1000 to make. As has been noted, a higher-quality tape may cost 100 or more times that amount. It may be possible to add some critical formal features and content to the local production to make it about as effective as the much more expensive one (Winett, Leckliter, Chinn, Stahl, & Love, 1985).

To summarize, Schramm's (1977) position, decisions about the use of media can be seen:

as a resultant of three decision vectors, a Task Vector, a Media Vector, and a Cost vector. That is to say, at whatever level the decision is made it is necessary to specify the task to be done, and to estimate the probable effectiveness of different media for doing them and the probable cost of using those different media for the objectives named. Thus the decision requires information from three different sources—pedagogy, economics, and media research and experience. (p. 264)

PROGRESSION AND FLOW OF COMMUNICATION INNOVATIONS

Schramm's framework alerts us to ask highly specific questions about the applications of new media. Another framework can inform us about the natural progression of communication innovations. That is, all present media were once ''new media.'' Examination of their development, dissemination, adoption, and refinement, as well as the past impact of any new media, can aid the understanding of contemporary media.

Bittner's (1980) introductory book on mass communication provided this framework by summarizing prior thought and research on the progression of media. Evidently, new communication have been introduced for a small elite, followed by a mass media period, and then eventuating in a more specialized, segmented media. Table 5.1 summarizes this progression for newspapers, magazines, books, radio, and TV.

Examination of Table 5.1 suggests a relatively consistent pattern of media and other new technology initially designed for an elite, followed by mass appeal and marketing, then followed by more specialization and segmented marketing. Note that this perspective also is compatible with a diffusion model (chapter 3), with the final step being similar to reinvention.

The introduction of PC's is a contemporary example that has quickly followed these stages. PC's initially were fairly expensive and targeted to an intellectual, economic, and professional elite. This was closely followed by a period of the development of less expensive, less intricate PC's for the masses. Undoubtedly, highly specialized PC's and software are right around the corner. The example of PC's also illustrates that modern marketing coupled with relative affluence can expedite the progression and that stages can overlap.

The progression of media development also makes it apparent that many contemporary analyses of new media, including this one, are time bound. Many of the forms, uses, and targets of new media will soon change as we progress from the elite, to mass, to specialized phases. Preliminary analyses can be quite shortsighted as when some new media have obvious inappropriate applications leading to their quick demise (see the following). However, if there is a relatively orderly progression and some similarity in development across media, then historical analyses may teach valuable lessons. For example, in the last sections of this chapter, a review of the development of radio and TV suggests centralization of power and influence despite (or, perhaps because of) certain regulatory approaches. Unfortunately, this history seems to be repeating itself with new media. Thus, there is a danger in too preliminary analyses, but also danger in failing to analyze past media innovations.

Dimmick and Rothenbuhler (1984) have taken another informative, but more ecological perspective on the succession of media. They noted that it may be possible to look at the effects of new media on the use of old media by studying past incursions. They used three variables, audience size, total resources (which are finite), and reallocation of resources, to examine this displacement process. Further, if a media is very specialized (e.g., movies), it may be easier to displace than a more general one (e.g., radio). Until recently with the advent of cable stations and other pay TV, movies, for example, always depended on consumers coming to certain places and spending money. It was relatively easy for TV to displace part of the time devoted to movies. However, radio, as TV developed, lost most of its national advertising, but greatly increased local advertising that largely was not on TV. Thus, movies found it initially difficult to find additional

TABLE 5.1
The Progression of Media from Elite, to Mass, to Specialized
Periods*

| | Periods | | |
Media	Elite Period	Mass Period	Specialized Period
Newspapers	—Early papers contain mostly commercial and political news.	—Penny Press, expanded as tabloids for masses with increase in advertising. —Mass newspapers expand after WWI with advent of syndicated news services. —Demise of individual owners, with ownership by conglomerates. —Some decline in circulation partly because of competition from other media.	—Computerization of operations allows for quicker presentation of news. —More specialization (e.g., different sections) of mass newspapers. —Computerization and satellite and laser systems allow for different versions of same newspaper for different segments.
Magazines	—Started after Civil War; catered to wealthy and diverse audiences reachable by railroad distribution.	—Increased distribution led to more advertising, lower price, a bigger market, and more advertising. —Demise of many magazines as TV allowed advertisers to reach larger audience.	—Mass magazines reappear but now geared to specific segments. —Computerization allows for different versions of magazines for particular segments. —Increase of specialized magazines for specific segments.
Books	—Originally, only for elite.	—Railroad allows for mass marketing of inexpensive paperbacks. —Books face competition from radio and TV.	—Hardbound and best sellers continue for elite. —Paperback books made more specialized by region and audience. —Computerization will increase specialization.

TABLE 5.1 (*Continued*)

Media	Periods		
	Elite Period	*Mass Period*	*Specialized Period*
Radio	—Limited availability for a small elite.	—Government control in WWI led to sharing of ideas and technology. —AT&T starts first "network" in 1920s by licensing stations and charging a fee for use of long-distance lines; organized advertisers. —Four major radio networks in the 1930s mostly characterized by popular stars and shows for the masses; national advertising. —Some affiliates still presented some local, specialized shows and local advertising. —By 1950s, TV reaching mass audience with national stars, shows, and advertisement.	—Radio again becomes more local, but with some national packaging of shows. —FM radio creates better sound quality and more specialized programs. —Special uses of radio because of qualities, e.g., low cost, use when engaged in another activity.
TV	—First experimental network began in 1940.	—By early 1950s, TV becomes mass media with mass advertising; entertainment and news. —Increased technical quality, but concerns about TV's program quality and impact. —Steady increase in TV ownership and time watched.	—Cable and satellite systems become more common. —More specialized stations and shows developed. —Two-way systems being developed. —Mass marketing of VCR's allows for more viewer control and program diversity.

*(Based on Bittner, 1980)

resources. Dimmick and Rothenbuhler (1984) noted that: "The key question . . . in determining the outcome of competition between industries revolves around the number and characteristics of consumers who choose to allocate their time and money to the various media alternatives" (p. 301). Thus, one way to assess the impact of mass marketing of PC's and computer games on TV viewing is to examine consumer TV viewing patterns prior to purchase. If viewing time is high, TV viewing (quantity) is likely to decrease given the finite resource of time. The effects of PC use on the viewing of select TV programs (quality) is less clear.

The ecological model provides one way to conceptualize and analyze media succession. However, the model can not really provide accurate long-term predictions, nor accurately predict outcomes where suddenly the societal distribution of resources is radically changed. This occur's through changes in regulatory policy (e.g., the break-up of AT&T), mergers, or when powerful new firms (e.g., IBM) suddenly enter a new arena and bring great resources from one area to the other.

However, the ecological perspective keeps a focus on the interdependency of behaviors. Change in one set of behavior leads to changes in other behaviors that have positive and negative effects. This basic point again calls into question panacea-like claims for new media.

OVERALL PERSPECTIVE AND KEY ISSUES

This introduction has served the purposes of providing an overall perspective for examining new media and addressing critical issues. These points are central to the discussion that follows:

1. The most probable scenario for societal change with the introduction of new media is the "modest" one. That is some forms of communication will be replaced by new media, whereas other forms will remain relatively intact. This suggests that attention be directed to the seemingly consistent progression of change and succession of new media.

2. Rather than passively accepting each type of new media, some proper skepticism seems in order. The media × task × person × resource analysis appears highly appropriate. These analyses should not just focus on technical and human factor aspects, but extend to the larger social context.

3. Conceptual and methodological aspects of the behavioral systems framework can be applied to analyses of new media. Although somewhat speculative at this point, given the dearth of research, the adaptability of the framework to other problems in information and behavior suggests applicability here. At the same time, perspectives and conclusions derived from others (i.e., McGuire, Atkin), should also have general applicability.

THE NEW MEDIA

Rice's (1984c) seminal social science book, *The New Media: Communication, research, and technology,* serves as a basic reference for a number of sections of this chapter. However, the objective here is to bring only key parts of the very detailed information presented by Rice into the perspectives of this chapter and volume. Thus, there is not any attempt to comprehensively review that book.

According to Rice, the new media primarily have changed the channel of communication, rather than specific content or purposes. However, if "the medium is the message," then it is apparent that a change in medium almost inevitably alters content and purpose.

The new media include PC's, videotext, and teletext, interactive cable systems, various computer games, videodiscs, electronic mail, computer conferencing, communication satellites, and office information systems. Major overriding dimensions of the new media are: speed of access; interactivity; the linking of communication and computer systems, i.e., "compunications," as well as the linkage of different media systems; variability in the time and place of communication; incredible capabilities for storing and arranging information, and blurring of distinctions between different media and technical and artistic endeavors. These major dimensions are captured in this extended quote from Rice (1984d):

> Optical fibers of spun glass, made from silicon in sand, brings worlds of sound and sight into our lives; the same laser beam used in optical fiber transmission, when used in holograms, contains enough information in any part of its message to recreate the entire three-dimensional image; a single strand of spun glass can contain nearly infinite bandwidth; and an hour's worth of information transmitted by these fibers would take nearly an eternity with most other media. . . . New ways of encoding, transmitting, distributing, and displaying information appear most overtly in the form of new communication technologies. For example, digital, as compared to analog, encoding dramatically increases the speed, accuracy, and volume of information that can be exchanged. It efficiently integrates voice, data, and video. It facilitates signal processing and coding techniques. It offers greater privacy and security. But more important, humans are beginning to communicate in new ways as well. New media . . . are blurring distinctions that seemed so clear and useful a generation ago. (pp. 33–34)

The key dimension of new media is interactivity between users of a system or between a user and the information in a system. For many new media (e.g., computer-mediated communication), the roles of sender and receiver become interchangeable. However, the exact definition of interactive is a bit fuzzy at this point. For example, interactivity can be between individuals on a system, but is also represented by the user's interactions with system designers and programmers who developed the system.

The sin qua non of new media is the microprocessor. This was preceded by the invention of the transistor that allowed for extreme miniaturization of electronic equipment. A microprocessor is a semiconductor chip or a set of two or more chips. The logic or "brains" of the computer is contained in the chips. The "information revolution," according to Rice, was made possible by microprocessors and memory chips, and the rapid decline in their costs.

Videodiscs exemplify the key dimensions. A videodisc can contain a tremendous amount of information. For educational and training purposes, videodiscs can be combined with a TV monitor, computer, and, perhaps, other control devices. The user can access a great volume of information in seconds, at most, that can be displayed in print, graphic, and pictoral form. For instructional purposes, content, questions, and learning branches can be completely individualized. Of course, all user responses can be automatically recorded.

Thus, there is interactivity, individualization, speed of access, the combination of systems, and different representations of information. However, bear in mind that creating videodisc programs is very expensive (J. Moore, personal communications, May, 1985); they are useable by only one person at a time, and it is unclear how learning and training generalize to nonmedia settings (Kiesler, Siegel, & McGuire, 1984), despite early hyperbolic claims (Broderick, 1982).

This underscores a general point made by Rice and Williams (1984). It is necessary with any media, but, perhaps, in particular new media, to differentiate between its usual content and its specific attributes. Presently, on videodiscs there may be considerable training content, but this does not mean that this current use best reflects the medium's best attributes and uses.

Two other aspects are important for understanding the uses and impacts of new media. Media can vary on the dimension of social presence felt by the user. Evaluations of media on semantic differentials can assess "unsocial-social," "insensitive-sensitive," "cold-warm," "impersonal-personal" dimensions. Data is limited at this point on social presence, but it appears to be an important aspect of any media system.

A second aspect that is often overlooked is that most people most of the time use media for entertainment (see also chapter 2). For example, Rice and Williams (1984) noted that in 1982 video-arcade users in the United States spent seven billion dollars on this pursuit; this figure was greater than the combined revenues of the movie and record industry. Videogames involve symbolic, mythic, social, and entertainment functions. The arcade situation also can make video game playing a public, even interpersonal and participatory, entertainment situation that may substitute (or succeed, from the ecological perspective) other social activities. Thus, videogames uniquely combine interactivity, social presence, social interaction, and entertainment.

However, at this point, it is not clear what effects a great amount of time spent on playing videogames has on learning and socialization outside the context of the game situation. Claims for spontaneity, increased eye–hand coordination, or preparation for computer use must be met with calls for evaluative data and concern on other fronts. For example, the learning and interactivity is restricted to what has been preprogrammed by others. Also, the content of the games often centers on violent action, with the games designed by males for the use of males. Obviously, many of these points are similar to those raised concerning the effects of violent TV programs (Rubinstein, 1983).

OTHER NEW MEDIA: EXAMPLES AND ISSUES

Other new media described at length by Rice (1984c) include electronic news-papers, computer-mediated group interaction, advanced word processing, multi-media teleconferencing, new library systems, and the large-scale introduction of PC's into schools and homes. In order to illustrate the applicability of the behavioral systems framework to the study of new media, specific aspects of the framework (e.g., implications of understanding behavior in context; acceptable research methods) are applied to the discussions and analyses of these select new media.

Electronic Newspapers and Behavior in Context

Dozier and Rice (1984) described electronic newspapers as "any system for distributing textual information on TV screens, where shelf life and manipulability of information permit direct competition with pulp newspapers" (p. 103). The primary attribute of electronic newspapers is the ability of the user to display by individual choice a subset of the available information on the screen. As newspapers become more expensive to print and distribute (as well as environmentally destructive), electronic news media becomes appealing. In addition, as noted before, newspapers are attempting to become increasingly specialized and segmented. The electronic newspaper can almost totally individualize their offering because readers can get what they want, when, and where they want it. Thus, electronic newspapers exemplify the cycle toward segmentation of a medium.

The development of electronic newspapers appears to have neglected a major perspective of the behavioral systems approach. That is, behavior must be studied in context. Dozier and Rice noted that much of the hardware and research revolve around utilitarian and human factors considerations. For example, videotext systems are often built around menu-driven systems that proceed from general to more specific menus. This may be a logical and precise way to approach access and information retrieval, but it may make it hard for some people to quickly find the information they want and also markedly reduce the pleasure derived from reading a newspaper. Most of the human factor studies have attempted to find the best entering system, format, and decision trees, and neglected aspects related to attractiveness, clarity, and enjoyment.

Consistent with the behavioral systems approach, the development of electronic newspapers may better proceed with an analysis of the settings, behaviors, and purposes of newspaper reading. For example, considerable time spent reading the newspaper may occur at the breakfast table with the major purposes being information and pleasure. Much additional newspaper reading may occur after dinner, in a comfortable chair, for the purpose of relaxation. The portability, adaptability to different settings, ease of access, and purposes may make electronic newspapers (in their present form) a poor vehicle in these settings. Settings for which the only purpose is quick access to the most up-to-date information may be more ideal for electronic newspapers.

Perhaps, for these same reasons, videotext systems have been slow to diffuse to the general public (Weaver, 1983). Important diffusion variables (chapter 3) such as relative advantage, simplicity, and compatibility seem to have been overlooked in relationship to how people read newspapers in specific settings.

Although studies on videotext systems suggest no extreme displacements of other media by videotext use, this result may be attributable to novelty (i.e., simply use videotext at first in addition to other media) and inadequate market penetration to make more definitive conclusions. Dozier and Rice concluded their discussion of electronic newspapers with points consistent with behavioral systems (e.g., how do people actually read news) and social marketing (e.g., how can videotext be designed to appeal to specific segments):

> The key to successful development of electronic micronewspapers is development of forms consistent with the type of play that characterizes the newsreading interlude. Vital to such play . . . is regular and consistent style or form of presentation. The indexing of information must become part of the subjective play of the newsreading interlude . . . (electronic) newspapers cannot be transformed into a task-oriented drudgery of data-base manipulation and intricate information recovery protocols . . . to do so is to take newsreading out of the realm of play and into the world of work and task accomplishments. Such systems will attract only nonpleasure readers; mature and pleasure readers will find little communication pleasure. (p. 125)

Computer-Mediated Group Communication and Social Psychological Considerations

Rice (1984b) noted that groups are the basic unit of social interaction in organizations and communities. They mediate the form, direction, and content of individual and interpersonal communication. Group communication via computer is relatively new and little research emphasizing social–psychological aspects is available (Kiesler et al., 1984). Presently, most computer-mediated interaction has changed two communication variables: (a) the channel is changed from face-to-face to computer print and graphics interaction, and (b) the content is shifted more to task-oriented interaction from social–emotional interactions.

Computer-mediated communication is most simply the introduction of the computer as the channel for sending, receiving, and storing textual and group discussion information. This medium allows for geographically dispersed individuals to interact simultaneously during real time, or at any time of a group member's choosing. The basic hardware and software is relatively simple: modems, a telephone line, terminals, at least one PC, and specifically designed programs for interaction, storage, and retrieval. Files in the system can be shared and worked on at any time. Messages and conferences can be public or private and involve individuals, or defined subgroups. A popular and burgeoning example of computer-mediated interactions is computer-bulletin-boards (see the following) now used for varying personal, social and entreprenurial interest.

Rice (1984b) delineated a number of potential weaknesses of computer conferencing including:

1. The written mode may be disliked for certain statements.
2. The speed and accuracy of typing may affect the interactions.
3. Direct interpersonal and nonverbal feedback is missing.
4. Participation rate in the groups may be infrequent.
5. Negotiations may become more rigid and less compromising.
6. Compared to face-to-face groups, leadership and the perceived need to communicate may be diminished.
7. Varying conference paths may develop leading to information overload and confusion.

What appears needed is some more research to delineate what tasks, decisions, groups, leadership, and tone (i.e., given limited emotional and nonverbal feedback) is most suitable to computer-mediated communication. At present, the strengths of this type of communication appear to be:

1. The ability to communicate with anyone at any time.
2. Possible maintenance of the group less by formal meeting times and places, but more by interest and motivation.
3. Facilitation of information exchange, processing of information, record keeping, and coordination of geographically remote members.
4. The development of more functional communication links rather than ritualized ones as in some face-to-face groups.
5. Perhaps, more equity of interaction because communication may be less bound by rank and/or social skills.

Kiesler et al. (1984) have started what may be at present the only programmatic, social, psychological research on computer-mediated communication. They noted that all types of information transfer and computer communication are advancing "like an avalanche" (p. 1123) and that computer-mediated communication is no longer for the few or the elite. However, the functions and impacts are poorly understood, such as, who uses these systems, for what purposes, involving what social psychological aspects with what individual and organizational impacts? Most of the research in this field has simply evaluated the efficiency, technical capabilities, and costs of a new media without addressing other dimensions. For example, they suggested that systems that can increase the communication rate may also change the status and hierarchical structure in an organization.

Kiesler et al. indicated that computer-communication had a number of distinct social-psychological qualities (see Rice's points, previously): (a) great speed, but no audio or visual feedback; (b) substitution of written text for other modes of communication; and (c) no strong etiquette on how to use the system. They then raised some key questions based on these points:

1. What does easy, rapid communication do? How does it change the quantity and timing of communication?

2. What does the absence of nonverbal feedback do? Is it efficient?

3. How do users compensate for the lack of audio and verbal cues? For example, how are compromises reached given the inability to use voice tone and eye contact?

4. Do these systems reduce charisma and status or are they retained or based now on other dimensions (e.g., facility in typing)?

5. Does the impersonal, socially anonymous nature of the communication have any effects?

6. How do these systems change cultural norms? Some examples here include the effects of the special language of the computer and its culture on the larger culture, and the effects of changes in real time, the spillover of work and home life, and issues in privacy (e.g., messages may be accessible by anyone).

Thus, from a social-psychological perspective, according to Kiesler et al. (1984) the major characteristics of computer-mediated communication are the absence of social context and widely shared norms:

> terminals and electronic signals convey fewer historical, contextual, and nonverbal cues. Electronic media do not efficiently communicate nuances of meaning and frame of mind, organizational loyalties, symbolic procedural variations, and especially individuating details about people that might be embodied in their dress, locations, demeanor, and expressiveness. . . . This situation, where personality and culture lack salience, might foster feelings of depersonalization. (p. 1126)

Kiesler et al., also felt that it was difficult to extrapolate from the introduction of other new technology such as the teletypewriter. This is because contemporary electronic communication becomes virtually discontinuous from former technology given time, speed, ease of use, fun, audience characteristics, and instant (print) feedback differences (however, see Table 5.1, where the analysis is at odds with this perspective).

To address some of the questions they have raised, Kiesler, et al., have done a series of experiments. The studies basically involve three people interacting on terminals in real settings. Of prime interest are patterns of interaction and decisions on present problems. Some studies compared face-to-face communication, anonymous computer, and nonanonymous computer interactions. Dependent variables included communication efficiency, participatory interpersonal behavior, and group choice.

Some general results from three experiments were:

1. Computer-mediated groups took longer to reach consensus than face-to-face groups. Computer-groups were as task-oriented as face-to-face groups, but exchanged fewer remarks in the time allowed. The use of the key-board took time, but these differences were not attributable to this problem.
2. Computer groups showed more equal participation and dominance of one person was less in computer groups.
3. Computer groups appeared to be more uninhibited and showed more choice shifts.
4. The general results pertained to novice and experienced users, i.e., not dependent on familiarity with the technology.

Kiesler et al., attributed these results to difficulties in coordinating the group and controlling discussion because of the lack of social influence and other feedback cues and a dominant leader. The lack of inhibition may also result from minimal nonverbal involvement and the absence of norms.

For future research, Kiesler et al. recommended basing studies on a framework emphasizing social processes and tests of alternative theoretical notions, and a focus on the critical issues of nonverbal involvement and (possibly) resulting uninhibited responses. They saw exciting applications in education, public affairs, and mental health, such as, long-distance collaborative work, interactive polling, and the development of personal, social support networks. Consistent with this volume, Kiesler et al. saw such theoretical and applied work being interdisciplinary. They also indicated that research must study impacts beyond the situation where the communication takes place. For example, it may be quite feasible to set-up computer-mediated support networks for the elderly, and monitor every interaction that takes place. But how such patterns of computer-based interaction relate to short and long-term health outcomes must also be assessed.

Computer Bulletin Boards and Behavioral Principles

Computer bulletin boards (CBB's) and computer networks are rapidly developing. CBB's have been designed for such diverse purposes as facilitating professional research interactions (Rice, 1982), to exchanging information on new software, to providing clinical health services (Walker, 1986). Basically, all that is required to start a CBB is a group of people at any number of locations with modems, communication and CBB software packages, and a printer. CBB's are obviously a subpart of computer-mediated communication, but presumably people have decided to communicate in this way for some mutual benefit and goal in some formal and informal ways.

The discussion here focuses on the use of CBB's for behavior change. Optimization of CBB's depends on an analysis of the uniqueness of the medium coupled with behavior change principles. For example, a least optimal way to use CBB's would be simply to have instructions, i.e., bibliotherapy, for behavior change. Not only is the approach, at best, marginally effective (Glasgow & Rosen, 1978), but using that format begs the question of why not simply sending out self-help manuals to interested people?

CBB's may provide a way to give:

1. highly individualized instruction based on individualized assessment;
2. frequent contact focusing on change strategies and specific assignments in which change strategies are tried within a successive approximation approach, and,
3. individualized and frequent feedback on such efforts.

Such contact, instruction, and feedback may be more extensive but less expensive, than face-to-face counseling. These interactions can also provide the bases for continual (data) monitoring of the individual intervention, and some external checks can be made to assess the reliability and validity of the self-reported data.

Preliminary study (Walker, 1986) indicated that although such an approach required considerable time for software development, once the system was in operation, minimal time was required to service over twenty clients in a stress management intervention. It was possible to individualize the program and provide frequent feedback. However, most importantly, there was some evidence for behavior change apart from the simple interactions with the computer. That is, recommended stress management procedures were used with reported (and, verified) reductions in stress. Such demonstrations of generalization across behaviors (i.e., from a mechanical and verbal computer interaction to a related behavior in an appropriate setting) and time are sorely needed.

CBB's also offer a way to involve the group in intervention so that the system operator is not simply performing individual counseling in a group context. For example, CBB members can be instructed on how to scan client files and also deliver appropriate support, information, and feedback. Such an approach approximates true behavioral group therapy (Flowers, 1979).

Finally, the research potential of CBB's is particularly intriguing. The content of every message (where not designated as private) and the particular interaction can be automatically recorded. Thus, it becomes possible to examine at a microlevel professional and peer interactions related to behavior change. Such research can help identify common elements of change related to different problems and interventions (Goldfried, 1980), as well as contributing to the understanding of how networks function (Danowski, 1982; Rice, 1982). A major problem in network analysis has been the suspect reliability and validity of the verbal reports of network members (Rogers & Kincaid, 1981). Thus, CBB's may offer a unique way to deliver service and study therapeutic process and outcome.

Word Processing and the Interdependency of Behaviors

Johnson and Rice (1984) noted that most of the study of new media has taken place in business organizations, perhaps because they have the monetary resources to try out new systems and must constantly make changes to remain competitive. However, adoption of new systems may be done rather blindly and without analyses of the tasks at hand, how such tasks are done, the potential for redisgn, the adaptability of technology, the interdependencies between different behaviors, and the effects of the new technology on individuals and the organization.

According to Johnson and Rice, the key resource in many organizations is attention. Information and information systems must be designed so that this scarce resource is more available for crucial and strategic tasks.

The introduction of word processing is an important innovation to monitor because it is seen as the first step toward the automated office of the future, and, hence, can supply some insights into the costs and benefits of such automation. Some interesting points emerged from these initial studies.

In most organizations, word processing simply has been substituted for typing. Therefore, clerical staff are the first people to have dealt with word processing and its simple substitution for typing misses the opportunity for changes in typical roles and the creation of new print information. Johnson and Rice (1984) suggested that to more thoroughly find out about new uses for word-processing, i.e., "reinvention" (chapter 3), it is more appropriate to interact at this point with the clerical staff and not the executives. Then too, if word processing is seen simply as a way to increase productivity in a narrow sense, then the potential of this innovation to create new ways to use media and to work will be stifled. "But good management of an innovation in information work can lead to increased effectiveness, successful accomplishment of organizational mission, and, perhaps even redefinitions of that mission" (Johnson & Rice, 1984, p. 176).

The emphasis on hardware development in word processing and its introduction to clerical staff as a substitute for typing has also missed a key point in systems analysis—the interdependencies between behaviors. It is impossible to have changes in one set of behaviors not affect other sets of behaviors. Likewise, some of these side-effects may be positive and others may be negative.

The observations of the author of his own university's introduction of word processing and PC's during the last 2 years have attended to the multiple effects of this innovation. Word processing and PC's have virtually replaced the typewriter during this period, but with mixed effects. For example:

1. Many faculty have their own high powered PC's and quality printers at home, which, in addition, are linked by modem to the university's main frame. Thus, at least at some universities, word processing may have different uses and impacts than in business settings where word processing may still be the province of clerical staff. Thus, more than ever, many faculty are doing their intellectual work at home and only being present on campus to meet classes and attend meetings.

2. Except for mainframe interaction, the advent of word processing and PC's seems to have decreased the dependency of some individuals on the organization. Some faculty now do not need support services (e.g., secretaries) and also can tap into data-bases far removed from the university. A modem also can make collaboration with people at diverse settings more possible, perhaps further reducing the need to interact with other colleagues in the university.

3. The introduction of individual PC's with word-processing capabilities seems to fit into, and enhance the academic, entrepreneurial model at universities. The individual advances based on his or her track record of publications and grants and contracts. Collegial collaboration, teaching, and service often are secondary considerations for evaluation. In the author's university (and I suspect in many others), a bottom-line mentality now exists (given economic contraction) with the mass delivery of PC's and other computer equipment introduced to increase productivity (i.e., recognition through publication, dollars through grants and contracts). The new technology may help to reach these productivity goals but, perhaps at the expense of quality time with students, collaboration with colleagues, and service to the university and community.

4. If more and more faculty do their own word processing, it becomes unclear what secretaries will do. Will the number of secretaries be reduced over time? Will the role of secretaries shift to more menial tasks (e.g., face-to-face and phone receptionist) or be upgraded (e.g., data-base management)? The fear of many support people is that they will be replaced by the machines.

This section has underscored the interdependent nature of behaviors. Change in one set of behaviors affects other sets of behaviors in positive and negative and, at times, predictable and unpredicable ways. The author's observations at his own university unfortunately suggest that relatively rudimentary system considerations (i.e., the interdependency of behaviors) have not been well addressed or studied prior to the mass introduction of word processing and PC's.

Teleconferencing: Behavior in Context, Interdependencies, and Cost-Effectiveness

Teleconferencing also is described as a "new media" even though the ideas about this innovation have been around for about 50 years (Svenning & Ruchinskas, 1984). Teleconferencing can take a number of forms and is being highly touted today. The technology and protocols are becoming more sophisticated, but less expensive. Adding to its appeal are its costs compared to the costs of travel (air and ground transportation, lodging and food) that have increased considerably in the 1970s, whereas at the same time, many firms have offices or business dealings at various geographic points. According to Svenning and Ruchinskas (1984):

> Teleconferencing is interactive, electronic communication among three or more people in two or more separate locations. All four teleconferencing modes (computer, audio, audiographic, and video) are communication tools that facilitate meetings among people in different locations. The geographic dispersion of many modern organizations and the need for groups of people in these varied locations to work together in a timely fashion makes teleconferencing an increasingly appealing alternative to face-to-face meetings and two-party phone calls. (p. 218)

Contrary to common perceptions, however, teleconferencing is still a relatively infrequently used new media. Svenning and Ruchinskas reported that a number of firms tried teleconferencing in the 1960s and 1970s, but discontinued the innovation because the systems had many technical problems, poor protocols for human-system interactions (e.g., procedures for participatory meetings), insufficient training for participants, high costs, insufficient management support, and limited assessments and evaluations. Currently, less than 1% of all organizations in the private business sector use teleconferencing on a regular basis, but renewed interest may lead to increased trials (Svenning & Ruchinskas, 1984).

From a diffusion perspective (chapter 3), it is not surprising that teleconferencing only has been slowly adopted. This is because:

1. It is complex. For example, the user must choose different modes and different combinations of these modes. Capabilities are also rapidly changing.
2. The cost and complexity requires individual, group, and organizational acceptance. An organizational "champion" is required.

3. The innovation may appear to be incompatible with prevailing rules and norms of conducting business.
4. It may not be much fun.

In defining teleconferencing, it is important to note that video conferencing is actually the least frequently used mode, whereas audio teleconferencing, far cheaper, is the most popular and frequently used mode. Different options, at different costs, exist for video from a constant picture of the audience to video switches coinciding with whom is talking. The most usual system is a two-way audio and one way video. Audiographic is the second most popular mode and may meet most business organization needs in this area.

Conducting cost-effective and cost–benefit analyses of teleconferencing appears to be more complex than the claims that its champions suggest. Analyses must take into account the ostensible goals of a conference, the secondary goals, and the distribution of costs. For example, conference goals may primarily be information transfer, information transfer and discussion to reach consensus, discussion and "brainstorming" to formulate new ideas and directions, or group and individual interactions to promote familiarity and trust for future meetings and other endeavors. Where conference goals mostly revolve around information transfer, it appears feasible to compare the cost-effectiveness (e.g., on knowledge gains by the audience) of face-to-face versus teleconferences. However, written materials or videotapes may replace either conference format for much less cost if the goal is simply information transfer.

The current protocols of one-way video, two-way audio teleconferences may not lend themselves to more personal, interactive formats and purposes. The author has participated in state-of-the-art teleconferences where the best description of the interactions would be "stilted." Too much focus may be on hardware, and too little on studying conference behaviors in context. Exchanging information only may not be very enjoyable, and teleconferences may miss the

TABLE 5.2
Face-to-Face Conference Costs

Parking for cars ($10 × 50)	$500
Air travel $300 × 100	$30,000[a]
Ground transportation $20 × 100	$2,000[b]
Lodging $50 × 100	$5,000[c]
Food $30 × 100	$3,000[d]
Cost of Conference Setting	$1,000
	$41,500

[a]Based on a mean cost from a midwest city to either coast.
[b]Shared limousine.
[c]A group rate.
[d]A minimum per diem for 3 meals.

TABLE 5.3
Teleconference Costs

Use of satellite (visual) ($1,000 an hour)	$6,000
Audio costs ($2,000 an hour)	$12,000
Site costs ($600 a site)	$3,400
Food (lunch) 100 × $10	$1,000
Cost of origination setting	$2,000
Cost for participants to travel to local sites ($20 × 100)	$2,000
	$26,400

main point of most conferences—to meet and interact with other people in order to form relationships to expedite diverse career goals. Simply put, the most significant conference behaviors and outcomes may have little to do with the formal presentations. These points suggest careful attention to the media × task × learner × resources framework.

It is possible to do some rudimentary cost comparisons of a face-to-face versus a teleconference where the primary goal is information transfer. This scenario entails 100 participants in a 6-hour (1 day) conference. The participants are from four distant settings and for the face-to-face conference must travel to the conference after work one evening and return the following evening. It is assumed that participants are at a professional level and will not be paid extra for their travel time. Costs also do not include conference preparation time.

Table 5.3 presents the costs of a comparable teleconference.

The costs for the teleconference are based on figures from Dr. Stanley Huffman, the Director of the Learning Resource Center at Virginia Polytechnic Institute and State University, a noted developer of teleconferencing. The present scenario would use the Westar #4 Satellite as an "uplink" and the Holiday Inn–High Net System as the "downlink". In this analysis, the teleconference seems more than one third cheaper.

The comparisons appear most viable for the information transfer conference. However, actual cost-effectiveness comparisons only can be done when an assessment is made of the real outcomes of different conference formats, i.e., information gain and later use of the information of at least prototypes of the face-to-face and teleconference (Levin, 1983).

These analyses would be remiss if other information transfer methods were not tried. Manuals and videotapes for each site would cost a fraction of either conference cost. Or, sending an instructor to each site to lead a local conference may cost as little as $2,000 ($500 per site).

Other issues arise than simply comparing costs even when the conference outcomes are the same. The resources to present the conference are distributed to different concerns. Most of the costs for the teleconferences are incurred for use of the communication technology. Minimal costs are for site use, travel to the site, and food. The primary expense for the face-to-face conference is for air travel, with lesser but substantial costs for food and lodging. Thus, changing from face-to-face to teleconferences means gains and losses for different industries and occupations. The long-term effects of resource transfer from one set of firms to another is less clear and demands societal cost-benefit analyses (Levin, 1983). This point returns us to the notion of interdependency. Large-scale changes from face-to-face to teleconferencing will have diverse outcomes on people and organizations far beyond the people and organizations implementing conferences.

Videodiscs and Social Learning Principles

Videodiscs mesh visuals, graphics, and print with the individuating and interactive capabilities of the PC. Thus, they are seen as highly appropriate for educational and training objectives, and as an adjunct to mass education that has sharply reduced interactive and individualized instruction (Bork, 1982). Videodisc instruction is also appropriate where visuals (and not merely a lecture, ''talking head'' format) are needed; and where a system needs to be suitable (via trees and branches) for use by people with varying levels of skill, knowledge, and motivation (DeBloois, 1982).

Brandt and Knapp (1982) further delineated when videodiscs might enhance instruction:

1. Where particular visual cues are important. For example, in diagnosing certain diseases, it is important for doctors to recognize a pattern of visual signs.
2. Where graphics are needed and a microcomputer cannot generate the needed graphics in a reasonable amount of time.
3. Where experiments or procedures must be demonstrated and where too much time, equipment, expense, or danger is involved for an on-the-spot demonstration.
4. Where learning requires combining both video and audio aspects, e.g., legal training in a courtroom.

Interactivity, a key aspect of new media, makes videodisc instruction different from merely viewing a videotape. Interactivity means at a minimum that the user has the ability to control how a presentation is viewed, with a complimentary response from the system (Woolley, 1982). Woolley (1982) states:

> The user, in effect, is given the power to alter or change the way in which information may be presented. Interaction by the user may take place as a result of a user decision; discrete instruction from the material being viewed; instruction from a teacher or instructor, or instructions from some auxillary source materials. The basic form of the interaction may be expressed through touch panels, keyboards, light pens, voice activation, or by simply walking away from the training

session. The entire process is characterized by both accuracy and overall speed of response of the delivery mechanism. (p. 149)

Producing a videodisc is quite different from producing a videotape (Bennion, 1982). Because the product is an interaction of visual, audio, and print media that is learner controlled, there must be many different branches. However, there usually is not need for a storyline (perhaps, just short vignettes or demonstrations) and only limited formal features such as dissolves, for example, are used in story lines for continuity between scenes. Also, the viewer is able to view scenes over and over again.

Videodiscs have also been developed for training of social skills, such as nursing care and sales. In these videodisc formats observed by the author, a trainee is presented particular scenes, e.g., an overly complaining patient, then asked to indicate (multiple-choice format) possible responses. The trainee is then shown the consequences of the response in an accompanying scene. Voice and print feedback and instruction then can indicate the positive and negative aspects of the choice with the trainee requested to make another response to the first scene, or move on to another. Depending on the pattern of responses, the trainee is able to advance at different rates.

For the most part, this author's response to these systems was mixed. The following are some subjective and objective reasons for this appraisal:

1. The systems were novel and fun to use, but it was not clear if these qualities were simply transitory.

2. The systems and training protocols generally did not follow accepted social skills training procedures (Eisler & Frederiksen, 1980). Most basically, at present there are few, if any, evaluations of these systems demonstrating efficient transfer of training, i.e., actual behavior change, in critical settings (Woolley, 1982).

3. There is not convincing literature that interactivy guarantees learning. Rather, the key mechanism may be enjoyment of the task, facilitating attention and practice (Woolley, 1982).

4. At present, demonstration, instructional videodiscs can cost as much as $60,000 to $100,000 to produce, depending on branches needed, available source material, and features of the discs (Willis, 1982). The cost may not be much for a business organization, but is beyond the reach of many human service agencies. However, replication of the master disc in large numbers is not expensive, about $15 each in lots of 50 (Wood, 1982). Thus, the viability of videodiscs depends on considerable front-end costs for production of many programs for consumer choice and costs for consumer procurement of systems. Once these costs are met, then distribution can proceed and bring down costs.

5. However, the videodisc systems are designed for individualized instruction (their strength), meaning they can only be used by one person at a time (their

weakness). Mass instruction by videotape may not be as effective, but it may be much more cost-effective.

6. Thus, videodiscs do have qualities for storage and retrieval of information and for education and training that can replace some print, audio, and visual media. But, it would be premature to call videodiscs a communication panacea (Wood, 1982).

Willis (1982) provided an important, cautionary overview that is highly consistent with one perspective of this chapter:

> As videodisc technology makes its way into the educational and industrial marketplace, the short- and long-term impact of preproduction formatting decisions is continually made self-evident. As a result, instructional developers are being reminded of a technological "fact of life": the selection of an appropriate medium can only be made after learner characteristics and formatting options related to media availability, cost, and capabilities are carefully analyzed. Too often, however, this "front-end" analysis is by-passed. The result is a poorly planned education product that may appear polished and useful but, in reality, fails to meet the goals that it was designed to accomplish. (p. 101)

Willis also discussed media innovations within a useful diffusion paradigm. Innovations go through three stages: birth, death, and resurrection. In the birth stage, the capabilities and specific applications are poorly understood. The new media is seen as a panacea and various appropriate and inappropriate applications are tried without any serious analysis. Because the innovation has been oversold and inappropriately used, many applications invariably fail, leading to the medium's death. Only after these failures, do developers step back and perform the kind of analyses that should have been performed in the birth stage. With these analyses, more appropriate uses are found for the medium and it is resurrected. "This cyclical process has been repeated with virtually every media innovation" (Willis, 1982, p. 101). Perhaps videodiscs and other new media are still in the birth stage. If so, a period of rejection can be anticipated, followed by more fine-tuned applications.

Social learning principles for skills training is the major point of input concerning the viability of interactive videodiscs systems. It was noted that these systems have the following positive qualities for training: (a) highly individualized format; (b) interactivity; (c) highly visual; (d) speed of access; (e) repetition and review. In addition, these systems can break down a set of behaviors (for example, courteous, but assertive nursing behaviors) into smaller segments, and it is clearly possible through formative research to closely tailor material to receivers and recommend behaviors in light of environmental constraints (e.g., the power of doctors over nurses). Thus, interactive videodisc systems, probably more than other new media, fit within the guidelines for effective media (see chapter 1, Table 1.3). However, despite this good, and probably purposeful fit, as currently used, these systems still do not reflect state-of-the-art training within social learning principles.

The major shortcoming entails the lack of real-life practice and feedback. Under present protocols, trainees may only acquire knowledge about behaviors, but not necessarily perform them. Behavioral modeling alone can be a somewhat effective behavior change strategy, but modeling with feedback and practice (participant modeling) can be much more effective. Participant modeling provides a person with a higher degree of self-efficacy than modeling alone (Bandura, 1977b). This is particularly the case where the behaviors to be enacted are not entirely simple (e.g., interpersonal behaviors) and where the response of others may not be exactly predictable (e.g., doctors to assertive nurses). For more optimal training, behaviors can be modeled; then role played; then tried out in real-life settings; results reported back to a trainer; adjustments made; behavior retried, and so on. In addition, training would follow a successive approximation approach in which more simple behaviors and situations (e.g., eliciting cooperation from a patient to change the bed) would be attempted first, and, if successful, followed by more difficult behaviors and situations (e.g., pointing out missed patient data to a doctor). This give and take process may be better, and perhaps less expensively, completed in a behavioral group (see Eisler & Frederiksen, 1980; Flowers, 1979).

Other important training problems involve issues in specificity, generalization, and maintenance. As suggested by the prior example, training can be most effective when it is highly specific, i.e., behavior geared to a particular situation. However, such specific training may limit generality and maintenance, such as somewhat different behaviors for different situations over time. Efforts at more general training (e.g., problem solving) have yielded at best mixed results. The trainee may know general strategies but have difficulty applying them to specific situations at a later time (Wilson & O'Leary, 1980). Finally, in all behavior change efforts, the most important problem, even when initial training is optimal, is maintenance. The following procedures could facilitate maintenance: (a) Real-life training in diverse settings with corrective feedback; (b) Training for nonoptimal responses, e.g., responses for refusals to the client's assertive requests; (c) Planned and frequent follow-ups on target behaviors.

It may be possible to build all these features into videodisc training programs. For example, assignments based on individual progress and data can be given with the person inputting the outcome of the assignment in order to produce tailored training and the next assignment. Then, too, periodic check-ups can be part of the protocol.

The major point here is that failure to provide for real-life and maintenance training will result in an expensive, but faulty program. As in other examples, there appears to be a need for meshing the hardware and software of the new media with behavioral systems principles. Simply using videodiscs for behavioral training may lead to their premature death.

Problem Solving by Computer and Artificial Intelligence: The Need for Behavioral Research Methods

An important article by Kleinmuntz (1984) put current interest in computer problem solving and artificial intelligence (AI) within four converging fields:

1. Studies on clinical versus statistical accuracy in predictions.
2. Information processing psychologists and other scientists emphasis on the ability of the computer to think.
3. A new focus on complex human decision making strategies.
4. The interest by physicians on formal approaches to medical reasoning.

However, the simple availability of the computer and the recognition by the 1950s and 1960s, that computers could do more than merely compute, is probably the most significant factor explaining the growth in interest in problem solving and AI. Some background on the four contributing fields is instructive.

1. Clinical versus Statistical Judgment. Over 30 years ago, Meehl (1954) demonstrated that intuitive judgments may not be as accurate as formal ones (e.g., using statistics). This position has been countered by others (Holt, 1958) who have argued that subjective judgments add a significant dimension to prediction and that machine-oriented assessment denigrate the clinician and patient. However, it appears to be the case, particularly for physicians, that they typically combine hard data from laboratory and other tests and make decisions based on specific rules and facts stored in memory. That is, this is exactly the kind of situation where computer analysis would be very useful.

2. Artificial Intelligence. This field also can be traced back to the 1950s with efforts to create psychological theories, i.e., simulation theories, of human problem solving using computer program statements as basic elements in theory construction (e.g., Newell & Simon, 1958). The theories and statements are intricate enough to simulate complex human tasks. For example, Kleinmuntz indicated that chess playing computer models can predict the moves a human would consider and all the problem solving behaviors associated with the choice. This basic approach has been incorporated into so called expert-systems that can sequentially perform a set of deductive steps that can lead, for example, to specific diagnoses and prescriptions for treatment. The system can learn in the sense that the course of each treatment and outcome becomes part of its data-base for subsequent diagnoses.

3. Behavioral Decision Theory. Kleinmuntz attributed the seminal work in this field to Savage (1954) who used Bayesian statistical theory as a way to combine subjective beliefs with objective data to then provide subjective probabilities. Subsequent to these developments was the application of this method to business, medical diagnosis, and policy decisions. Much controversy in the field exists on the accuracy of subjective probabilities and how errors in probabilities affect decision making. Considerable work by Kahneman and Tversky (1984) has shown how subjective probabilities can be markedly influenced by certain information processing heuristics. Nevertheless, research continues in this field with the computer a necessary part of studies given the vast amounts of data handled in this work.

4. Formal Approaches to Medical Reasoning.   Interest in developing formal, but simplifying, approaches to medical diagnosis also started in the 1950s. Guides and other heuristics were used to indicate symptom complexes and diseases that a patient did or did not have. Through an elimination and matching process, a diagnosis could be reached. This cumbersome approach was formalized with the use of symbolic logic, conditional probability, and value theory. Obviously, the use of computers was needed to handle the enormous number of possible complexities. But even today, the number of permutations are challenging to computers so that the possible combinations of symptom-disease complexes are reduced by using hierarchical structures (of complexes).

Given these developments, it would appear that the medical profession would readily embrace computer-based clinical decisions. However, Kleinmuntz indicated that this has not been the case. Computers have been involved in complex activities; for example, they can play chess as a good chess player does, which requires knowing about 1,300 patterns (Simon, 1979). However, masters and grandmasters must know about 50,000 patterns. Because of the stakes involved in medical decision making, computers must perform at the grandmaster level—a level of proficiency, that according to Kleinmuntz, is reachable in the near future.

This will be possible because:

1. The data base, hospital files and case material is becoming computerized, and automatically entered by physicians and staff using relatively standard programs.

2. With this computer-based system, a large variety of statistical analyses (e.g., on symptoms complexes, diagnoses, treatment, and outcomes) can be done.

3. There are presently several computer-based medical records systems used to assist in diagnosis, management of cases, and prognostic evaluation of tests and other diagnostic methods. Beginnings have also been made in expert systems for particular diseases (e.g., glaucomas) that will state a probability for confirming, denying, or nondetermined based on the input.

4. Various other computer systems have been developed for use in emergency rooms, cardiology, and internal ailments. All such systems depend on the viability of the computer programs, the expert clinicians who are being simulat-

ed, or mathematical modeling of a large data base. The simulation and mathematical modeling approaches both seem, according to Kleinmuntz, acceptable and can, indeed, complement each other.

Thus, Kleinmuntz concluded that computer-based, diagnostic systems are becoming more sophisticated and applicable in a number of domains. He indicated further that if funding in medical applications had been as rich as in other areas of application—defense—that computer problem solving in medicine would be much further developed. What is the next stage in this development? Although controversy exists in the AI field on how to construct intelligent machines (i.e., design them on formal mathematical logic or as people think—which does not usually follow mathematical logic), there is agreement that the goal is to teach computers to go beyond the mere facts, i.e., to have common sense. What Kleinmuntz has predicted is that the various spin-offs from AI research will be applied to diagnostic problem solving in a new, more sophisticated, and perhaps, more versatile and accurate approach.

Applications of AI seem very promising, however, one major problem is illustrated in the discussion of a derivative of AI, expert systems. Although to date most of these applications have been for military purposes, more systems will be developed for medical diagnoses and even for decisions in human service agencies (Schoech, Jennings, Schkade, & Hooper–Russell, 1985). According to Schoech et al. (1985), a simple definition of the workings of expert system is that they:

> contain user and system generated facts, inference schemes, and a knowledge base comprised of expertise such as that contained in the rules-of-thumb experts use in making a decision. These systems mimic human decision making by using familiar processes such as identifying patterns, drawing intermediate conclusions, and combining conclusions into a major decision. The capacity of expert systems to analyze user presented facts using a large body of human expertise, to detail the rationale for the decision made, and to learn from use offers great potential for assisting and training human service professional decision making such as that which occurs in the professional-client interaction. (p. 83)

Obviously, the most crucial input to the expert system is the knowledge, rules, and heuristics supplied by the experts. And, it is at this crucial point where behavioral research strategies could be most beneficially employed, but where they appear not to be used. For example:

1. Reliability data must be generated between independent experts (interexpert agreement) on recognizable stimuli patterns, diagnosis, prognosis, and treatment. Where agreement is low on material (i.e., less than 80%), there is clearly a danger in incorporating that material into the system. Expert systems that use unreliable inputs are, at best, limiting the system to mimicking the processes of one expert.

2. The efforts to decipher the expert processes so they can be inputed, may be tedious and time consuming, but it appears that these efforts only rely on verbal reports. That is, an expert may be asked, ". . . given symptoms "A", "B", and "C", it means _____? You would, therefore, use X treatment based on this stimulus pattern and its likely course." Simply to obtain this information for many possible stimulus configurations is quite difficult. But, what is needed is to again assess in another way, if the same expert responds the same way to the stimulus configuration (intraexpert agreement). But, this is still only verbal report. It is further necessary to verify that when confronted with the pattern in real-life, the expert's behavior conforms to the separately obtained verbal report. This appears not to be done.

3. Once the expert system is in operation, it should be independently run for a time in overlap fashion with the experts. This would be for purposes of reliability.

4. Even when inputs are obtained following reliability methods common in behavioral research, it is necessary to conduct validity studies. For example, experts may agree between themselves, and verbal reports may correspond to actual expert behaviors, but the knowledge-base may be invalid. That is, a stimulus pattern may reliably receive a particular diagnosis and treatment plan, but the treatment may not be effective. The expert system then simply continues the ineffective practice!

5. A final point follows from this last point. A danger in expert systems is the continuation of expensive and/or ineffective service delivery. The expert system may bring the guise of innovation to a service delivery mode that itself needs to be modified. The best examples here are within medical practices. Expert system for diagnosis may expedite some diagnostic processes and make such processes available to remote services. However, the expert system in this example may have little to do with two important elements of problems in cost-containment in health care, i.e., the emphasis on an expensive, high technology treatment approach with minimal emphasis on prevention (chapter 6).

Thus, behavioral research methods may lead to more accurately designed expert systems. However, more critical questions may involve perpetuating ineffectual systems with the introduction of new technology.

SPECIAL ISSUES IN NEW MEDIA

In this section, four special issues are discussed: (a) how new media and other high technology will affect employment patterns in the future; (b) the effects of PC's and other new media on children; (c) how new media may change communication theory and research; and (d) new ways of defining and measuring productivity in the information age. A final, and longer section, addresses in some detail issues concerning new media's relationship to centralization of power and control, and free-market versus regulatory approaches to increasing access to media and diversity of images and information.

Employment Patterns

New media and the growth of high technology have fostered a public image of a large growth of well-paid jobs in sparkling, clean white-collar palaces. This image (or more likely, hope) has led to many debates and dialogues about the need to restructure education along more technical lines in order to prepare students for the high-tech future. Undoubtedly, there is some basis for optimism about employment opportunities and educational change. However, this chapter's adoption of the modest change scenario suggests caution in being overly optimistic about employment in the future and radically restructing the content of education.

Levin and Rumberger (1983) issued an extremely sobering report entitled: *The Educational Implications of High Technology* (1983). Their analyses of education needs and growth in the high technology sector indicated these trends will probably lead to:

1. Expansion of the *lowest* skilled jobs at a pace far greater than expansion of high technology jobs.
2. Diminishing the skill requirements of many jobs in the U.S. economy.
3. Many jobs *not* requiring more analytical and communicative skills.
4. But, the education system should start stressing these skills more because these skills will help people deal with changing political, economic, social, and cultural institutions in the future.

These additional points were made: (a) A wholesale switch to high technology education was *not* recommended; (b) Education should stress preparing people for skill changes and education they will need in their adult lifes.

This report is highly consonant with the points made about analyses of new media. It is necessary to step back and study trends, uses, tasks, costs, and markets before leaping to conclusions. One other important point is also illustrated by the study of Levin and Rumberger. As diffusion of innovation researchers have belatedly discovered (Rogers, 1983; chapter 3), innovations have positive and negative consequences. One basis for appraising an innovation involves equity considerations, and unfortunately, high-tech education and careers and the evolution into the information age may increase the distance between the "haves" and "have-nots."

A further example of this last point is an analysis of working at home using computers and other telecommunications equipment. Olson and Primps (1984) pointed out that where an individual had special skills, was in demand, and where the job was characterized by autonomy, work at home reinforces autonomy and self-control of work. However, where an employee skill was not in demand, and where the employee had few other work options due to family constraints, the job may well be designed to reduce autonomy and may involve reduced compensation relative to similar work performed on-site. For example, word processing at home may become the province of part-time female employees, essentially working on a piece-work basis with reduced or no benefits. Working at home may further increase stress from social isolation, overlapping responsibilities for child care, loss of valuable home space to work equipment, and a further demeaning of particular kinds of work as "women's work." The analysis by Olson and Primps is an important and sobering counterpoint to Toffler's (1980) euphoric notion of the "electronic cottage." It is also a reminder that serious contextual analyses must replace dazzling, hyperbolic claims.

Computers and Children

Chen (1984) pointed out that we are now at a point comparable in the use of computer technology by children as we were with television when Schramm, Lyle, and Parker (1961) issued their ground breaking study. Chen reported that just as children quickly took to TV, they have taken to the microcomputer. In the 1950s, little was known about the effects of TV, and similarly today we know little about the effects of microcomputers on children.

It is important that such studies begin because microcomputers are rapidly diffusing. By 1983, Chen reported that 8% of homes in the United States had micro's; 42% of elementary schools, and 77% of high schools. Doubtless, at this point, the household and elementary school figures are much higher.

TV and micro's have different economics and have been perceived quite differently by our society. People do not pay directly for network TV shows (except nominal fees for cable systems), but do pay through their continual exposure to commercials and increased costs of products. TV shows and commercials are geared primarily to adults. However, most people perceive television as inexpensive and free. The educational value of commercial TV is somewhat dubious and it took TV almost 20 years to get into educational TV such as PBS.

In contrast, the costs of micro's are relatively high and are generally more than a TV and VCR. The latter can be used by many children (in a school) at one time, however, this is not true of micro's. There are also the costs for specific programs and hardware in order to update any system. However, many micro programs have been geared to an "educational" market (the quotes simply mean that labeling a program educational does not automatically equate to learning outcomes).

Research on children and micro's is still in the very early stages, but has not followed past TV research. Micro's are seen as positive, and until recently (e.g.,

Wright & Huston, 1983), TV was almost always seen as negative. For example, there does not seem to be much emphasis in the micro research on antisocial behavior even though some fears have been voiced about the violence in video games.

Instead, most of the research on micro's has focused on cognitive learning. Children are seen as active, engaged, and thinking, i.e., a perceptive information processor and "user." This is in stark contrast to how children are portrayed in TV research. There, they are viewers, passive recipients of images, noise, and information (see chapter 2). It is basically a media-effects model. As was seen in chapter 2, however, TV research is finally broadening and starting to see children in more active interaction with TV. Also, some of the TV research is beginning to adopt a developmental perspective that seems to be a necessary approach for research on micro's and children.

Chen pointed to some important issues in the use of micro's and directions for future research. He expressed concerns about sexism: do girls get as much encouragement as boys to use micro's? Are violent videogames made by males for males perpetuating stereotyped behaviors? Equity concerns were raised: is the spread of micro's not really reaching poorer children, thus increasing distance in knowledge skills, and earning power between segments?

Research needs revolve around development of an interdisciplinary perspective and studies on combinations of new media to optimize educational and learning outcomes. Chen also cautioned that much TV research has had little impact on programs (chapter 2). Basic and applied research on software must learn from this past failure of TV research by more directly attempting to influence developers and marketers of educational software.

New Research Strategies

Rice and Rogers (1984) called for new research methods to investigate the new media. One approach entailed the complete integration of formative research product design, and evaluation processes, most reminiscent of intervention research in psychology (e.g., Hersen & Barlow, 1983). When different facets of research are done by different parties, this may decrease bias, but with some real costs. For example, useful "pre" data may then be limited. In addition, separating research functions may not allow for the continual redefinement and redesign of an innovation based on data-feedback.

It is difficult to introduce new media in a controlled manner that can enhance the external generality of evaluation research. This is because often only certain departments, programs, and people will adopt new media. At best, the researcher may have to use non-random designs.

Typical research experiments implicitly or explicitly use simplified, linear causal models. Rice and Rogers recommended approaches that emphasize both processes and outcomes, explore varied techniques (e.g., participant observation as well as archival data), and take a systems approach to analyzing impacts of new media. For example, it would be instructive to know how word processing changes the work environment and how these changes then feed back into the use of the technology.

According to Rice and Rogers (1984), computer-based new media also open up unique opportunities for automatically collecting highly detailed and reliable data:

> such systems also provide information about how a medium is used and what it transmits . . . Computer-monitored data can indicate actual usage of the system after the new medium has been implemented. These data may provide a direct measure of user behavior, may complement attitudinal and reported use data, and can be used in ongoing processual and quantitative research to supplement some of the qualitative analyses. Computer monitoring of an information or communication system consists of the automatic logging of the type, content, or time of transaction made by a person from a terminal with that system. (p. 94)

Such automatic recording of use data can greatly facilitate different kinds of behavioral research. For example, it is possible to obtain transactional data (what happened when, where, and by whom) and temporal data (the flow of interactions, time spent in different activities) using only a few simple demographic (e.g., terminal and user ID), boundary (e.g., start and end time), program (e.g., commands used), network (sender and receiver), and content indices. An incredible amount of aggregate and fine-grain individual data can be obtained for all manner of evaluation and impact studies.

Rice and Rogers indicated that the advantages of computer-monitored data were:

1. The possibilities for analyzing data from many people over time.
2. The reduction of response bias and demand characteristics endemic to more obtrusive data collection methods.
3. Experimental control possibly could be gotten over variables such as the order of commands, receiver feedback, etc.
4. Communication networks can be more easily investigated (compared to self-report; see chapter 3).
5. Longitudinal studies can be done ending the reliance on problematic cross-sectional studies.

However, Rice and Rogers noted there are disadvantages to computer-monitored data:

1. The tremendous amount of data collected equates to the need for time and money for someone to manage and analyze the data.
2. More expertise may be needed to handle such volumes of data.
3. More theory driven research may be needed to discern what types of data to collect to be used in what ways.

4. Researchers and firms may become too entranced with the reams of objective, ''hard'' data and forget that how people think and feel about their interactions may be just as, if not more important, than only indices of use.
5. The type of data available may be constrained by the system designers so that data and outcomes may not generalize to other systems.
6. The collection of such data raises a host of ethical issues, e.g., invasion of privacy.

However, one hope of research with the new media is that it will enhance the possibilities of true systems innovation and research. Rice (1984c) states:

> Precisely because the new media facilitate and can structure human communication interactively, they necessarily will affect how individuals and groups communicate. However, increased understanding of these potential effects can lead to wiser and more appropriate decisions in design, choice, application, and use of such systems . . . Thus, ''effect'' is not necessarily deterministic and is likely interactive; it may involve the effect of developers and users on the media as well. (p. 101)

Productivity in the Information Age

Rice and Bair (1984) made the case for developing a new perspective on productivity in the information age. Most models of organizational productivity subtract inputs from outputs, and this simple approach may not work in this new era where already more than half the GNP revolves around the handling of information and where information workers represent more than half of the labor force.

Rice and Bair called for a shift in conceptualizing productivity that recognizes some key differences between information and material-based work. These differences include:

1. Information is not time or space bound. It is only constrained by existing hardware to transport it.
2. Information's worth can increase as more people use it, or it can lose all its value when others obtain it (e.g., information on hardware or a program that comes into the public domain).
3. Quality and timeliness of information is critical, but these aspects of information are not generally objective; they are determined subjectively by the producer and user.
4. Information must be in a form so that the scarce managerial resource of attention is properly focused.
5. The speed and efficiency of information delivery often is not as important as its effectiveness, i.e., produce certain outcomes. Effective communication is seen as the key to productivity.

Thus, one major point is that adoption of office communication technologies may not translate to increased productivity as measured in increased sales volume or dollars saved, and that thinking of productivity only in terms of dollars in and dollars out, may not always make sense. However, some aspects of organizational functioning may be amenable to simple input–output analyses when, for example, new media allows for less time to do a task (increases control); makes for more timely interactions, as when meetings are performed better because all parties have up-to-date information; formerly manual functions are automated (e.g., sending copies of reports to branch offices); time and energy to transfer information from one medium (e.g., print paper) to another (e.g., modifiable print on a TV monitor) is eliminated, and when "shadow functions" (unproductive time associated with a task, such as failure to get the right person on the phone) are reduced or even eliminated.

Although these types of benefits and a number of others (e.g., freedom from geographical and time constraints; a wider, accessible data-base) appear to accrue from new organizational communication systems, Rice and Bair noted that these documentable time and dollar savings may not be the most important outcome of these innovations. Rather, improvements at one level of an organization may represent opportunities to improve performance and develop new directions and initiatives at other levels of the organization. New opportunities may or may not be recognized or acted on. It would be a mistake, however, to simply try to quantify the cost of new equipment and staff training time to a bottom-line account, e.g., as when the cost of introducing PC's and word processing is compared to increased contract or grant acquisition in a university. The opportunity for new projects and missions may only show some beneficial impacts at some future point. For example, as the faculty adopt word processing in all phases of their work, the decreased amount of faculty time and secretarial time versus the cost of the new equipment can be examined with regard to the number of articles or chapters per year produced, and contracts and grants obtained before and after using word processing. However, this would miss the point that word processing is not just a substitute for the typewriter. Rather, word processing could present the opportunity for distant collaborations and new ways of constructing manuscripts that could yield qualitatively different sorts of outcomes than prior work.

ISSUES IN CONTROL AND CENTRALIZATION OF POWER

This book has been concerned about issues of power and asymmetry of influence. The ecological perspective described in the prior section serves to remind us that with media development and succession, we are often dealing with social, economic, and political issues entailing shifts in power, resources, and influence. One example is how much national and state elections depend on television, and much less so on other media and grassroots (interpersonal channels) organizations. The party that can enhance its media image, and continually has the resources to expertly design messages with large exposure, is likely to win. In fact, the morning after the debacle of the 1984 election, Fritz Mondale on network television, largely attributed his loss to his poor media image and his poor deportment on TV (Today Show, November 8, 1984).

Mondale also faced the impossible marketing task of using mass media to attempt to appeal to very diverse demographic and political segments. For example, disavowals of traditional liberal policies could be made to one audience seen face-to-face. But the disavowal would likely appear on the evening news and be seen by the liberal segment he was separating himself from. He then would later have to mount other appeals directed to the offended segment, which, of course, would be seen by the first segment. The major point here, however, is that politics today depends greatly on the control of TV images and messages.

The introductory sections of this chapter traced how media succession entails issues in the centralization of power and public access. For example, it was noted how conglomerates came to control newspapers and how newspapers came to depend more and more on news services (see Table 5.1). Prior to these developments, many newspapers had more personal control and particular points of view (not always constructive, e.g., "yellow journalism"). More recent years have seen the relative homogenization of the news and centralization of the news and other media as the same corporations can now own many newspapers, magazines, and radio and TV stations (Le Duc, 1982).

The purpose of radio and TV networks is centralization of resources, and control of the product and distribution system. Thus, networks are capable, because of their tremendous resources and control of distribution, to provide frequent and, at times, extravagant or incisive programs, and rapid and comprehensive news programs. However, homogenization of the product and the inability of diverse groups and interests to be represented on network media in a sustained and serious way (i.e., as differentiated from less popular, acceptable positions being displayed on talk shows) has occurred. Quite obviously the costs of advertising on network TV also severely limit the types of messages that are seen.

Federal regulations demand that a certain amount of broadcast media time be devoted to public service announcements (PSA's) and that affiliates run a regular schedule of PSA's with commercials. Various groups, government, and non-profit organizations compete for PSA time. However, many affiliates can approve, disapprove, or modify PSA's and they are only bound to put PSA's in spots that have not been sold to commercial interest. TV is run as a free-market institution and affiliates must make a profit to survive. Hence, some PSA's can appear at odd times, and almost certainly out of prime time. Poorly targeted PSA's seem worthless.

Likewise, the "Fairness Doctrine" deemed that radio and TV were bound to present all sides of a controversial issue. This has been more recently (1974) watered down. Bittner (1980) states:

> each station is not required to provide "equal" opportunity for opposing views. . . . [it] does not require balance in individual programs or a series of programs, but only in a station's overall programming [and] there is no assurance that a listener who hears an initial presentation will also hear a rebuttal. (p. 333)

One bright spot in the decentralization of media was the Federal Communication Commission's (FCC) requirement that cable TV systems permit local access for at least one of their channels so that local organizations could present locally originated programs to subscribers. However, in the deregulation fervor of the 1980s, this regulation has been watered down (i.e., FCC, 1984 regulations). In deference to the deregulation position, cable systems are also subject to a complex web of state and local regulations. But, except for rate issues, many cable systems now seem to have bypassed the local access issue (Don Le Duc, personal communication, February, 1985).

Obviously, there is a need for some balance on the regulation of some media. On one hand, mass media are supposed to have freedom from government control as guaranteed by the constitution. On the other hand, the broadcast media use limited resources and are in need of some regulatory control to assure more equal access, e.g., for political viewpoints. One critical question is whether the apparent diversity provided by new media will obviate the need for regulation to provide access and diversity. A brief history of other new media and current trends can help answer that question.

Le Duc (1982) noted in his article that:

> In the world of Washington, "the trend" seems mightier than the truth. New approaches to old issues are in constant demand so that yesterday's policies can be blamed for today's problem. Thus, for example, it is no longer fashionable to view regulation as the remedy for all inequities in the marketplace. Instead, it is now considered proper to view the marketplace as the remedy for all inequities in regulation. (p. 164)

Thus, it should not be assumed that current inequities are to be solved by the free-market approach, but it should not be assumed either that a return to prior regulation is the answer. The key questions are: (a) whether new technologies provide a degree of access and diversity so that true competition exists, thus obviating the need for regulation, and (b) what past implementation of new technology may tell us about diversity and serving the public interest, or centralization of power. The second question is addressed first by examining the development of radio and TV.

According to Le Duc, radio flourished in the 1920s and 1930s with over 700 stations in operation. More than half soon affiliated with the major networks and the networks only accepted the most powerful stations. Thus, local stations soon became, for the most part, outlets for network programs. As noted in Table 5.1, radio survived the introduction of TV by offering more specialized stations and programming, for example, FM stations. However, many of these stations actually offer only prepackaged programs and syndicated news and feature programs with infrequent use of local news and weather. The number of stations may have proliferated, but it is deceiving to think of this proliferation as meaning diversity. Prepackaged programs limit audience control and the diversity in programming, according to Le Duc, may be similar to the "choice" provided between Mac-Donald's and Burger King.

TV was originally conceived to be a local medium, and in the 1940s over 2,000 TV broadcast channels were assigned to different communities. One objective was to not repeat the network experience of radio. However, TV stations developed primarily in large markets where affiliation with a network seemed probable. Local and independent stations gradually developed, but then (1950s) and now, these stations mainly offer reruns of network fare. Thus, the history of radio and TV suggests a tendency toward centralization and decreasing diversity.

In an attempt to increase competition in television, the FCC in 1972 authorized telecommunication corporations to compete with ATC nationwide (ground) distribution systems with satellite and (other) ground systems. In the same year, the FCC issued rules for developing cable TV firms in major broadcast areas. Home Box Office (HBO), however, was the first to link these two developments together. For its programming, it used a domestic satellite system and leased a distribution channel from each new large cable TV system. Thus, HBO bypassed the AT&T system and local station outlets. This combination of satellite and cable has obviously spread (e.g., superstation and other cable stations).

Presently, there are now a growing number of domestic satellites for TV and radio service on a nationwide basis, numerous cable systems, and many stations equipped to receive and distribute different program channels. In addition, video playback devices are selling at a phenomenal rate (New York Times, March 3, 1985, p. 1); teletext series are increasing; direct broadcast satellites (DBS's) can bypass local affiliates and directly deliver programs; low power TV stations allow for coverage of local events; pay TV stations are available, and microwave systems can be used in areas without cable TV. Will these innovations not create diversity and competitiveness? The answer may be "possibly not" if attention is given to what actually is seen and who owns what.

According to Le Duc (1982), licensing regulations, rather than the marketplace, "compels broadcasters and the copyright owners of film and syndicated features to allow cable use of this material in return for a fee the cable system must pay into a reimbursement pool" (p. 175). However, this regulation does not increase the number of different programs, but rather allows their showing at a time different from that of the affiliate station. Likewise, with pay stations, it is possible to see a feature film (generally) after its run in movie houses, but before being shown on networks. This may generate more money for the film industry, perhaps creating more diversity. However, for the most part, pay stations may simply provide another opportunity to see existing material.

Cable systems now offer a number of advertising supported programming (e.g., ESPN) and some programming not yet self-supporting. Although this may be a promising area for diversity and competition, it is possible that networks will start to use these special stations as a way to bypass local affiliates. For example, ABC and Getty Oil produce ESPN. It is also unclear if microwave systems and DBS's will truly offer original programming.

In the field of videodiscs, RCA, the parent company of NBC, dominates the American market. It has cross-licensed CBS to use its standards. Most basically, the broadcast networks have moved into cable system ownership, cable networks, videodisc marketing, and DBS operation. The main problem, according to Le Duc, is that the focus of regulation has been on individual broadcast stations as if more stations or outlets could provide more diversity. Regulatory policy has failed to address the problem of control of broadcasting, film, and music, mass entertainment, by the three networks, five feature film distributors, and seven record distributors. They stand between the program, music, and film producers and the distribution channels. Cross-media ownership and cross-licensing agreements keep various information, entertainment, and art forms within the control of a limited number of corporations. By limiting itself to the program outlet and not the program supplier, the FCC has failed to create a competitive marketplace for ideas.

The FCC has not attempted to maintain a particular type of programming in an area and has rescinded its own authority in requiring radio stations to offer any amount of news or public affairs programming. The FCC has not regulated program offerings under the guise of "free speech." However, Le Duc (1982) concluded that this has been contrary to a 1969 Supreme Court ruling in which Justice White declared that:

> it is the purpose of the First Amendment to preserve an uninhibited market place of ideas in which truth will ultimately prevail, rather than to countenance monopolization of that market whether it be by the Government itself or a private licensee . . . It is the right of the viewers and listeners, not the right of the broadcasters, which is paramount. (p. 177)

As for approaches to create more diversity and competition, Le Duc noted that faith can not be put into new telecommunications technology alone. Rather, legal and regulatory principles must be developed. Some guidelines included:

1. The FCC should restore aspects of the Fairness Doctrine and maintain reasonable access requirements.

2. Regulations requiring cable systems to allow local access, but since rescinded, should be reinstated (Le Duc, personal communication, February, 1985).
3. The source of competition must be seen as program content, not merely in channels of delivery.
4. The rights of artists and the public and those of the merchandisers must be differentiated. Currently, the emphasis has shifted to the rights of the merchandisers.
5. A comprehensive set of policies must be developed to ensure a marketplace of ideas.

Other major issues concern the power and range of some new media. Satellite, not cable, is the major technological innovation in television (Wigand, 1982). Direct satellite broadcasting overcomes terretrial barriers and can offer local autonomy in broadcasting, flexibility, a large range of coverage, and improved signal quality and reliability at lower cost. Signals can be received by less developed countries, and distance and isolation have been removed as obstacles to communication.

However, great debates are now raging. Countries with different cultures, philosophies, and social mores from the United States and other Western countries can have their sovereignty easily violated by DBS's. For example, it is conceivable that workers in undeveloped countries could receive United States programs via satellite, given the spillover of communication. Thus, DBS's have great potential for providing news, education, and entertainment to virtually any remote area. At the same time, it provides another way for the more powerful to influence others without their consent.

Two-way cable systems, such as the Qube system provide new interactive educational, entertainment, and even medical capabilities. For example, heart patients can safely sleep at home when they are hooked into a two-way system that monitors their heart. Also, two-way systems provide another vehicle for centralization of power and influence. It becomes possible to know exactly what is viewed, when, and to key-in on other viewer response patterns. This, in turn, allows for greater advertisement and program specialization and segmentation with, perhaps, some invasion of privacy and greater influence.

CONCLUSION

This chapter has deliberately taken a rather restrained, even at times skeptical, approach to the review of new media. One purpose was to serve as a counterpoint to many other hyperbolic accounts. New media are seen as having vast potential to improve the quality of life. Although by adopting a ''moderate change scenario,'' the opinion is that new media will not replace all old media and other forms of communication. Organizational structures and living arrangements are likely to change partly as a result of new media. But, probably in the near future, change will not be as dramatic as some have predicted.

The new media, as any innovation (chapter 3), must be carefully designed and evaluated prior to introduction, but even then can produce a host of positive and negative effects, some anticipated and some not. Key concerns are worth repeating here.

1. Assessment/Evaulation.   A straightforward model (task × participants × resources × medium) has been offered as a framework for examining new media. Whereas some new media have unfortunately been pushed into application too soon (resulting in their "death"), better researched applications must adhere to this general model. In some cases (e.g., training in social skills), much simpler and less costly approaches seemed available (video tapes, small groups vs. videodiscs). In addition, studies in new media must be interdisciplinary. As an example, the psychology literature would predict marginal effectiveness with more complex skill training with videodiscs, because such approaches often do not include in vivo practice and feedback.

This point underscores another application, research, and evaluation issue. No matter how sophisticated the hardware, or the software's ability to automatically record individual responses and interactions, there is still the need to investigate processes and behaviors outside the new media setting that may be attributable to the use of new media. And input for new media (e.g., expert systems), must be based on acceptable reliability and validity methods.

Additionally, analyses of new technology must be made in light of cultural, social and economic contexts. This point was particularly well illustrated in the analysis of job and educational requirements in the years ahead. Few people will have high paying, high-tech jobs, and the "electronic cottage" can easily become a prison, not a site for creativity and liberation.

2. Access, Equity, and Control.   Many accounts of new media emphasize new possibilities for access, perhaps more equity in access to technology, and decentralized control of technology and communication. This simply may not be true, and is certainly not universally true. Indeed, the history of the advent of former new media suggests centralization and decreased diversity. New media may also increase the distance between "haves" and "have nots", for example, access to computer training in schools; ability to pay for information services. The growth in the information sector may also promote many career possibilities for the elite, while leaving the masses behind in an ill-paid service sector. The natural progression of media may also mean that the masses will have the mundane new media (e.g., some video games), while the elite will be attended to with specialized technology and programs.

The hope of decentralization of power and influence with new media may not be a reality at all. For example, new technology has the capability of accumulating incredible data banks on people. Many new media are simply being obtained

by conglomerates already involved in media. New media (e.g., satellite communication), also has the capability of directly influencing people across geographic
boundaries who may or may not want to be influenced in particular ways.
Although the political climate at this time (1985) may not favor new regulatory
policy, marketplace policies may fail to promote diversity and competition. A
change in the political climate may lead to a reexamination of regulatory policy.

3. Values.   The points in this section are not meant to be totally pessimistic.
Rather, they are meant to underscore the main point that innovations have
positive and negative impacts, and that they should not be blindly accepted as
automatically good. For example, perhaps there is some skepticism that should
be added into the studies of PC's and children. PC's have been accepted as
"good", but it can be asked, what is happening to those children's social
development who spend hours with their PC's?

The overriding issue is societal values. Do we really care about equity in
access, a true marketplace of ideas, or a more even distribution of income? As
emphasized by Rice (1984a), new media may create opportunities to do things
differently—they do not automatically mean we will do things differently. For
example, whether organizations only pursue a narrow-vision bottom-line, or
expand their horizons as a result of new media, is a value (and economic) issue.
Whether AI is applied mostly to defense or becomes more entwined with health
and other quality of life concerns is a question of priorities and values. Rather
than just focusing on the intricacies of the technology, perhaps it is time to
redirect the agenda on new media and other technologies to the discussion of
these basic value issues.

6 Information and Health Behavior: Futile Attempts or Small-Wins?

OVERVIEW

The topic of health behavior provides an unusual opportunity to develop a contextual perspective for the use of information strategies to promote behavior change. This is because there is a very large, contemporary literature that has studied health behavior at many different levels. For example, there is a literature on life style and health (Matarazzo, 1982), economics and health (Fielding, 1983), and community structure and health (Catalano, 1979). However, recent years have seen the behavioral sciences particularly emphasize life style and individual factors (e.g., responsibility) at the expense of analyzing diverse systems that influence health behavior (Winett, 1983; Winkler, 1982). Health behavior has often been viewed within the ''contextless'' approach discussed in the first chapter.

One purpose of this chapter is to provide balance to contemporary behavioral science health literature by seriously and extensively developing a contextual approach. A strong case is made for an environmental position that seeks to understand health behaviors within diverse systems.

However, when an environmental position is developed in a convincing manner, it also can be extremely intimidating. Understanding the numerous constraints to effectively change health behaviors and practices can become an intellectual exercise that leads to a paralysis of action. The tasks and barriers appear insurmountable, and attempts at intervention, therefore, futile. Constraints may well be insurmountable and interventions futile if change is looked at and approached as an all or none process.

In the second part of this chapter, the examples of change follow Weick's (1984) ''small-wins'' strategy. None of the strategies is seen as totally solving the problems of health—an impossible task—or even totally solving the more limited health problem for which the strategy is designed. Rather, the strategy is workable and should yield some meaningful health outcomes that can serve as the building blocks (small-wins) for other endeavors.

The illustrative subject matter in the second part of this chapter at first appears quite disparate because a common approach and analysis has infrequently been given to these different practices, behaviors, and problems. Thus, the examples include intracellular response to environmental information mediated by neurological processes, i.e., psychoneuroimmunology; the effects of physician counseling on patient health behaviors; supermarket interventions to promote nutritional purchases; corrective advertising to create a more healthy marketplace, and community–media-based preventive health programs. Although these topics are quite different, the common theme consistent with the contextual perspective is change within a system (e.g., physician practices, advertising guidelines), as the necessary antecedent in providing new information flows to positively affect health behaviors. In these examples, an attempt is also made to apply the communication model (McGuire, 1981) and knowledge base (Atkin, 1981) described in detail in the first chapter to information flow and health behavior effects.

Prior to this exposition, it is appropriate to develop a background and framework for understanding health behaviors. The purpose of these sections is to ask and to partially answer the seemingly simple question of, ''Where do healthy and nonhealthy life styles come from ?''.

BACKGROUND

This lengthy section attempts to answer that simple question. It also tries to provide balance to recent work in behavioral health that has overemphasized individual responsibility and contributions to health at the expense of examining system influences and constraints on health behavior. Matarazzo (1980, 1982, 1983) has written extensively about the role of individual behavior and psychological approaches to health behavior modification. He has discussed how the health-care system has conquered long-standing diseases (e.g., tuberculosis) during this past century. Yet, the cost of health care has continued to increase— from 4.5% of the gross national product in 1950 to about 10% in 1983 and higher in 1984–1985. It is the cost and its containment that are the focus of discussions of health care today. But, where have these costs come from and what can be done about them? According to Matarazzo (1982):

> Health care in the United States is expensive in part because our citizens, speaking themselves or through third-party payers, have opted to pay for intensive care and renal dialysis units in hospitals, neonatal heart surgery, computerized axialtomo-

graphy (CAT) scanners, and many other costly diagnostic and critical-care life support services. My criticism is not directed at such defensible costs but instead at the inordinate costs that are associated with preventable health conditions: those associated with one's life style. These latter, unnecessary costs must be addressed by psychologists and representatives of the other disciplines interested in individual behavior. (p. 1)

During the last 80 years, health-care practices (one must note here, primarily public health and not medical care; Hanlon & Picket, 1984) have reduced or eliminated tuberculosis, influenza, measles, and poliomyelitis. At the same time, there have been increases in lung cancer, major cardiovascular diseases, drug and alcohol abuse, motorcycle and alcohol–automobile-related injury and death. Morbidity and early death now appear more attributable to what have been called *life-style factors*. The implications of this label (stating the strongest case) are that: (a) there are direct and/or substantial links between ''life-style'' risk factors and later morbidity and mortality rates; (b) practices such as smoking, and alcohol and drug abuse are subject to individual choice and are modifiable by individual initiative or individually-focused intervention; (c) system influences on these practices need not be seriously addressed for effective policy and intervention, and that, (d) the formerly successful public health model may no longer be appropriate. Thus, Matarazzo (1982) stated that:

focusing some of this country's investigative, educational, and professional talent and resources on *changing the behavior of individual Americans* will reduce the human and financial costs associated with a number of preventable conditions. Today's indefensibly high health expenditures will therefore drop as well. National leaders of various persuasions agree that the costly toll from heart disease, cancer, and so on can be materially reduced. (p. 5)

My argument is not with most of the end-state behaviors (e.g., smoking), although there are still many questions here (Kaplan, 1984), but rather how to understand the origins of these practices and ways to approach their modification—which may or may not directly focus on individual citizens.

There are two basic and apparently forgotten tenets: (a) health behavior change may require a renewed emphasis on central planning and social responsibility, and that, (b) the traditional public health approach may need to be resurrected (Hanlon & Picket, 1984).

Knowles (1977) is one author who is frequently cited as starting the call for the focus on individual responsibility. It is instructive to reread one of Knowles (1977) key quotes to see that he has been misinterpreted, or at least, not completely quoted. For example:

Over 99 percent of us are born healthy and made sick as a result of personal misbehavior and *environmental conditions*. The solution to the problems of ill health in modern American Society involves individual responsibility, in the first instance, and *social responsibility* through public legislature and private volunteer efforts in the second instance. (p. 58, italics added)

Thus, Knowles was actually suggesting a balance in understanding the origins of detrimental health behavior (i.e., individual and environmental factors), and a balance in approaches (i.e., individual and social responsibility.) A return to a public health model and some deemphasis of individual interventions may help to achieve this balance.

Most current and popular approaches to health behavior change are not truly public health efforts. Thus, various smoking cessation, exercise, stress management, and even wellness programs, generally are delivered in a clinical fashion to relatively limited numbers of people. Recent analyses suggest that when they are delivered in this way, such interventions appear only to be marginally effective and can be quite costly (Kaplan, 1984). Delivering these types of interventions through the media to the population-at-large dilutes effectiveness, but results in a more favorable cost-effectiveness ratio (e.g., McAlister et al., 1982). But these educational and skills training efforts tap only one aspect of the public health model.

Runyan, DeVellis, DeVellis, and Hochman (1982) made the distinction between more psychological and public health approaches quite clear by first citing a classic case in public health that illustrated the empirical and environmental emphasis:

This empirical approach is exemplified by John Snow's work, first reported in 1855. Based on several years of mapping the distribution of cholera cases in London, Snow observed that patterns of disease occurrence were associated with the use of a specific water source, the Broad Street pump. Drawing upon the fruits of his extensive and systematic data collection, Smow devised a simple yet effective intervention which prevented the further spread of cholera. He removed the pump handle. (p. 171)

This example still illustrates the key elements of the contemporary public health model:

1. The effort was triggered by the identification of a health problem or concern.
2. The population, not specific individuals, was the unit of interest.
3. The investigation of the problem and choice of solution were based on empirical means, i.e., epidemiological research.
4. The emphasis was on prevention of the cause of the disease rather than ministering to its victims.
5. Once an appropriate intervention action was identified, it was implemented directly, without (at times) complete understanding of causal mechanisms.

6. Actions were carried out not by individual decisions and voluntary compliance, but through regulatory action at the environmental-community level.

The original public health model was developed to understand infectious diseases, but its basic framework remains useful for understanding and ameliorating other health problems. The host in the model refers to individuals susceptible or vulnerable to the disease or problem. The host can also refer to the entire population. The agent was originally conceived of as germs, but now can be considered as any number of environmental factors. The environment refers to all other aspects of the process in question. For example, we may be particularly concerned with one kind of work stress, but we need to study and then modify that work stress within the context of the modern, highly automated work setting. The model is now considered to be interactive, not linear (Hanlon & Picket, 1984) and has been expanded to consider an array of biologic (e.g., genetics), environmental (e.g., radiation level), organizational (e.g., accessibility of services), and behavioral (e.g., drinking) factors. Ecological (Catalano, 1979) and interbehavioral models (Morris, Higgins, & Bickel, 1982), with their emphasis on multiple, interrelated causes are similar to the public health model. As noted in the first chapter, the behavioral systems model is also similar, but more contextual than interactive systems models. The public health model is also different from some medical models of singular causality and does not seek to understand processes at the individual level; it is more concerned with extra-individual influences.

Runyan et al. warned that although the use of psychological perspectives and procedures to focus on life-style factors in health has some use, the individually based interventions are not entirely appropriate. They have appeal because such procedures appear to be scientific and effective (although, this is questionable; Kaplan, 1984) and their development has (not surprisingly) coincided with the reemphasis of individualism in the 1970s and 1980s (as opposed to collective well being and action as a societal norm).

Runyan et al. (1982) also warned that:

Although these individually targeted efforts clearly have their usefulness in alleviating some of the problems of individuals, the attention *solely* to *host* factors to the exclusion of the agent (e.g., modifying nicotine content in cigarettes or salt in packaged foods) or the environment (e.g., enforcing air pollution standards or providing diet alternatives) is neither consistent with the public health approach nor likely to be the most effective solution for achieving improved health of the population. (p. 178)

This writer is in essential agreement with Runyan et al. and the next section performs, albeit in a sketchy way, some of the analyses Runyan et al. and Hanlon and Pickett suggested. However, two qualifications are offered here. First, to be able to effectively perform mass, individual interventions, requires considerable effort at the system (institutional) level. For example, to have networks feature prime-time programs on personal health would entail major changes in the nature of American television fare. Thus, it can be simplistic to discuss individual interventions and also system interventions. Second, it is unrealistic to expect wholesale change in large systems in a short time. It is also unrealistic to expect scientists who are trained and comfortable working at the individual level to suddenly become system designers and political crusaders. It is more realistic to think in terms of some change in activities and level of analysis, and development of some strategic interventions, i.e., "small-wins."

BEHAVIORAL SYSTEMS FRAMEWORK

Health paradigms need to explicitly delineate influences and constraints on behaviors. The deceptively simple question asked in this chapter is, "Where do healthy and unhealthy life styles come from?" The behavioral systems approach does not neglect or discard what is within the person, i.e., "host susceptibility." It is assumed that any environmental influence is mediated by a range of interactive, intraindividual genetic, biological, cognitive, and behavioral-skill variables. Indeed, the first illustration focuses on the role of patient perceptions in activating immune system responses. However, the primary focus of concern is the broader environmental influences in which health-related behaviors are enacted.

The purpose of this section is not to comprehensively review every potential environmental influence on health, an impossible task, but rather to briefly review a number of different kinds of environmental influences on health to illustrate this perspective and provide a basis for analysis and intervention. The discussion is started with a familiar influence, the interpersonal environment, then moves toward larger influences more relevant to population-based health efforts.

Interpersonal Environment

There is some evidence that the nature of a person's interactions with family, relatives, friends, and coworkers can have health protective, and possibly health–promotional benefit (Gottlieb, 1983). Recent work has gone beyond initial epidemiological studies that showed a relationship between social isolation and illness, and social support and health (e.g., Cassel, 1974). For example, a long-term follow-up of participants in the Alamenda County study showed that social connectedness (i.e., being married, belonging to a church; Berkman & Syme, 1979) was an independent risk factor and health protector. More recent work has been concerned with delineating aspects of social support that may buffer stress (Cohen, 1983). Critical aspects of social support may include the perception that it is available and the provision of the availability of nontangible (e.g., empathy, advise) support. This notion has wide intuitive appeal, suggests exciting preventive programs, and has resulted in an avalanche of papers and studies. However, the consensus is that this concept remains somewhat conjectural and that person, interaction, and network aspects of social support are exceedingly complex (Heller & Swindle, 1983).

The faddish aspect and inherent complexity of social support research can be acknowledged. But what seems most important and revealing is that social connectiveness (or lack thereof) seems to crop up as an influential variable in a range of research (Felner, Jason, Moritsuger, & Farber, 1983; Gottlieb, 1983). If future research continues to provide evidence for the relationship of social support to health-related behaviors, then both individual and population-based analyses need to examine further this variable. This is even more true if future research shows that social networks can be developed or modified for health promotion or restorative purposes, a research direction that has already begun (Hirsch, 1980, 1981; Wellman, 1981).

General Informational Environment

Information that is available to citizens in a variety of forms can have a marked impact on health behaviors. For example, regulatory reform has had as one objective, the freer distribution of information on foods, cigarettes, medicine, and availability and price of medical services so that consumers can make better informed choices in their health practices (Pertschuk, 1982). Recent attempts to roll back information disclosure laws by portraying them as invasive and paternalistic or harmful to business must be met by the evidence that consumers appear to like and increasingly use available information in health choice. In some instances (advertising), readily available information has created a more competitive health sector so that certain services have become less expensive and available to more people (Benham, 1972; Benham & Benham, 1975; Pertschuk, 1982). The provision of free and easily accessible information is at the heart of democratic systems and free-market economics. Here, the focus turns to the broader information context, particularly the television media.

As noted in chapter 2, the advent of television assuredly influenced health behaviors. For example, the presence of television has changed family and other social interaction and activity patterns, and not surprisingly, has also changed aspects of sleep (Comstock, 1980). Most attention, however, has been focused on the more direct effects of the medium and its messages on health behaviors. The content and form of television can only be understood from the perspective of its major mission, which in the United States is to deliver the largest possible audience to advertisers (Cantor, 1980). Thus, television programming is the vehicle to maintain viewership of advertisers' products, with the eventual goal of increased consumption of products. Therefore, cartoons can deliver children to advertisers, and violent shows can also deliver adult population segments. The arguments concerning health and media include: (a) the nature of the specific program content (e.g., violence) and its effects on behavior (e.g., aggression; Liebert, Sprafken, & Davidson, 1982; see chapter 2); (b) the nature of the products typically advertised during particular programs geared to particular population segments (e.g., heavily sugared cereal; a succession of beer commercials), and (c) the more pervasive and, perhaps, insidious picture provided of health and well being (i.e., consume more); the frequent depictions of nonhealthy and unsafe behaviors (e.g., reckless driving), and a view that health problems are individually based, cannot be prevented, but even when serious, are easily fixed (e.g., recall "Marcus Welby").

A medium virtually controlled by advertisers' dollars makes arguments about not tampering with the "free-market" of the medium or interfering with First Amendment rights a bit ludicrous, and recent years have seen attempts, some successful, to modify program content, e.g., with regard to violence (Liebert, Sprafkin, & Davidson, 1982), or eliminate certain products from advertisement such as cigarettes (although some claim cigarette companies have actually monetarily gained from this ban; Pertschuk, 1982). Recent years have seen a burgeoning of interest in the development of pro-health, media-based programs and communication campaigns (Maccoby & Solomon, 1981; see chapter 4) and even a 24-hour a day cable TV health network ("Life-Time") has been started. These efforts are seen as one small way of trying to balance the availability of correct health information. One caveat is that many of these programs may only focus on the personal aspects of health behavior, and thus, continue the distorted picture of individual causality and blame for health risk. The second caveat is that in this country, for health programs to have wide impact, they must be supportable through advertising, a situation that suggests that programs depicting social, economic, and environmental, much less media causes of ill-health, may not be commercially viable.

On a population level, we are alerted to the fact that the media can reflect and maintain distorted health information and beliefs. However, the promise is that the media can become a major vehicle for health promotion and health care.

Ecology of Cities

It is impossible to understand and modify health behaviors and practices without some regard to the organization and ecology of our population centers. Large cities, as the major place of work, can be seen as a result and perhaps, remnant, of the earlier industrialization that required the centralization of mass operations and people (Catalano, 1979). The advent of the automobile, a determined highway policy, a rising middle class, and a federal policy to make the American dream of home ownership an inexpensive reality, created the suburbs (and, later exurbs) and the commuting society (Sarason, 1981). These arrangements have had profound effects of health behaviors in some obvious, and not so obvious, ways.

Many writers have documented the plight and numerous problems of the poverty stricken population segment left and contained in the central cities. Substandard housing, crowding, unavailable services (e.g., groceries), health care, and prevailing despair and powerlessness result in health statistics comparable to some of the poorest developing countries. These same conditions result in levels of crime, violence, and addiction, at times, compatible with a war zone (Catalano, 1979). These points are not meant to be an exposé or a way to arouse guilt. Rather, they serve to remind us that in our analyses of the interplays of individual characteristics and behaviors, and environments and health outcomes, for some population segments our focus must be more on the environment. Against the overwhelming barriers to good health ennumerated previously it makes little sense to explain poor health outcomes as a result of individual deficits or lack of responsibility (Rappaport, 1977). As long as the conditions remain, the health statistics will remain the same.

Although this first focus has been on the entrapment and poverty of one segment of our society as a long-term result of urbanization (which is not to say that some similar conditions do not exist in some rural areas), the centralization of work and the creation of suburbs have had effects on health practices of the broad middle class. One effect has been the detachment and lack of connectedness when many communities became bedroom communities where people (until recently, mostly men) slept and engaged in some leisure and consumption in between commuting and working. Suburban communities are characterized by age and income segregation and, for some, social isolation (Dolce, 1976). Perhaps a larger effect for those commuting substantial distances to work is to create a level of stress and time commitment that is ironically at odds with the historical movement to humanize work and reduce the hours of work (Nollen, 1982)!

In this analysis, it is essential to understand how work and its schedule determines the ebb and flow of peoples' lives, and the daily life of cities (Robinson, 1977). It is the schedule of work that dictates when people will arise, when they will eat, when they will socialize, and when they will sleep; it is the schedule of work that determines when and where there will be massive traffic jams and unacceptable air quality. It is the schedule of work and living and commuting patterns that determine the availability of time and constraints on engaging in some health-related behaviors. For example, in one of the author's studies on alternative work patterns conducted in Washington, DC, which is actually not an extremely large city, it was found that the average time spent at the worksite was 8 hr 30 min per day; however, 2 hr 30 min per day were spent on the average in commuting and related activities, meaning that about 11 hr per day were spent on the average in work-related activities (Winett, Neale, & Williams, 1982). Recent studies have documented the stressful aspects of commuting each day (Stokols, Novaco, Stokols, & Campbell, 1978) but the sheer amount of time involved in work placed constraints and costs on engaging in other behaviors.

For example, examining some very fine-grain, time-allocation data collected from detailed time-activity logs from participants in the alternative work schedules project, on the average this young ($x = 33$ years), middle-class sample of people who were parents of younger children, minimally ($x = 10$ min per day) engaged in one key health behavior, such as exercise. Our eventual interpretation of this finding was not within the current health psychology paradigm of individual deficit and responsibility. Rather, it was noted that the time devoted to commuting, work, the family, and sleeping and eating, did not leave much extra time. Time became a scarce resource and precious commodity. To devote an hour a day to exercise had some very high costs and constraints attached to this resource expenditure. Some proposed solutions to this problem were seen in recent worksite health programs (e.g., being able to exercise at the worksite during lunch hour; Wilbur & Garner, 1984); allowing for reduced work hours (e.g., 6 hours per day) during life cycle periods requiring considerable family time (Lamb & Sagi, 1983), and efforts to decentralize work settings and make them contiguous with living centers, particularly as the nature of work changes in our society (Nollen, 1982).

The arrangement of our urban areas and the time involved in working in our society are only two examples of how the ecology of our society forms and constrains health-related practices. The examples are used not because they are the best or are more inclusive of other factors, but because they are familiar to us and serve to remind us that health analyses and intervention strategies must focus on the environment as well as the host.

Economic Influences

The prior section has noted some of the health-related outcomes of poverty, but in this section, the purpose is to examine more broadly the economic influences on health care practices, i.e., economic policy and health-care economics. The recent, pervasive and purposely planned, and deepest recession since the depression (Piven & Cloward, 1982) has had one favorable outcome in the behavioral sciences; it has resulted in some important research connecting change in the economic environment to health practices and outcome and thrust the behavioral sciences into a major policy debate of the day. For example, Catalano and Dooley (1983) have greatly refined the earlier epidemiological techniques of Brenner (1973) who demonstrated a relationship between economic downturn and aggregate measures of poor health outcome by carefully assessing economic change, intervening mechanisms, and individual health outcomes. One conclusion of a study, actually conducted during a relatively good economic period (late 1970s), was that for the middle class, economic downturn did result in job and financial difficulties, which in turn increased the probability of ill-health incidence and health risk. Thus, their work provides the linkages missing in some earlier research.

Liem and Ramsay (1982) noted that considerable economic and social welfare policy has been developed on the notion that there exists a certain underlying, but benign, level of unemployment. Given this belief, the true social and psychological costs of unemployment have never been calculated, much less been a part of economic policy. In their research, they document that for some groups, unemployment seems to result in clinical (mental health) symptomotology that may have large, long-term person, family, and community costs. They also point out that in the United States where health-care benefits are attached to employment, the loss of employment automatically imperils the person and his or her family.

Thus, the work by Catalano and Dooley, and Liem and Ramsay is supported by other investigators (see Felner, Jason, Moritsuger, & Farber, 1983), and, of necessity, forces prime emphasis on economic policy analysis and intervention.

However, it is equally important to assess the role of economic variables within the health-care system itself. Most recent attention has been directed to health-care cost-containment as data indicate that health-care costs continue to increase at a rate much greater than inflation and that health costs now amount to more than 10% of our GNP (Matarazzo, 1983). Of major concern has been the fee for service and an insurance system that prevails in the United States offering no incentive for providers to focus on preventive health measures and provisions for supplying the least expensive services (Navarro, 1976).

In his review of health-care regulation, Fielding (1983) well elaborated on disincentives for cost-containment in health care:

Several features of the medical marketplace encourage government regulation. Salient among them is the lack of incentives for major participants in the system to constrain costs. Consumers are insulated from the true costs of their health care by third party reimbursement systems that finance nearly 70% of expenditures on personal health care services. Employers, who assume a greater proportion of total health care costs by providing health insurance for employees, are able to deduct insurance premiums as a business expense, reducing their tax burden. A study in the Congressional Budget Office indicated that in 1982 the health care tax expenditure from employer contributions to health insurance premiums amounted to $23 billion—$16.5 from income tax deductions and $6.5 from payroll tax deductions. Physicians, who act not only as the providers of care but as the purchasing agents as well, face equally strong disincentives to be cost conscious. Third party reimbursement has diminished the concern physicians had about the financial impact of the services they ordered on their patients. In addition, reimbursement incentives favor more costly, technology-intensive health care services over the practice of less costly, prevention-oriented medicine. (p. 91)

Regulatory policy has attempted to influence the distribution, price, quality, and delivery of health care. Over the years, a number of alternative health models have been proposed (Roy, 1978) including the expansion of health maintenance organizations (HMO's) and other prepayment plans. In HMO's, the primary incentive is to keep people well, because a fixed prepayment is all the money available to provide a complete range of services to the enrollee. Presumably, if the person is kept well through more attention to preventive services, the costs to the HMO decrease. Whereas HMO's have not developed as quickly as expected and there are still many questions about HMO's (e.g., the possibilities of excluding from a plan too many people with expensive preconditions or even promoting under utilization of services), and some continued political opposition, burgeoning health costs have made the HMO concept more attractive.

Most health-care costs are now paid through third-party mechanisms, i.e., health benefits/insurance and entitlement programs (Medicare and Medicaid). Although for most Americans, this has resulted in the minimization of the financial hardships of long-term illness or other catastrophic events, it has also resulted in a situation where neither patients or providers have any incentive to contain health costs. Thus, the true and escalating health insurance costs are both delayed in time and distant in place and saliency, meaning that such costs are often not seen as directly resulting from current practices, and have minimal effects on provider or patient cost containment behaviors; they have the apparent effect of increasing costs. Various proposals have been put forth to change this situation principally through empirically testing the effects of plans that require differential cost sharing by health-care consumers (Newhouse et al., 1981). Other proposals call for more emphasis on a free-market approach in health care by allowing different health plans to openly compete with each other. However, such competition would need to be regulated (Fielding, 1983). Finally, another approach involves further government regulation by the specification of acceptable fees for particular service. Fielding noted that preliminary results of these studies suggest cost savings of several percent. However, the health insurance issue has another major question that links economics and behavior.

"Health insurance" is an interesting misnomer because health policies generally only pertain to illness, disability, or death. Although the value of preventive approaches has been documented (Matarazzo, 1983), they generally are not paid for by health insurance. There are historical and economic reasons for this system (e.g., see Navarro, 1976), but the main results for consumer and provider has been the gross overemphasis on expensive diagnosis, treatment, and rehabilitation, and a neglect of prevention. In the search for understanding why people are not healthier or why simple preventive practices are not more widely engaged in, one must come face-to-face with health care economics. It is unlikely that people will act counter to economic contingencies. The attractive part about HMO's is that this concept and organization of services recognizes this fact and seeks to change contingencies to foster health and well-being.

OTHER ENVIRONMENTAL CONSIDERATIONS

At the outset, it was stated that the function of these sections was not to delineate every possible environmental factor related to health, but to highlight some areas that make us question the prevailing paradigm in health psychology, that for the most part views health behaviors out of context. Concepts and data showing the interplay of health behaviors with interpersonal networks, the media and information environment, the organization of work and cities, and economic factors were chosen because they represent different aspects and levels of analysis. The direct connection in each area of behavior and context was apparent. In this section, a few current concerns are noted, in less detail, to broaden the perspective already developed, but without any claim to the exhaustiveness of the exposition.

Regulation

One of the major debates in governmental policy in recent years has been the role, enforcement, and effectiveness of governmental regulation. Two examples are the policies concerning regulation and enforcement of toxic waste procedures, and debates about the clean air act. Although exact knowledge concerning dosage levels and exposure needed to significantly increase health risk (particularly at more typical levels) are not always clear, there seems less debate about effects given more extreme and long-term exposure to certain toxins. Indeed, recent and apparent politically motivated attempts to roll back such regulations in the guise of increasing industrial productivity (e.g., see Pertschuk, 1982) have been countered by framing the regulations within a public health perspective (New York Times, 1983). There appears to be ample evidence that inappropriate toxic waste disposal has current and long-term radiating effects on health through the seepage of toxic wastes into our ground water supply (Ashworth, 1982). Recent efforts have taken these health risks seriously, and also have attempted to develope standard means to compare the cost-effectiveness of different interventions and regulations, i.e., a "wellness years" index (Kaplan & Bush, 1982).

Just as fluoridation and vaccination programs have had large-scale effects on health, now as in the past, current environmental and consumer regulations are needed to foster health on a population basis. For example, whereas smoking prevention (Evans et al., 1981) and smoking cessation programs (McAlister, 1981), and programs to change dietary habits (Maccoby & Solomon, 1981) are valuable and becoming more effective, their ultimate effect on actual health outcomes is minimized in places where simply breathing the air may be equivalent to smoking a pack of cigarettes per day, or where knowledge about, and choice of foods is limited by restricted information flows and other policies.

Nature of Work

Considerable interest through the years has focused on the nature of work and health outcomes. One connection with the brief prior section on regulation is the various health and safety regulations that are under recent attack. Whatever is the eventual outcome of the debates concerning the degree of regulation needed, it is apparent that specific work conditions (e.g., work involving asbestos) greatly increase health risks. In conjunction with other health risks (e.g., smoking), certain working conditions dramatically multiply the chance of disability and early death (Matarazzo, 1983). These connections have been made through the years, but it remains to be seen how much focus there will be on occupational health and safety.

In addition to the extreme examples of increased health risk from particular kinds of work, recent interest has focused on the stress and strain caused generally by work, with such stress seen as a precursor or concomitant of detrimental health behaviors (e.g., alcoholism and drug abuse) or other stress-related diseases (e.g., a range of psychophysiological problems). In this case, we are not only addressing high stress occupations, such as air traffic controllers, but the more pervasive day-to-day stress caused by increased automation of work, and alienation from the processes and products of work. One possible interesting and very valuable secondary outcome of changes toward more participatory management practices to increase productivity may be a decrease in alienation and stress, and hence a decrease in job-related health problems.

Recent research has focused on the health costs of extreme work schedules, i.e., shift work. Shift work may actually increase because the large capital investment needed for the new technology industries virtually demands some round-the-clock operations. Recent data also indicate that shift work is most prevalent in a population segment already under considerable stress, i.e., dual-earner families with young children (Presser & Cain, 1983). The interactions of shift work with family patterns and health costs, however, remains unclear.

What recent research has made clearer is that shift work can radically interfere with an individual's circadian rhythm, creating a plethora of predictable sleep, mood, eating, and interpersonal problems (Czeisler, Moore-Ede, & Coleman, 1982). An important behavioral system intervention has involved changes in shift rotations in light of biological principles so as to reduce aversive health outcomes of shift work (Czeisler et al., 1982).

Regulations on health and safety and shift work draw us heavily into the world of work as important ground in analyzing antecedents of ill-health and potential protective interventions.

Safety

Safety regulation has been alluded to in the prior section, but here the focus is on one set of safety practices that have enormous potential individual costs and tremendous documented societal costs. The practices involve safety restraint in automobiles. Not wearing a seat belt or improper (or no) child restraint is a major health risk. Recent attempts to increase use have included psychologically-based incentive interventions to increase seat belt usage (Geller, Paterson, & Talbott, 1982) and the passage of laws (of different scope and contingencies) to promote increased use of appropriate child restraints and fine for nonuse (Seekins et al., 1985). The psychological and legal approaches are important but should not distract us from one of the original impetuses for the consumer movement, i.e., the effects of automobile design on safety (i.e., Ralph Nader's first issue). Some aspects of current design (e.g., air bags and passive restraint systems) can be further modified in ways to reduce the injury and death toll of accidents.

Political/Ideological Context

The preceding sections make the case that health-related behaviors and practices are the product of a range of environmental influences, from interpersonal networks to payment mechanism for health care to the arrangement of work in our society. Throughout this background section, there were also some allusions to the political nature of these environmental influences. For example, radically different views of the role of government regulation in health and safety are likely to result in quite different outcomes. In this section, some aspects of the overarching political context are further discussed.

In some respects, a system perspective that is concerned with interdependencies is at odds with some political positions. For example, an extreme laissez-faire position tends to depict individuals as free to choose various paths of self-interest, relatively unencumbered (Friedman & Friedman, 1979). Presumably, everyone acting in self-interest will result in the greatest collective good, i.e., the "invisible hand" of Adam Smith. Particular kinds of regulation and other government interventions are seen as undermining the workings of a free-market economy.

The system position stresses constraints on behavior and interdependencies of actions that may, or may not, be for the collective good. Thus, the laissez-faire position seems to contradict emerging conceptions of human behavior and the workings of society. The word "emerging" was purposely used in the prior sentence to reflect the fact that the dominant American (psychological) paradigm has been the paradigm of the contextless individual (Sarason, 1981). This paradigm, not surprisingly, closely parallels a number of tenets of laissez-faire capitalism, e.g., an individual free to choose. American behavioral science has, for the most part, followed the country's political traditions, and also been used as an instrument of policy, for example, how and what to focus on in health programs.

Recent swings to this more conservative position have resulted in some deregulation (with presumably some health consequences) with the original rationale of "freeing" people, i.e., "getting government off the backs of people." The apparent support for certain regulations such as clean air measures suggests that a large segment of the population may not share the conservative position on this issue and sees the close relationship between environment and health.

However, as Hanlon and Picket (1984) noted, arguments about the role of institutions in health and disease go back to the founding of the United States. For example, Hanlon and Picket (1984) indicated:

> In the century during which the American colonies drew together and eventually formed a federation of states, little progress of a public health nature was made. Recognition must be given, however, to at least one notable person of that period. The multifaceted Dr. Benjamin Rush wrote that political institutions, economic organization, and disease were so interrelated that any general social change produced accompanying changes in health. Regretfully there are still many today who seem unable to grasp this simple concept. (p. 30)

An even more basic and current ideological battle concerns the issue of "rights" versus "duty and responsibility" in health care (Winkler, 1982). This issue is intertwined with political beliefs and conceptions of human behavior, but has come to the forefront because of the continuous escalation of health-care costs in the face of decreased resources to fund health care. An extreme rights position sees access to good health care as a basic entitlement of a citizen regardless of cost. An extreme "duty and responsibility" position sees health in large measure being related to individual initiative and choice and, thus, has some compatibility with some conservative ideology. Thus, one simplistic connection made is between the relationship of health risk behaviors, life style, and morbidity. The greatest causes of morbidity today are seen in behaviors such as smoking, drinking, overeating, or poor dietary practices, with disease potentially preventable (Matarazzo, 1983). These behaviors are largely seen as a product of individual choice (Fuchs, 1975). Government can supply information and education to promote prevention and better health choices, but in the end the ultimate responsibility for health belongs to the individual.

Obviously, there is some truth to this position. People can and do make health choices, but this chapter has emphasized that they are choices made under environmental influence and constraint. In addition, the responsibility and duty perspective can and has been used as a rationale for deregulation in health and safety, decreases in environmental protection, and for the defunding of health care.

One of the greatest tasks in this decade is to strike a balance between the rights and duty position. Society cannot continue to pay for more and more health care, or have every aspect of life regulated. Even within constraints people can and do make relatively free choices that greatly influence their health. There seem to be certain basics in health care and environmental protection that should be the entitlement of citizens, and certain health choices that are not really choices at all.

This section was not meant to reduce the tension between these positions, much less solve the issue. Rather, the section was meant to show how overarching, ideological concerns shape analyses of health behaviors.

A BRIDGE TO INFORMATION/SYSTEM INTERVENTIONS

Whereas a behavioral systems and public health perspective can make good conceptual sense, the movement of this position into the everyday concerns of analysis and intervention can be quite intimidating for most behavioral scientists. This is not only because such a perspective means interactions and complexity, but it points toward analysis and intervention in organizations, communities, and institutions. This is unfamiliar turf to many of us. The conclusion then is that smaller scale efforts are futile and lead to a paralysis of thought and action. Although there are some recent exceptions (e.g., Maccoby & Solomon), it is probably true that the likelihood of behavioral scientists routinely becoming involved in macro-level interventions is not great.

Fielding (1983) has also provided a warning about the effectiveness of health interventions that essentially do not modify the prevailing system:

> It is as if we have hooked several 50-foot tug boats, each powered by a three-horsepower engine, to a 1000-foot ocean liner and have been surprised not to have seen them turn the ocean liner around. We display amazement when the liner's wake capsizes the small crafts. (p. 114)

Although it is apparent that there is not a solution to the dichotomy between theory and belief and reality and system constraints, there do seem to be many reasonable compromises when the issues of levels and type of analyses and intervention are addressed.

Problems can be conceptualized at different levels, such as, individual, small group, small setting, organization, institutional, community (Rappaport, 1977), and one key for behavioral scientists in the future may be to raise our level of analysis one notch and develop strategies at the intersection of individual/group, and group/setting/organizational level. Such analyses and interventions must realistically examine and plan for system constraints. However, this need not mean that the behavioral scientist believes that the entirety of the cause and solution to the problem rests at that level of analysis or intervention, or the approach is absolutely optimal (Rappaport, 1977).

Weick (1984) has effectively made this point: we may be better off breaking down problems into manageable parts with manageable solutions. The strategy of small-wins is more realistic and helps to overcome inertia created by analyzing problems and solutions in their entirety. Small-wins can also add-up over time to large wins.

The examples that follow examine how effective use of information in various systems can lead to positive health outcomes. The examples are diverse and include intracellular (immune system) response to neurologically mediated information; physician counseling on preventive health practices; supermarket information; regulatory information remedies, and community information campaigns. In each example, effective information can be framed using principles, evidence, and strategies described throughout this book. Clearly, none of the examples represents the health panacea. However, each approach in a small-wins sense can help to promote more positive health behaviors. And, one win can lead to others. For example, positive patient response to one type of information starts to beg the question of how other aspects of patient care can be modified. Consumer response to a well-planned, but simple, supermarket information intervention counters positions claiming that food purchase practices are not modifiable and suggests other regulatory and intervention strategies.

INFORMATION EFFECTS AT THE INTRACELLULAR LEVEL

Norman Cousins' books (1979, 1983) have dramatized that a person's perception of their own health and illness, the degree of control a person's feels they have over their own health behaviors, and the information and feedback provided by others, may remarkably effect the course of a disease or other bodily afflictions. Some writers (e.g., Weil, 1983) have suggested that Cousins' experiences and other documented phenomena (e.g., healing warts through psychological means, for example, by "suggestion") seriously call into question the philosophy, culture, training and techniques of Western medicine. For example, Fitzpatrick, Hopkins, and Harvard-Watts (1983) state:

> The characteristics of Western medicine as a cultural system are now familiar. It aspires to even more precise understanding of the mechanical functioning of the body in normality and disease. Explanations of the ways in which medicine achieves therapeutic benefits are increasingly based on the isolation of discrete effects of specific interventions. The pharmacological agents are viewed as acting by specific pathways on particular target organs. Nevertheless it is now widely accepted that on average one-third of the therapeutic improvements obtained by modern medicine have to be attributed to non-specific mechanisms unrelated to the mode of action of administered treatments. (p. 502)

Thus, specific medical interventions may not act as originally thought. This is because any medical regime interacts with social psychological variables. However, simply describing the latter variables as nonspecific factors, or a placebo response, will not advance the health knowledge base. Person and environmental variables must be specified and their effects on diverse health outcomes assessed.

Research is needed to substantiate and further evolve the broad, emerging conceptions of health and disease (e.g., Antonovsky, 1979) and scientific system approaches to the study of social psychological effects on health (e.g., Schwartz, 1982). A most exciting conceptual and empirical development is the new field called *Psychoneuroimmunology* (Ader, 1981). A schema that defines this term and captures this model is shown in Fig. 6.1.

Cunningham (1981) explained the model in this way:

> The whole organism is an open system in dynamic interaction with the environment. We need ultimately an overall theory connecting social, psychological, and somatic events. The individual adapts to his environment, two of the most sophisticated kinds of adaptation being development of mental and immune memory. This raises an important point: the exchanges which take place between environment and organism are transfers of energy, but even more interesting involve transmission of *information*. Memory is information about specific aspects of the environment. (pp. 610–611)

Thus, one possibility is that there are differential internal responses to different kinds of information mediated by a person's ideas, beliefs and expectations

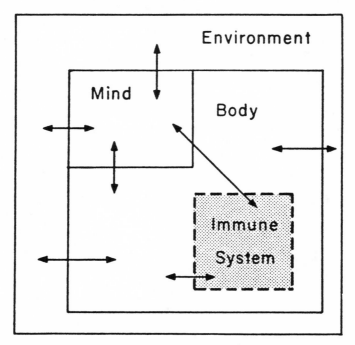

FIG. 6.1.   The interactions between immune system, body, mind, and environment (Cunningham, 1981).

(e.g., degree of perceived control), emotional state (e.g., distress), and the environmental context. Such internal responses appear able to influence the course of health and disease states. These linkages are best shown in Fig. 6.2.

Advances in this field are being rapidly made (Jemmott & Locke, 1984) so that it is safe to say that any specific empirical work mentioned here will have been extended by other investigators by the time this book is in print. However, several points will be made by way of illustration. The degree of control, real or perceived, exercised over environmental stimuli, i.e., "stressors," appears to play an important role in coping with stress, and the eventual effects of stress on the immune system (e.g., Frankenhauser, 1979; Laudenslager, 1983). That is, how stress is perceived, how information is framed, can eventually affect immune system responses.

Kiecolt-Glaser and her colleagues at Ohio State University have probably done the most sophisticated chain of studies in psychoneurimmunology. The studies are unusual in that Kiecolt-Glaser, a psychologist, has been able to focus on critical social psychological variables, whereas Glaser, an immunologist, has provided the state-of-the-art immune system assessments. Their work illustrates the value of interdisciplinary collaboration, an approach to investigation emphasized throughout this book. The following are some key points from their research, most of which has used prospective designs:

1. The immune system's response helps to govern the body's defense against infectious and malignant disease.

2. Common everyday stressors, not just traumatic events or stressful life events, affect immune system functions (e.g., Kiecolt-Glaser, Spelcher et al., 1984). Psychological distress may be the most critical kind of stress.

3. An important variable modifying responses to stress is the degree of social connectness. However, Kiecolt-Glaser has advanced the intriguing, but often

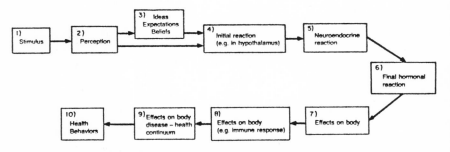

FIG. 6.2. Some of the levels through which an environmental stimulus, perceived by the mind, may affect events in the body and eventually health and behavior (Cunningham, 1981).

vague, research in social support by identifying (and measuring), loneliness as a key dimension. (Glaser, Kiecolt-Glaser, Spelcher, & Holliday, 1985; Kiecolt-Glaser, Ricker et al., 1984).

4. These environmental, social and somatic connections were illustrated in a study with medical students. Those students scoring high on a loneliness scale showed lower levels of natural killer (NK) cell activity in a blood sample drawn on the first day of final exams compared to a baseline taken one month previously. Those scoring low on the loneliness scale did not show this change. NK cells appear to have ". . . specific and preprogrammed antitumor and antiviral activity . . . [and] have been shown to be of vital importance in preventing tumor development and spread" (Kiecolt-Glaser, Garner et al., 1984, p. 9).

5. These findings have been futher further replicated. For example, in a sample of 28 newly admitted psychiatric patients, the 14 scoring highest on an indice of distress had significantly poorer DNA repair in lymphocytes (Kiecolt-Glaser, Stephens et al., 1985). Most carcinogens apparently induce cancer by damaging DNA in cells and producing mutant cells. The ability to repair DNA cells may be critically related to the incidence of cancer. Another study with medical students further showed that loneliness modulated the stress from final exams (Glaser et al., 1985). A measure of herpes virus showed increases to stress, but again students scoring high on a loneliness scale showed more increase than those scoring lower on the scale.

6. Simple social psychological procedures may modulate cellular immunity. For example, measures were taken of the percent of helper/inducer T-lympho-cytes in medical students (Kiecolt-Glaser, Glaser, Strain et al., 1985). Large reductions can produce immunodeficiency. Stress (exams) produced declines in the ratio. However, half the students had received relatively standard relaxation training for a month prior to exams. Those students actually practicing relaxation training showed a lower decline in the helper/inducer ratio. In a better designed experiment with geriatric residents of an independent living facility (Kiecolt-Glaser, Glaser, Willinger et al., 1985), it was found that residents receiving relaxation training (as an active coping skill to exert control over stress) showed at the end of a month's training (three times a week for brief sessions) increases in NK activity and decreases in a measure for herpes simplex virus. These results were in comparison to a control group or a group only receiving social contact.

7. These studies generally provide evidence for central nervous system (e.g., perception of environment; information availability) mediation of immune system functions. Acute stress and distress appears to be immunosuppressive and may be associated with important dysfunctions at the molecular level, e.g., DNA repair. Simple relaxation training, and, perhaps other social psychological strategies may provide important stress buffers for some immunologic functions. These points are also consistent with Cousin's (1979) emphasis on the health-enhancement qualities of positive emotions.

It is important to include the caveat that much of this work is in the beginning stages. Longer term investigations, or studies with at-risk populations, may better qualify the relationships of social-psychological factors to health and disease (see McQueen & Siegrist, 1984; Palmblad, 1981). However, the current work by Kiecolt-Glaser and others illustrates the value of multilevel analyses and investigations and seems quite supportive of these points:

1. A health, medical approach that excludes serious consieration of social psychological and milieu variables is not only short sighted, but probably not as effective as it can be.

2. A person's perceptions, derived from past experiences (e.g., degree they feel alone) and the environmental context (e.g., degree of personal control afforded) can greatly color informations input, so that in the worst case, immune system functions are decreased.

3. The provision of more positive frames for information about health and disease states, and a higher degree of control concerning stress and health behaviors, may result in beneficial health outcomes.

4. Appropriate investigations in this field can include the impact of critical aspects of information delivery, e.g., frames, vividness, types of messages.

Thus, treatment that conveys a realistic degrees of hope and provides personal control may yield surprising outcomes, unexpected from conventional Western medicine (Cousins, 1979, 1983). And health information that emphasizes positive approaches to health and personal control, coupled with long-term and immediate environmental supports may help to create what Antonovsky (1979) has called a ''sense of coherence''—an enduring feeling about the predictability of internal and external events and general confidence in the future—that may be a prime mediator of health.

Although, at first glance, studies in psychoneuroimmunology may seem like one of the little tugboats described in Fielding's quote pertaining to the immovability of the ocean liner, this may not be the case at all. By conducting scientific studies and issuing guarded conclusions, these studies are meeting the medical establishment on their own terms, with methods and outcomes that cannot be ignored, i.e., a small-wins approach. As the two figures from Cunningham indicate, these studies, as their most basic contribution, are providing a true multilevel systems approach to health and disease. This development can be seen as the continuation of ecological approaches in medicine and public health, but, perhaps in a more sophisticated direction than before (Catalano, 1979). The most basic connection to the theme of this book that this area of study provides is that it is possible to see how information, framed by environmental context and person mediation, potentially may have profound effects on internal events and external health behaviors.

PHYSICIAN COUNSELING

The prior section suggested that a physician's role behaviors, as differentiated from particular medical interventions, may have much to do with the course of an illness. The instillation of hope and the provision of personal control seem to be key variables. This section focuses on more specific, and direct efforts by physicians to impart preventive health information.

The first question to ask is why would a physician provide such information? In an HMO, physicians and the firm benefit by keeping people healthy. That is, there usually is a set yearly prepayment to cover all medical expenses. Presumably, if it costs more than that sum to care for an enrollee, the organization losses; if it costs less, the organization benefits. However, it must be kept in mind that most patients are still seen within the fee for service system where payment is made by third parties, with ostensibly little reason for either physicians or patients to be concerned about cost, and perhaps, preventive measures. The following are some incentives for private physicians to become preventive health counselors:

1. Because preventive measures are becoming more valued by the general public, the physicians who offer such services may find themselves gaining new patients, i.e., it may make them more competitive.

2. A patient population for a given physician that is more knowledgeable and healthy may expedite service. That is, the physician may be able to see more patients in less time, thus, increasing income.

3. Providing an alternative service may relieve boredom and "burn-out" partly attributable to seeing many patients on a daily basis who have only minor problems. For example, in the author's community, family physicians may see as many as four-to-five patients per hour, and close to 100% of these encounters can be considered "routine" (Hendricks, personal communication, February, 1985).

Even within the fee for service system, there may be some identifiable incentives for physician, preventive health counseling.

From the perspective of information effects, there are a number of aspects of physician counseling that can make it an almost ideal situation. For example, with regard to independent variables:

1. The source is very credible and of high status.
2. Attention and comprehension can be maximized by the situation and nature of the message.
3. The message can be very specific and tailored to the individual patient's present state of health, receptiveness, education, and life style.

4. The channel of delivery is interpersonal, and that can be enhanced by print, audio, or visual media.
5. The situation and context also are favorable since the physician and patient can be alone and information may be imparted at a very "teachable moment", e.g., after a patient receives an examination and has heightened health concerns.
6. Counseling can be formulated to focus on immediate and long-term behaviors with intermittent contact and feedback possible within the context of the usual service.

With regard to dependent variables:

1. Exposure and attention can be assured.
2. Comprehension can be assessed by physician and patient questions with the message reworked to achieve a high comprehension level.
3. Specific techniques (e.g., diet and exercise plans) can be provided or behaviors modeled (e.g., taking heart rate), thus, enhancing initial behavior change.
4. A gradual approach to long-term behavior change can be constructed with feedback and reinforcement available from the physician and staff.

Physician counseling also has the advantage of providing help to nonselected individuals on a massive level. Few people actually avail themselves of the many commercial and nonprofit health programs (e.g., smoking cessation) in a community. Those who do so may be a highly self-selected sample whose problem may be particularly recalcitrant (Schacter, 1982). Physicians could routinely provide this type of service to virtually all of their patients.

Russel and his colleagues (Russel, Wilson, Taylor, & Baker, 1979) have written extensively about physican counseling and have shown the worth of low-cost, low-level physician-based intervention. Their study targeted all the smokers who attended five different family practices in London over a four-week period. Over 2,000 smokers were assigned to one of four groups: (a) a control group who simply had their names taken for follow-up; (b) a group who completed questionnaires on smoking habits and attitudes; (c) a group that completed the questionnaires and were advised by their physician to stop smoking; (d) a group that completed the questionnaires, were advised to stop smoking, were given a leaflet entitled "How you can give up smoking", and were warned that they could be followed up. Of the original sample 88% were available for follow-up at 1 month. At this follow-up 7.5% of the persons in group four had stopped smoking. Only 3% of the control group had quit. At 1 year follow-up 5.1% of group four subjects were still not smoking compared to only 0.3% of controls.

There are a number of important implications of the Russel et al. study. The follow-up data indicated that the greater number of persons who stopped smoking in group four was due to "motivating more people to try to stop smoking rather than increasing the success rate among those who did try'' (Russel et al., 1979, p. 231). In addition, persons who stopped smoking reported doing so because of the advice. The effect of the follow up and leaflet added little long-term effect, however, the effects of the advice were visible almost immediately. Even though the 5.1% success rate is substantially lower than the 20–25% success rate claimed by some stop-smoking clinics the results are nevertheless impressive. Russel et al. projected that if all 20,000 general practitioners in Great Britain adopted the simple procedure demonstrated in this study, there could be as many as one-half million additional ex-smokers in Great Britain in a year's time! The cost per ''cured'' smoker would be considerably lower than that of the withdrawal clinics.

There seem to be many ways to make physician counseling more effective. In a review of studies on physician counseling, for example counseling that follows patient completion of a Health Risk Appraisal (HRA) form, it was very difficult to discern what was meant by counseling (Israel, Hendricks, Winett, & Frederiksen, 1983). Generally, it appeared to be some exhortation and advice (as in Russel et al.). It is not surprising that this simple antecedent strategy is only marginally effective. However, within the daily routine of the physician, and with little or no extra time, it appears possible to provide much more specific information in verbal and written form, and to have staff follow-up patients and give additional tailored information, feedback, and reinforcement (Israel et al., 1983).

The potential of further intensive, investigation here is shown by the results of a demonstration study by Israel et al. (1983). Considerable formative research was done to find an HRA form that was comprehensive, yet could be filled out in a few minutes in a waiting room. It was also found that by varying the directiveness of what the physician said to the patient, and by using a highly visible office display, it was possible to activate patient preventive health behaviors. Without the directiveness of the physician and the prominent display, there was no patient behavioral response.

Physician counseling may become an effective intervention when the approach is supported in its development and enactment by social marketing, communication, and psychological principles. The approach is consistent with the emphasis on system change in that the focus is change in physician behavior and not solely patient behavior.

NUTRITIONAL INFORMATION PROVIDED BY A SUPERMARKET CHAIN

In chapter 7 on information and consumer behavior, it was noted that it may be in the interest of the firm to take a proconsumer stance and promote nutritional purchases within the store. In this section, the best known effort is described here in detail. The purpose is not only to detail the project and indicate the outcomes, but also to discuss how similar efforts can become more successful.

The "Foods for Health" program was a joint effort involving Giant Foods, Inc. and scientists at the National Heart, Lung, and Blood Institute of the National Institutes of Health (National Heart, Lung and Blood Institute, 1983). It serves as a good example of private and public sector cooperation. The project was based on pilot work (Zifferblat, Wilbur, & Pinsky, 1980) showing that prompts at the point of food selection in a cafeteria and vending machines could alter food selection of Institute employees to a significant (i.e., statistical and health criteria) degree. The Institute scientists were interested in seeing if this approach could work on a large-scale. At the same time, Giant Foods believed that helping shoppers make more nutritional purchases would benefit their shoppers and the firm (e.g., by increasing customer loyalty and attracting new customers).

The project, conducted from October, 1978 to October, 1979 in 90 giant food stores in the Washington, DC (experimental) and Baltimore (control) areas, had these basic assumptions:

1. Knowledge of nutrition is somewhat limited, thus, resulting in less than optimal purchases.
2. If consumer awareness and knowledge of nutrition was increased then consumers will implement purchase and dietary changes, i.e., a hierarchy of effects model.
3. Point of purchase information is an effective way to increase awareness, knowledge, and eventually, behavior.

Unfortunately, the hierarchy of effects, causal chain model when used as more than a heuristic, and the effectiveness of prompts and in-store displays, are both questionable. In addition, it appeared that other than the pilot studies, little formative research was done to assess typical consumer beliefs and knowledge, their connection to actual food purchases, and the efficacy of the particular strategies used in the project.

The central theme of the project was that given the facts, "you decide." The primary information vehicles were the *Eater's Almanac,* a series of four-page brochures distributed every 2 weeks within supermarkets and companion supermarket shelf tags called "Shelf Talkers". In the 26 issues, the Almanacs provided facts about heart disease, cardiovascular risk factors, and nutrition. They identified research questions that remained unanswered, but gave seasonal suggestions for food selection and preparation, such as holiday and summer meals. From the points discussed in the first chapter on effective media, the almanacs seem ineffective because their information is too complex and vague. However, the shelf tags were placed directly below designated products to provide information at the point of selection. Presumably, the almanacs would be taken home and read.

Other promotional devices included radio spots, newspaper ads, in-store banners, window signs, and in-store posters, all tied into the almanacs. Over the course of the project over 2 million almanacs were distributed. Importantly, however, most aspects of the program only focused on awareness and knowledge.

The evaluation assessed the feasibility of the approach, i.e., in-store nutritional education and private–public sector cooperation, awareness and use of the program by shoppers, reported nutritional knowledge and food habits, actual food purchases in the supermarket, and general interest in and dissemination of the program to other organizations. Evaluation instruments included telephone surveys and questionnaires with representative samples of Giant food store shoppers and food purchase data generated by the computer-assisted check-out system in 10 DC and 10 Baltimore stores matched on demographic and sociological characteristics. There were also some unobtrusive observations made of shoppers.

Overall, the findings indicated great public and professional interest in the project; extensive and smooth cooperation between the representatives of the private and public sectors; some small, but significant, changes in knowledge, but no actual change in purchase pattern.

A closer examination of the project description and data in the rest of the report showed the following:

1. At the outset of the project, only one (i.e., Giant), of 20 food retailing chains contacted would meet all the requirements of the project, e.g., the experimental design and extensive promotional materials.

2. The use of radio spots, newspaper ads, window signs, and banners was also quite extensive and strategic and continued throughout the program.

3. The major emphasis of the almanacs was not on general nutrition, but more focused on reducing fats, cholesterol, and calories in the diet (a positive aspect of the almanacs).

4. The computer-assisted check-out system monitored 246 items that were eventually reduced to nine categories (e.g., eggs, milk, salt). The categories did represent ones frequently noted in the almanacs, although fruit and vegetable purchases were not monitored.

5. Although 45% of the DC sample indicated they read the project materials, so did 35% of the Baltimore sample, i.e., there were problems with the self-report measures and/or there was contamination in the Baltimore stores.

6. At the outset, over 70% of the DC and Baltimore samples could correctly answer key items about the fat/cholesterol content of food and relationship of dietary fat to serum cholesterol.

7. It was not clear what percentage of people actually read the almanacs.

8. The gain in knowledge was only about 8% to 10%, and education level was related to knowledge.

9. At the end of the program, about 90% of the DC and Baltimore (control) survey respondents endorsed nutritional beliefs highly consistent with the project's goals.

The results of this program warrant some detailed discussion. In the history of health promotion programs, this program was developed at the "first dawn." That is, it is easy to criticize the project based on the informative experiences of this one and other projects, and in light of more recent emphases on social marketing and behavioral outcomes. It is clear that more formative research was needed to assess the knowledge, beliefs, and behaviors of the target population. Given the findings on knowledge and beliefs in absence of the program, or prior to its outset, it is apparent that the hierarchy of effects model was inappropriate. Much attention needed to be directed to strategies to promote behavior change given (already) adequate knowledge. In addition, an analysis of food shopping behavior suggests that in-store prompts and displays (unless very specific, targeted to certain items, and instrusive) will probably not be an effective behavioral intervention in supermarkets, at least as far as promoting changes large enough to be pertinent to health outcomes. A highly simplified approach using out-of-store media, particularly TV, is advocated in chapter 7. In addition, the potential for specifically tailored feedback via the computerized check-out system is also discussed.

The need to focus and simplify the approach taken in the Food for Health project is captured by this quote by the National Heart, Lung, and Blood Institute (1983):

> in the 26 Eater's Almanacs and 23 shelf signs, a great deal of information and general food selection and preparation principles were presented. This information was illustrated by specific foods, but the consumer then had to apply this information amongst the 10,000 to 40,000 grocery store items and individualize the messages to their own food preparation techniques. (p. 49)

The "Foods for Health" program can be summarized within key information variables that were apparently *not* well attended to:

Message. Over-emphasized quantity; vague and complex messages (e.g., diffuse nutritional education; "you decide"); lack of specificity.
Channel. Too much reliance on print media; faulty assumptions on use of materials and point-of-purchase signs.
Source. Presumably high credibility (U.S. government), but unclear what consumer perceptions were of Giant Food's role.
Receiver. Little formative research to understand consumers, segment market, and target messages.

Destination. Unclear purchase behavior changes, e.g., changes were focused on many kinds of purchases.

Conceptualization. Inappropriate causal chain; most of focus on knowledge and awareness; too little analysis of competing information and environmental constraints (e.g., use of information to deal with 10,000 to 40,000 store items). *Goals.* Unclear, unrealistic expectation of change across types of purchases.

Thus, it may be the case that a simpler and much more focused approach could be effective. For example, it could be stated with some degree of scientific confidence that a diet high in complex carbohydrates is healthier and can be cheaper than the traditional Western high fat and protein diet. The consumer can then be shown foods to increase and those to decrease, without much further elaboration (i.e., nutritional education). This simplified approach follows some aspects of the author's work in energy conservation where consumer response was shown, and will be experimented with next by the author with food purchases (Winett, Kramer, Walker, & Malone, 1985).

Some very recent evidence to support this position comes from an evaluation of the effectiveness of specific shelf tags used in Giant food stores to indicate foods low or reduced in sodium, cholesterol, or calories. According to Dr. Alan Levy (personal communication, September, 1984), a psychologist who performed the evaluation for the Food and Drug Administration (FDA), the program solely consisted of the shelf tags. There was no other persuasive, promotional materials. The FDA allowed Giant Foods to experiment with the special labels. The approach was based on the evidence from the first project that many consumers are aware of dietary-health links. Because knowledge was not the issue, it was decided to merely help an informed segment choose the right products.

Levy, Mathews, Stephenson, Tenney, and Schucker (1984) reported that in about half of the targeted items, there were statistically significant shifts in the rate of product purchases in Washington, DC stores (experimental) compared to Baltimore stores (controls) of about 4% to 8%. Although this effect was not large, and the health benefits of such a shift in product selection are open to question (Kaplan, 1984), Levy indicated that this change was about what might be expected from pricing or other promotional strategies.

Obviously this is a very simple, portable approach. One hope is that the success of this program will encourage other food concerns to adopt more consumer-oriented policies. More generally, these results indicate the need for careful consideration of Schramm's (1977) classic information medium × task × cost framework. In the supermarket study, a very simple, inexpensive prompt was all that was necessary to yield some behavior change for (albeit) fairly knowledgeable consumers in a relatively low-involvement situation.

INFORMATION FLOW AND REGULATORY POLICY: THE USE OF CORRECTIVE ADVERTISING TO COUNTERACT DECEPTIVE ADVERTISING

This section highlights the uses of corrective advertising. This is an important area of health concern. For example, billions of dollars each year are spent on nonprescription drugs (e.g., sleep medications), most of which have little or no documented effectiveness (Lee & Zelenak, 1982). Additional billions of dollars are spent on foods that typical consumers may believe are nutritious, e.g., fruit drinks, because they are so named and promoted. In actuality, using the example cited, their primary "natural" ingredients may be water and refined, white sugar!

Wilkie, McNeill, and Mazis (1984) have traced the development and outlined critical issues in corrective advertising as promulgated by the Federal Trade Commission (FTC). The original objectives of corrective advertising were to provide a remedy for deceptive advertising thereby aiding consumers and competitive firms, to deny the offending firm any future benefits from deceptive ads, and to serve as a general deterrent. The approach was developed in a more liberal era (early 1970s), but even then, there was some strong concern that the FTC had overstepped its bounds by intruding into the market system in a highly punitive manner. However, in the spirit of the times, several noteworthy cases in corrective advertising were completed focusing on:

1. Profile Bread's claim that its bread helped in weight loss because it contained fewer calories than other breads; actually, only the slices were thinner.
2. Ocean Spray's claim that its cranberry juice cocktail had more "food energy" than orange juice or tomato juice implying more nutrients and vitamins; actually, it only contains more calories (i.e., it is mostly sugar and water).
3. Listerine's claim that its mouthwash deterred germs and, hence, helped with colds; actually, there is no evidence to support this claim.
4. Hawaiian Punch's advertising approach that used the jingle, "seven natural fruit juices in Hawaiian Punch" and showed natural fruits; actually, the punch is a fruit *drink* because it's major ingredients are sugar and water and contains only between 11% to 15% fruit juice.

The development of corrective advertising is fraught with legal, political, economic, and social, psychological difficulties. The FTC's mandate, to provide a "fair competitive and consumer environment" (Wilkie et al., 1984) is sufficiently vague as to make unclear whether the FTC can enter into this new realm. Obviously, as the political climate changes, the FTC's mandate changes. If it is decided that the FTC can demand corrective advertising, it must do so in a prospective way that is essentially nonpunitive (although it is also unclear what this term means), bears a relationship to the degree of violation, does not infringe on the First Amendment rights of the firm (commercial free speech), and must be done in a nonburdensome, but effective way. To make matters worse, exact social, psychological criteria for deception have not been clear (Engel & Blackwell, 1982).

Wilkie et al. traced the development of corrective ads within a highly charged adversial environment. Generally, corrective ads that were ultimately implemented represented years of legal maneuvering and eventual compromise. A major problem has been in the corrective ads implemented. Because most of the hearings focused on legal questions and were conducted by lawyers, the issue of actual consumer effectiveness was rarely, if ever addressed empirically, but rather apriori—as is typical of the legal process. The form, content, extent, and medium for the corrective ad campaign was not based on consumer or communications research.

Wilkie et al. (1984) reported that when corrective ads have been evaluated, when delivered in a realistic contexts, i.e., within an ad shown during the course of a regular TV program, the effects on such simple measures as recall (and, very early in the causal chain), are very weak. For example, in the case of some Listerine ads, the correction amounted to about 5 seconds of a 30 second spot. Here, according to Wilkie et al. (1984) is how this type of ad eventually played:

> A final twist occurred when Listerine placed the required disclosure into effect by creating advertisings first "corrective, comparative commercial". Mouthwash marketers had discovered that an onion theme was a useful symbol for evidence of product power. Listerine's corrective commercial featured two couples, with each husband finding himself having "onion breath". Each used mouthwash, one trying Scope and the other Listerine. After sniffing her husband's breath, one wife stated that she hadn't known that "clinical tests prove Listerine fights onion breath better than Scope". The other replied, "we always knew". The corrective disclosure had been placed midway in the 30-second spot as follows: while [Listerine will not prevent colds or sore throats or lessen their severity] breath test prove Listerine fights onion breath better than Scope. (p. 22)

Obviously, this example indicates that corrective ads should be developed and evaluated prior to enactment of the final FTC decision. However, pursuing a course of effective corrective ads faces important obstacles: an ad cannot be so strong that it is disproportionately damaging to the firm; there is a lack of motivation by firms, and in some instances the FTC, to implement effective ads; and, there is difficulty of specifying, prior to evaluation, the exact parameters (e.g., medium, content, duration) of an effective ad.

Wilkie et al. recommended more input into this process by psychologists, consumer behaviorists, and marketers. Another companion approach is to allow the experts, the firm's advertising agency, to develop ads and demonstrate effective impact to levels predesignated by the firm and the FTC. For example, it may be required that corrective ads must continue to run until it is empirically shown that 90% of the product's users have the correct information.

The discussion of corrective ads is an important reminder of how the information and regulatory environment impacts on consumer expenditures and health in certainly a nontrivial way. For example, consumers fully induced to follow the advice of many ads will end up wasting their money on ineffective drugs and other medications and buying worse than worthless "natural" food products. The lack of information flow in health care results in a noncompetitive market where prices are inflated (Benham, 1972; Benham & Benham, 1975).

The author is at odds with the approach advocated by Wilkie et al. and favors a more definitive, stronger approach. Counter ads can be designed and field-tested by expert communication professionals and consumer behaviorists. Dependent measures must move much further down the causal chain. At a minimum, it appears reasonable to assess a corrective ad's impact on behavioral intention, for example, consumers do not intend to buy Listerine to prevent colds. I do not consider this a "punitive" action that denies commercial free speech. Further, changes in regulatory policy are needed so that prime-time media access is provided for health education spots. Spots can explain the effectiveness of different drugs, the meaning of certain food items, and the contents of food. Professionally designed and strategically placed spots can somewhat diminish the asymmetry of time and money devoted to commercial versus noncommercial information and provide some countervailing power to consumers.

COMMUNITY HEALTH INFORMATION

The final example in health information attempts to influence health behaviors on a community level—the Stanford Five City Project (FCR: Farquhar et al., 1985). The social marketing approach for this project was described at length in chapter 4. The purpose here is to describe the objectives, design, and methods of this project.

At the outset, it is important to note, as others have for the forerunner Three Community Study (Leventhal, Safer, Clearly, & Gutmann, 1980), that in actuality, the Stanford Community Studies are better thought of as mass individual efforts supported by local media and organizations. That is, the approach entails supplying information and programs through Stanford initiated efforts supported, and eventually conducted by local media and organizations. The FCR generally does not attempt to change community structure (e.g., hours of work, commuting patterns) or other commercial policies (e.g., availability of certain foods), although such outcomes are possible and should be documented. If the reader feels that structural and policy change is the core of community programs, then the Stanford projects are community in name only, and the definitive community study has yet to be done. However, the Stanford projects probably do represent the best that can be done with an information approach within current political and economic constraints.

The FCP is a multifactor, 9-year, risk reduction study. It extends the earlier effort by bolstering the community organization component and including independent population surveys to assess cardiovascular disease (CVD) morbidity and mortality across a wide age range. It focuses on factors related to increased CVD risk-elevated arterial blood pressure, cigarette smoking, elevated plasma cholesterol, obesity, physical inactivity, and type A behavior.

The explicit goal of the program is a 20% reduction in the Framingham multiple logistic measure of risk in representative samples of persons 12 to 74 years old in the two communities receiving the intervention. Such a risk-reduction appears modest. However, this level of risk decline is hypothesized to lead to a decline in CVD morbidity plus mortality in persons aged 30–74 that is significantly greater in the intervention cities than in the comparison cities. Another goal is to develop cost-effective and generalizable methods that can be used in other cities to control chronic diseases.

Beyond the specific targets of the intervention, it is hoped that it will be learned how to: design and use informational materials; effectively use various media; develop cooperative arrangements with community organizations to achieve common goals; establish and maintain mutually advantageous relationships between a community and a university; and apply behavioral principles in a practical way.

The media efforts in the FCP are varied and extensive. TV and radio are used to promote attitude and knowledge change and to instill motivation. The print media is used to provide more detail on behavior change with distribution of materials through direct mail and existing organizations. The educational efforts began with the airing of an hour-long Heart Health Test, i.e., general risk reduction information. This was followed by 6 to 10 shorter programs, with some of these beginning as still shorter (3–5 minute) segments on local news programs covering smoking cessation, cooking, exercise, and weight control. In addition, about 100 different PSA's have been (or will be) developed as well as many brief radio announcements and five-minute programs. Efforts in the print media include a weekly newspaper column and kits for (individual) guided behavior change for smoking cessation and nutrition. Radio and print media use English and Spanish. At this point, every household in the intervention community has received four print products; over 100,000 booklets and pamphlets and a larger number of less expensive print materials have been distributed.

Although many of the materials and programs originate from Stanford, as the project progresses, an increasingly larger proportion of products and activities will rely on community resources for collaborative products and distribution. This seems absolutely essential if the program is ever to be transportable. To achieve the long-term goals of behavior maintenance, from the beginning of the project community programs emphasizing interpersonal contact are used. The interpersonal programs are delivered through the health department, community colleges, schools, voluntary agencies, health agencies and hospitals, providing multiple programs in multiple settings. Thus, the approach reflects the two-pronged media (for attitude and information change) and interpersonal influence (for behavior change) model long advocated in communications (see chapters 2 and 3), but obviously the most critical test is long-term behavior change.

There are constant efforts made to formulate programs based on target audience data, and to pilot and redesign media and programs. Farquhar (1985) states:

> Formative research begins with a clear definition of objectives, including the intended audience and the change to be achieved (increased knowledge, use of a new recipe, etc.). The next stage is "concept testing" where the general idea is evaluated for its validity. For example, do people use cookbooks to obtain new recipes? Next the specific content and format are defined and evaluated for clarity and effectiveness. After materials are introduced, they are "tracked" to see if they reach the intended audience and are effective. We employ a social marketing model to guide our formative research. (p. 12)

Although many of these formative research stages use surveys and focus groups for evaluation information, a major advance has been made. Recognizing that these methods only rely on self-report, behavioral data is collected using small-scale experiments comparing the acceptance and impact of different materials.

The overall evaluation of the intervention includes numerous behavioral measures (e.g., smoking, activity) and physiological measures (e.g., lipoproteins, blood pressure). Epidemiologic surveys, which do not depend on vital statistics that may not be clear-cut and reliable, include population rates of total and CVD mortality, fatal and nonfatal myocardial infarction, and fatal and nonfatal strokes. Whereas it would be interesting to assess other non-individually based changes (e.g., aggregate data on food product availability and sales), as in the forerunner project, these data apparently are not part of the evaluation plan.

Although it is worthwhile to debate whether or not the FCP is a "true" community program, the debate should not detract from these points:

1. The FCP probably represents the state-of-the-art for informational interventions given the current political and social environment and economic constraints.

2. The large volume of carefully and expertly developed health materials does entail some countervailing effort to the larger and also expertly developed commercial media partly responsible for less than healthy practices.

3. The goals of the project seem realistic and not grandiose. FCP is not a panacea, but does appear to represent another small-wins approach.

4. The overall evaluation is eagerly awaited to assess the initial efficacy and particularly the generality of the FCP model.

CONCLUSION

Will these information-based, small-win strategies make any difference in health outcomes? Is each strategy, to use Fielding's (1983, p. 114) words, just a little tugboat trying to move a gigantic ocean-liner? Or will strategies complement each other and, perhaps synergistically, impact on health? Will strategies be effective, i.e., change provider, commercial sector, and consumer behavior, but miss these points: (a) poverty and environmental influences may still override and constrain personal behavior change (Hanlon & Picket, 1984); (b) some of the targets of these efforts (dietary and activity patterns) appear tenuously related to health outcome (Kaplan, 1984); (c) long-term hospital care, the hospital industry, and the public's infatuation with high (medical) technology will still escalate our nation's health care costs (Matarrazo, 1982)? Rather than ending on an emphatic note, it seems more appropriate to say that these are questions that will be addressed, if not answered, during the next decade.

7

Behavioral Systems Approach to Information and Consumer Behavior: Economic, Legal, and Communication Aspects of Effective Information Remedies

> *As a society, we claim to value citizen sovereignty and the responsible exercise of informed choice. This is a value that lies at the core of our faith in the possibility of a democratic society. It is a precondition for the success of our political system, as well as our economic system. We are also concerned, properly, with the inequities that arise when information is asymmetric, when sellers gain a bargaining advantage because they possess greater knowledge than the buyer. We see informational remedies as part of government's responsibility to redress this imbalance between producers and consumers. . . . While consumers may theoretically not be willing to pay for information they are not accustomed to using, the very provision of that information may serve to educate consumers in its beneficial use. Consequently, the* ultimate *value of information to consumers is much higher than the initial value.*
> —Pertschuk, 1982, p. 149

This chapter focuses on the topic of information and consumer behavior. It best illustrates this recurrent theme in this book: Multilevel and interdisciplinary analyses as a basis for using effective information variables. Because the topic of information and consumer behavior is very broad, it is necessary to focus this chapter around several issues and perspectives:

1. The position is taken that the power of unorganized, individual consumers to influence market forces and corporate practices is miniscule in comparison to the power of large corporations to influence market forces and consumer behavior (Galbraith, 1973, 1983). The free-market balance between the power of the

seller and the countervailing power of the consumer is mostly seen as an illusion or convenient myth. This is because large corporations (in contrast to smaller companies and businesses that do actively compete with one another in a free market) can effectively control and limit competition, while at the same time they can control and stimulate (to an imperfect degree) consumer demand through massive, multimedia advertising that they alone can afford. Because of this "asymmetry," it is "government's responsibility to redress this imbalance between producers and consumers" (Pertschuk, 1982, p. 149). However, the myth is not extended so that information is seen as the sole or best remedy to limited consumer power. Informational approaches are only one of several potential interventions that may be enacted in concert with other approaches (e.g., regulations on use of particular terms and standards for foods plus effective information campaigns).

2. If informational approaches are to be part of the basis for restoring balance between seller and buyer, an approach consistent with our "free-market" economic and political traditions, then such an approach must be effective. Most approaches affecting consumer decisions with information have, at best, been marginally effective, and most often, ineffective. Policies and programs to aid consumers have inexpertly followed cognitive and advertising models (e.g., Hilkie & Nelson, 1984). It is argued that the field must develop a behavioral systems perspective in order to understand consumer behavior and to develop effective interventions. A behavioral systems perspective for consumer behavior combines microeconomic, communication, marketing, social learning, and behavior analysis principles.

3. However, a behavioral systems approach, if it is to have any impact on consumer policy, must be developed in light of economic and legal realities. This does not mean that a viable approach must subscribe to prevailing economic myths (e.g., rationale man, sovereign consumer). Nor does this mean that the approach given the asymmetric market can not be strongly pro-consumer. What is being called for is an approach that is, in reality, powerful enough when combined with other interventions to actually create conditions for a "free market" to operate. This approach should appeal to conservatives who see most solutions to economic imbalances in bolstering the free market, and to liberals who more readily may seek government intervention on the side of the consumer.

THE RISE AND PAUSE OF THE CONSUMER MOVEMENT

The title of this section comes from Pertschuk's book and is an extension of points 1 and 3 just mentioned. Pertschuk is a former chairman of the Federal Trade Commission (FTC). It is important to keep in mind that the FTC, established in 1914, has as its most basic goal, the policing of unfair competition

(Engel & Blackwell, 1982). Thus, the major goal of the FTC is to make sure that the market remains competitive. Part of making the market remain competitive entails restoring power to the consumer. However, Pertschuk made it clear in his book that the methods to do this in the 1980s and 1990s are likely to be quite different from what they were in the 1960s and early 1970s.

The consumer movement of 20 years ago was fueled by an unusual coalescing of personal, social, and political forcers—the emergence of an indefatigable, charismatic (to some) leader, namely, Ralph Nader; the acceptability of anti-business/antiestablishment views and their institutionalization, and the intervention of courts and legislators to create equal opportunity, justice, and fairness for all citizens, but particularly, for the poor and powerless. It is not likely that such factors will again fuse in the near future.

But, during the rise and fall of the consumer movement, some important lessons were learned that are most relevant for a different era. If these lessons are appreciated and form part of the basis for another consumer movement, this contemporary movement may be more powerful than its predecessor. This is because these are practical concerns and because, "unlike social issues, consumer issues tend not to be broadly divisive" (Pertschuk, 1982, p. 135).

The lessons that were learned are consistent with the perspectives of this chapter and of this book. It is now seen that any regulation must be scrutinized carefully prior to implementation and must be evaluated carefully once in place. Regulations must be thought through before there is any intervention in the marketplace. Who will gain and who will lose through the intervention? What are the inequities (e.g., to certain firms) that will result from the intervention? How much will consumers really gain from the remedy?

Any new rule or regulation, must, where possible, be consonant with market forces to the maximum extent. For example, how can complying firms gain most? Or, can compliance and benefits to the firm be best realized through performance standards (i.e., outcome) and not design standards (i.e., process), which may cost firms dearly and be difficult or impossible to enforce?

Thus, an overarching lesson was respect for cost–benefit analyses and market forces. However, this should not be construed as blind acceptance of economic reality coupled with moral indifference. Pertschuk (1982) states:

> We have learned that we must be accountable for the costs and burdens of regulation. But, we will not concede that the economist's useful but imperfect tool of cost–benefit analysis dictates policy judgements on what is right and what is just. (p. 138)

The greater appreciation for evaluation and use of market forces also extends to the consumer's side and use of regulations and information. Will the rule or remedy adversely affect competition (e.g., perhaps, only the largest corporations can comply) and undermine the consumer? Will the regulation preserve freedom of informed individual choice to the maximum extent possible consistent with consumer welfare, or in the guise of consumerism, actually constrain choice? What are relevant criteria (e.g., hazardous products, infrequent purchases, high cost) for instituting mandatory standards versus applying the remedy of informed consumer choice? It was learned that certain standards, when coupled with information, could drive market forces, as when mileage ratings helped push the demand for fuel efficient cars or when nicotine and tar ratings increased the search for lower tar and nicotine cigarettes (but at less than hoped-for benefits):

> Far from being a weak incentive, information in the hands of motivated consumers can prove far more potent in channeling market forces than fixed standards. (Pertschuk, 1982, p. 148)

Within the framework of lessons learned, a more definitive schema is presented for the criteria for developing, implementing, and evaluating information, standards, and regulations.

CONSUMER USE OF INFORMATION AND PUBLIC POLICY

If part of a restoration of balance involves developing effective consumer information systems, it is important to know how consumers seek out and use information. Seeking out information is called *information search* in consumer behavior and microeconomics. It often has been assumed by public policymakers that the task of creating information remedies is relatively simple because consumers will seek out objective information prior to purchase, particularly of expensive items. According to Beales, Mazis, Salop, and Staelin (1981):

> However, . . . consumers engage in very little overt search for information even for expensive products such as major appliances and furniture. . . . This lack of active search is often noted why government, either through regulation or direct disbursement of information, has failed in the hoped-for impact on consumer behavior. (p. 12)

The questions are: When do consumers need information? Why do consumers seemingly engage in so little information search? What conditions could increase information search and use of that information?

Beales et al. (1981) identified six conditions under which consumers may need different information. These, in turn, can be divided into a need for consumer education (general knowledge) and consumer information (specific knowledge of products; see Crosby & Taylor, 1981).

Education needs are: (a) understanding of the functioning of consumer markets (e.g., how ads are used to induce consumer identification with a product); and (b) general information on the advantages and disadvantages of various products (e.g., nutritional information about what are high fat foods and alternatives). Information needs are: (a) product alternatives to fill particular functions (e.g., the advantages and disadvantages of heat pumps versus wood stoves); and (b) quality information on particular brands (e.g., as supplied by *Consumer Reports*) (c) prices of competitive products; and (d) terms of sales (e.g., as with return policies).

Information search is also usually divided into internal search and external search. In internal search, the type of approach most frequently used, the consumer searches previously acquired information from memory. External search involves actively seeking new information from personal inspection, from sellers as in advertising, or from third parties such as government or consumer magazines. Internal search can consist of a review of actively acquired information from external search sources and/or from use of a frequently purchased product. If the information obtained from external search and frequent purchase of the product is reliable and salient, then "the collective purchase decisions of consumers based on this source may be sufficient to maintain the competitiveness of markets for frequently purchased products" (Beales et al., 1981, p. 12). But, consumers often do not have considerable experience with many brands or product alternatives. Thus, their information sets often are limited. Further, some purchases (e.g., alterations in plumbing) are one-shot affairs not allowing for comparisons to past experiences.

Internal Search

Beales et al. also noted that most consumer information is acquired in a highly passive way. Television commercials, billboards, and informal communication with friends seem to be the main sources of consumer information.

Most of this information acquisition comes about during low-involvement learning (Engel & Blackwell, 1982). For example, an avid TV viewer may acquire bits of information about hundreds of products through watching thousands of ads that are at most of only mild interest. Occasionally, an ad may make a large impression because a stimulus is unexpected or novel. The consumer was still in a low-involvement state, but the qualities of the stimulus cause it to be noted and remembered. Bettman (1979) termed these occasions *interrupts*.

A danger in low-involvement, passive information acquisition, is that the consumer is nonfiltering and nondiscerning. For example, in a high-involvement state entailing external search, a consumer may closely scrutinize various ads and counterargue against various points. In a low-involvement state, counterarguing generally does not occur with the result that the consumer may have a more positive feeling toward the nonscrutinized information!

Because search is internal, with information that forms its basis often acquired in a passive way, what are the implications for consumer policies directed toward assuring that consumers have an adequate amount of marketplace information?

Because consumers have (or think they have) considerable information available from internal search, many consumers will not be motivated to seek out third-party or government information.

If this is the case, information that is available must be easy to find, see, comprehend, and remember. However, a danger in creating simple information is that it may be inaccurate for the individual consumer (e.g., when average energy information is discrepant with their home, behavior patterns, or climatic conditions).

Information available to the consumer through internal search may be inaccurate. Thus, information presentations must not only be simple and assimilatable, but also be capable of overcoming false beliefs. For example, in much of the author's energy conservation work, we had to overcome the belief that winter energy conservation meant "freezing in the dark" or elaborate home retrofitting (reinsulating).

Because time and effort is involved in external search, consumers may have some accurate information for some items, but only from a limited sample of items. For example, they may know, based on shopping in three stores, that "Store A" has the lowest price on "Brand E" aspirin. They may not be aware that "Store B" has its own house brand aspirin that is identical in content to "Brand E," but costs only half as much.

Because most consumers get most of their information from ads, there is an important "watchdog" function that must be performed by government and the industries themselves as far as accuracy and deception (Engel & Blackwell, 1982). Accuracy and deception criteria must be applied to more than just verbal and print content because visual content and context can distort meaning.

In designing third-party or government information presentations, it is important to consider the information processing mode of the consumer. If the message will primarily be received in a low involvement state, then detailed information is probably precluded. However, if the presentation can be made to appear novel, then "interrupts" are possible, and more detailed information can be presented.

It is necessary to examine the familiarity of consumers with certain product class information, the nature of information presentations, and the information seeking of consumers. For example, consumers presumably are very familiar with different soft drinks, their price, availability, and their nutritional value. However, despite their frequent consumption, individuals may not be interested in finding out more about the product. Consumers may lack basic nutritional knowledge (Schucker, 1983), claim great interest, but still not seek out nutritional information unless it is presented in a simple, vivid way.

Thus, this section indicates that there are many variables to consider in light of passive consumer information acquisition and the reliance of most consumers on internal search. Beales et al. (1981) summarize this point with an additional sobering conclusion:

> Empirically, we know very little about the limits of the complexity and quality of information that can be absorbed passively, the retention of such information, or how the mode of presentation and the nature of the information itself might affect these limits. (p. 14)

External Search

External search can be accomplished through three information sources: (a) direct inspection of products; (b) disinterested third parties; and (c) seller-related sources.

Inspection

Inspection of products, perhaps in a simpler era, was a preferred mode for external search. Today, however, with a myriad of products, brands, models, types and accessories, it has become virtually impossible, given time, effort, and knowledge constraints, for the typical consumer to carefully study all salient alternatives before purchasing. At most, consumers can engage in a "satisficing" operation where only a limited number of alternatives are examined (March & Simon, 1958).

Many consumers will not compare even a limited number of alternatives, but base purchase decisions on certain screening heuristics that may or may not be related to quality. One prominent screening heuristic is price—with the assumption that higher price means more quality. Or, for a product that consumers may feel (such as bread), its texture may be altered; in this case, preservatives and air are added to make bread soft and, hence appear fresh. This latter example suggests that sellers may exploit consumers' focus on superficial screening devices as signals of quality. For example, the author is familiar with a high-priced soft drink that is expensive and is promoted as natural, healthy, and connected to sports—these are high-status screeners. The drink contains 10% juice (because it is a "drink") with the rest of the content consisting mainly of sugar and water. It could sell for half of its current price and more accurately be seen as another junk product.

When signals or screening heuristics are accurate, there seems little reason for concern. Where they are not, as in the example just given, there is a need for standardized performance measures, disclosures, and information that must be based on an analysis of what signals and heuristics consumers use for different products. For example, are the signals and heuristics based on advertising information, popularity (market share) of the product, or length of time on the market? The regulatory, educational, and informational effort must supply the consumer with understandable standards and useable heuristics. This is an important area of study and seems to possess the capability of bolstering the power of the consumer.

Disinterested Third Parties

Use of disinterested third parties can be an excellent means for external search. One approach is for a consumer to hire an expert to help in product selection, inspection, and purchase. An expert may be particularly useful for expensive products. For example, a skilled and reputable mechanic can help in all phases of buying a used car. Thus, the expert is hired by the consumer and acts in the consumer's best interests.

Another example of disinterested third parties is periodicals such as *Consumer Reports*. This magazine provides independent and neutral testing and analyses for quality, durability, and price of a wide-range of products. As a group, these periodicals have little or no incentive to distort facts or steer consumers toward certain products. Given the advantages of this type of information and format, government could help to stimulate the sale of such periodicals and also develop its own through the FTC and the Consumer Product Safety Commission.

If such periodicals are so valuable, why are they not consulted more often? And, why, in general, is there so little external search (Wilde, in press)? Some of the reasons are as follows:

1. It takes time and effort to do so.

2. The value of such consultation may or may not (no comparison experience) be apparent until after the purchase is made.

3. Consumers often limit their search to a few seemingly feasible alternatives and may not want to investigate many alternatives.

4. Information may not be individually tailored to a particular consumer's tastes and needs. To do so, would require a much more complex reporting format. To some extent *Consumer Reports* does this when it presents a detailed matrix that analyzes alternatives across many attributes.

Given these points, it is not surprising that most attempts to design and implement third-party information services have failed. Further, with few exceptions, the marketplace does not appear capable of supporting such services. If the information is perceived as a "public good" (see the following), then government support may be justified. Aside from government interventions to support the system, according to Beales et al. (1981), a sophisticated approach using communication principles and up-to-date hardware is needed:

> One of the major difficulties facing third-party sources is the high cost of delivering relevant product information. Consequently, there is a need for efficient systems

that deliver information that is tailor-made to specific consumers and viewed as reducing rather than increasing the consumers' cognitive efforts. Such systems will have to incorporate the advances in both new hardware technology and consumer information processing research. For example, third-party sources might take advantage of technological breakthroughs that enable the use of home television sets on displays of pertinent information. Research on information processing and communication would be useful in developing a format that simplifies the consumer's decision making task. (p. 18)

Third-party information may also go through more normal channels of delivery such as ads, retail store newspapers, and news articles. Unit price information and point-of-purchase nutritional ads are additional examples. The consumer, in a sense, "hires" the store to provide this information. Retailers may have some incentive to provide neutral information. It may make the store or chain appear to be "pro-consumer" (which it may be), and thus, increase patronage. Also, many store managers may not care what brands are bought as long as the products are bought in one particular store.

Again, many points already made throughout this book about information presentation format come into play here. Third party information must be simple, usable, and effective. Government can become involved in supporting third-party information by funding research on communications, information processing, and consumer behavior. One such program to do this existed in the National Science Foundation, but has been disbanded during this "pause" in the consumer movement.

Another exceedingly important point, consistent with this chapter and book, must be made. If third-party, government-supported information sources are to provide any countervailing power to the consumer, they must be expertly designed within an overall social marketing framework. Beales et al. recommend detailed evaluation studies in communication and message development before information campaigns are widely developed. An overall social marketing perspective can assure that messages are effectively designed for and used by particular population segments.

Seller-Related Sources

Seller-related information, distributed through many mediums, could provide the least costly source for external search. However, seller-related information is inherently one-sided and mixes factual information with nonfactual persuasive appeals. Beales et al.'s discussion of seller-related information presented additional points also consistent with this chapter and book. Ads are much more than sheer print or verbal content. Ads are devised to imprint associations of a product with an image, to set up certain impressions, and to embed the brand name in the consumer's memory.

Most of the work on regulating deceptive advertising has focused on its factual content. Rarely, if ever, have regulators examined how ads use images and other persuasive appeals, which may be the key to ads' impact. If the purpose of such regulation is to protect the consumer then "regulators must be at least conversant with advanced communication technology in order to gain a better understanding of the information environment in which consumers operate" (Beales et al., 1981, p. 19).

POLICY APPLICATIONS

There are a number of policy implications based on the analysis of internal and external search processes. Much of the information consumers have is obtained in a passive, low-involvement state, and the source of this information is primarily seller-related. There are so many ads in different mediums that the consumer usually has few incentives to seek out more neutral information. Indeed, because of the persuasive nature of ads, their sheer number and the consumer's limited ability to sift through all of them and delineate accurate and exaggerated or deceptive information, the consumer may believe he or she has a storehouse of trustworthy information. This is generally not the case.

Further, evidence of wide price dispersion on the same or similar products (e.g., Devine, 1978; Devine & Hawkins, 1972; Maynes & Assum, 1982) in different retail stores appears to support Stigler's (1961) thesis that such data are reflective of market ignorance. In light of rapid changes in product lines, differentiation within products, frequent price changes, and managerial control, the likelihood of accurate market information is low. Minimal accurate information for the consumer increases the probability of pricing inefficiency and resource misallocation.

Given this situation, policymakers are urged to stimulate the development of alternative information sources both within ads and through other means. Comparative ads can be a reasonable source of information if enough comparisons are made on relevant attributes. More encouragement can be given to present simple, straightforward accurate information in ads. Once enough of these ads were done, they may become the norm so that the consumer first expects accurate, simple information in an ad.

Clearly, investigations are needed on the nonprint/nonverbal aspects of messages. Perhaps, research similar to Wright and Huston's (1983) work on formal features of television can be undertaken. If information disclosures are to improve consumer purchase decisions, then government agencies must become more expert in designing such messages, much as educational TV programs must effectively use the formal features of TV.

Government intervention may also be needed to aid the development of third-party sources of information. It may be that such services may be better construed as a public good supportable through taxes. Because much information is available through ads, third-party sources must start from the position that they are in steep competition from sellers for the attention of consumers. Therefore, the emphasis is on research to make sure third-party sources can compete and do have some impact. Such information systems can be based on the behavioral system framework developed later in this chapter.

WHEN, WHERE, AND HOW TO INTERVENE

The preceding sections made a strong case for alternative sources of information, particularly from neutral third-party sources, as a way to enhance the power of the consumer. However, it is not always clear when information remedies should be undertaken, under what circumstances, and how best to do this. Regulatory and information policies are hardly the major purview of behavioral scientists so that economic and legal issues predominate (economists and lawyers generally make up the lead staff of regulatory agencies). Further, note Pertschuk's cautionary points in the beginning of the chapter on ''lessons learned'' during the last 20 years, principally those suggesting study and care before intervening in the marketplace.

In another important and frequently cited companion paper, Mazis, Staelin, Beales, and Salop (1981) attempted to integrate economic, legal, and consumer behavior perspectives into a framework for evaluating information regulation (for a focus on legal aspects, see Beales, Craswell, & Salop, 1981). The overriding principle, consistent with Pertschuk, is the assessment and comparisons of costs and benefits on when, how, and where to intervene (often compared to nonintervention). Their three major principles to maximize benefits and minimize costs were ''Incentive Compatibility'' (economic), ''First Amendment'' considerations (legal), and ''Communication Effectiveness'' (consumer behavior). Based on these principles, the authors outlined a ''Remedies Continuum'' from least to most restrictive of market forces. It was suggested that government always turn to the least restrictive approaches first.

The reader will recall that traditional microeconomic theory postulates that both buyer and seller are endowed with perfect information. It is the buyer's task to differentiate between the offerings of different sellers and the seller's task to accurately judge different consumers' needs. In a free-market situation, the forces between buyer and seller are purported to be in balance via information feedback (''signals''). The basis of most consumer regulatory policy comes from this perspective (and convenient myth). Government intervention is warranted when an informational market failure exists, for example, when consumer decisions are based on false or limited information. Buying under these conditions sends inappropriate feedback to the seller. For example, the seller may perceive that their product is first-rate when, in fact, it is not. Intervention can help improve consumer decision making, enhance product quality, and reduce prices. Thus, the major objective of intervention is to restore competitiveness to the marketplace.

For some products, particularly those involving frequent purchases and obvious feedback (the cleanser did not clean), the market may be self-correcting. In many other cases, infrequent purchases are made or the feedback is nonobvious or too delayed. For example, this may be particularly true with food that *does* involve frequent purchase:

> Without nutritional or ingredient information consumers would be unable to purchase products based on "health" considerations. Trial and error could be used, but this is an inefficient process since it is difficult to associate changes in health status . . . with consumption of particular food products. (Mazis et al., 1981, p. 13)

Another condition for government intervention is when there is no incentive for the seller to provide consumer-protective information. For example, there were few incentives for cigarette manufacturers to list health risks and warn smokers not to use their product.

A third situation for which there may be important benefits associated with intervention are cases where substantial positive externalities exist. Positive externalities provide benefits to many beyond the individual consumer. For example, the availability of simple third party information may only benefit the motivated consumer who seeks that information. In the future, other consumers may learn to use such information. The information might also eventually effect sellers so that higher quality or lower cost products are available.

> In this sense, information is similar to traditional public goods such as national defense or lighthouses, where the private demand for such facilities accrue to everyone. In this respect, the free market solution would not be optimal. (Mazis et al., 1981, p. 13)

To illustrate this point further, another example is given. Most consumers will not pay for general nutritional education and specific nutritional information on different products. However, the provision of such information, delivered in an effective way, over time may affect product availability, consumer food selections, and the eventual health of our collective citizenery. In addition, dietary links to disease (whose treatment is subsidized and expensive) indicate large externalities and a justification for government intervention (Tracy, 1980).

Conditions that warrant intervention and potential benefits have been outlined, but what are the costs of any intervention?

1. There are costs associated with compliance with the remedy. For example, the seller may have to develop special labels or broadcast corrective ads. Obviously, these costs may be passed on to the consumer.

2. The costs of enforcement can be very high. For example, if verbal disclosure is required by salespeople on warranties and terms of a cooling-off period, it would be prohibitively expensive to even observe a sample of such transactions.

3. There may be unintended side-effects to both the buyer and seller. For example, comparative ads may be very expensive to make. Their proliferation may further confuse issues as all alternatives will not be compared with one ad.

Mazis et al. then expanded on their three principles: economic, legal, and consumer behavior, to maximize the benefit to costs ratio.

1. *Incentive Compatibility.* The basic notion here is that the remedy can be constructed in such a way that litigation is avoided and the seller will benefit from compliance. For example, when standards were promolgated for miles per gallon for a company's fleet of cars, it provided a simple means for consumers to discern fuel efficiency and for manufacturers to benefit who could meet and surpass standards. Thus, incentive compatibility approaches rely on consumer sovereignty and seller incentives.

2. *First Amendment Protection.* The major premise here is that remedies should adhere to the provision of an unimpeded flow of nondeceptive, commercial "free speech." The objective here is to maximize the flow of ideas in the marketplace. Thus, this criterion is in accord with the first principle and the one to follow.

3. *Communication Effectiveness.* If the remedy of information disclosure is to accrue any benefits, information must be developed that is readily available, and which promotes awareness, comprehension, and active use. Information must be constructed in such a way that not just one element (e.g., an ingredient's label), but the entire information environment, (e.g., TV ads, store displays) is considered. This means that "government agencies must approach the problem in much the same way as sellers designing a marketing campaign" (Mazis et al., 1981, p. 14). Because most government agencies involved in regulation are not equipped to do this, it was suggested that sellers be given the task of designing and implementing disclosure until the standards are met and the situation rectified. However, the criteria of such standards are of critical importance (Wilkie, McNeill, & Mazis, 1984). Simply changing consumer "recall" or "recognition" may be unacceptable (see the following).

From all three perspectives, the goal is to use the least restrictive approach and have information remedies go only far enough so as to restore competitive forces, i.e., to restore "free-market" conditions. Mazis et al. developed three major classifications for information remedies on a continuum from least to most restrictive:

1. *Remove Restraints on Information Flow.* The objective is to make available information previously unavailable or only available through extensive and unrealistic search processes. A prime example of this strategy involves allowing professionals to advertise their services and prices. The goal is to increase competition via reduced information search processes, and hence increase quality, lower costs, and, perhaps spread availability. A frequently cited success of this approach is the reduced costs (40%) of eye examinations and eyeglasses in states where ophthalmologists and optometrists can advertise (see chapter 6). Of course, a danger of this approach is that advertising information will be deceptive, thus requiring governmental surveillance and regulation.

2. *Enhance Information Flow.* The goal of this middle-ground approach is to permit greater consumer search by the development of information standards and disclosures. Standards can include definitions of terms (e.g., "juice" vs. "drink"), particular grades (as in meat) and metrics (U.S. Recommended Daily Allowance—"RDA"), terms for sales (e.g., cooling-off periods and time to test a product), or differentiation of services (e.g., separating filling eyeglass prescriptions from the original examination and diagnosis). This approach depends on consumer awareness of the meaning of different standards and terms and an effective communication campaign needs to be developed. Some observation and enforcement of regulations is also required.

3. *Restrict Information Flow.* This is seen as an approach of last resort and may often come face-to-face with first amendment issues. Examples of this approach include bans on certain product claims, which may involve a single seller (e.g., banning Listerine when it claimed to prevent disease) or an entire industry (e.g., cigarette ads banned from TV and radio). This approach may also have to be activated where disclosures will not work. For example, frequent attempts have been made to limit the advertising of cereals containing mostly sugar on children's TV programs. This approach has been taken because it is doubtful that young children would be influenced by messages indicating that a diet high in sugar is not good for them. However, this is an empirical question that can only be answered if counterads as skillfully made as the cereal ads are widely distributed.

CONCLUSIONS AND REGULATORY/INFORMATION FRAMEWORK

By combining the two articles, a regulatory/information framework can be developed based on critical points that were raised. These points are summarized in Table 7.1.

TABLE 7.1

Main Points of the Information Search and Information Remedy
Framework from Beales et al. and Mazis et al.

Democratic principles and free market economics depend on the free flow of information and active consumer search.

Consumers do not engage in extensive external search.

Consumers obtain information in mostly passive ways and later use internal search. Such information is limited and may not be accurate.

External search must compete with internal search which is simpler and less costly.

Extensive external search is difficult given a wide array of products and stores.

Screening heuristics used by consumers may distort product inspection.

Third-party information sources must be based on modern communication and marketing principles if they are to be effective.

Seller-related information may be expertly developed but often is biased in presentation.

Government intervention appears needed to develop effective third-party information sources.

Research needs to be directed to the format, medium, visual, and nonverbal aspects of messages.

Information remedies for market imbalances must be developed within economic, legal, and consumer behavior perspectives.

The goal of intervention should be to increase competitiveness in a way that maximizes benefits and minimizes costs, where possible, in the least restrictive way.

Sufficient externalities may warrant intervention so that information is construed as a public good.

Information remedies entail costs including those involved in compliance, enforcement, and unintended side-effects, and such costs must be minimized.

Maximization of benefits can accrue if information remedies offer compatible incentives to sellers, aid in the flow of information, and are effective for consumer behavior change.

Information approaches should restore competitiive forces where possible by removing the restraints on information flow and enhancing information flow.

In summary, the articles by Beales et al. and Mazis et al. provide a framework for information remedies in the marketplace. The thrust of their position, as well as earlier points noted from Pertschuk, is that: (a) more effective third-party sources of information are needed; (b) the provision of more information is most compatible with economic, legal, and consumer behavior perspectives; (c) such efforts can be supported by government as public goods; but (d) involvement and benefits to sellers must also be considered; (e) such remedies need to be constructed within state-of-the-art communication and marketing approaches.

The last point has been made many times in this chapter. However, it is the contention here that communication and marketing approaches must overlay principles of consumer behavior derived from a new conceptual paradigm and empirical (field) research. The rest of this chapter seeks to develop a behavioral systems approach to consumer behavior that can provide those principles with supporting data.

A BEHAVIORAL SYSTEMS APPROACH TO CONSUMER BEHAVIOR: PROBLEMS WITH A COGNITIVE APPROACH

In reviewing a considerable amount of literature in ''consumer behavior,'' the author has been struck by the fact that very little of this literature has to do with actual behavior such as buying particular products. Instead, most of the literature focuses on cognitive processes, e.g., information processing. It is as if the typical consumer is lost in thought before proceeding with even the most mundane purchase (''low-involvement'' decisions). However, the review of search processes suggests that this may not be even the case for more expensive infrequent purchases (''high-involvement'' decisions)!

Theories of consumer behavior have put person variables first—at the expense of context. This is the same point made in the first chapter and the two schemas in that chapter which depict the different perspectives are relevant here. Oddly enough (and most disturbing for a behaviorist), when behavioral perspectives have been introduced into this field, they have been offered apologetically as a simplistic approach, and have mainly shown how operant principles can be used by sellers to manipulate consumers (e.g., Rothschild & Gaids, 1981). Trying to study the reciprocity between environment and behavior is anything but simplistic, and a behavioral systems analysis can assuredly be used in the service of consumers as well as sellers.

The predominant propositions of cognitive approaches are that the critical variables entailing choices and decisions are best studied and isolated at the cognitive level, and that changes in cognitions relate to change in behavior (e.g., Mazis & Staelin, 1983). Behavior may be ultimately mediated by cognitive processes, and more cognitive interventions can influence behavior (Bandura, 1977a). However, this is not the same as saying that cognitive processes must be the figure and all else is relegated to the ground, or that cognitive interventions are the most effective behavior change strategy. A behavioral systems approach reverses the figure and ground.

An age-old problem studied in psychology has been the relationship between information, attitude, affective change, and behavior change, i.e., analogous to a ''hierarchy of effects'' model (McGuire, 1981). The best that can be said at this point is that sometimes there may be a relationship between these variables (McGuire, 1981).

It is apparent that recall and information (e.g., typical dependent measures on the effectiveness of ads) are easier to change than intent and actual behavior.

This is one reason why an exclusive focus on cognitive processes is not an optimal approach (e.g., as advocated by Day, 1976). For example, in Bettman's (1979) often cited book on information processing and consumer behavior, the reader is hard-pressed to find any study demonstrating the flow-through for information processing change and behavior change. This is also one reason why laboratory studies on decision making (e.g., Kahneman & Tversky, 1984) are not very impressive from a behavioral systems perspective. Demonstrations showing that an alteration in word phrasing influences perception and checking-off a preferred choice on a paper and pencil form is neither convincing nor exciting consumer research from a behavioral systems perspective!

These laboratory studies on decision making do provide some insight into important variables of the stimulus medium (e.g., how information is framed and organized). But these principles must be tested in real life settings. In addition, the focus of these studies represents only a portion of the phenomena of interest. The focus on cognitive processes is obviously necessary, but not sufficient. For example, analyses of behavioral and setting parameters are seen as critical and interactive with cognitive processes (Winker & Winett, 1982).

It must be emphasized that a return to a "black-box" approach is not being advocated. What is being said is that cognitive processes and individual decisions are always embedded within a context that must be understood in its own right, which may have far more influence on consumer information processing and choice than is represented in current literature.

In defense of cognitive approaches, it appears that applications of cognitive positions in consumer policy are at best piecemeal and unsophisticated. For example, a recent FTC paper (Hilkie & Nelson, 1984) presented a case of "predatory advertising," wherein a dominant firm presumably attempted to diminish the entry of a new firm into the market by increasing advertising. At times, the advertising of the dominant firm was purportedly similar to the new firm so as to create information overload and reduce differential memory. Evidence to support the predatory advertising of the dominant firm was data on TV ad exposures and viewer recall. This reviewer could not discern a consistent pattern in the data. Nor, is it clear how important potential exposure and recall are as far as influencing purchase decisions. Finally, the strong positions taken in the article on information overload overstepped current opinions (Engel & Blackwell, 1982). The kindest conclusion is that the case seemed to lack a coherent framework for understanding and influencing consumer behavior.

Somewhat parallel to this case, and one type of information remedy, are cases whereby corrective advertising is deemed appropriate (Wilkie et al., 1984). Specific examples of corrective advertising are given in chapter 6. What is debated here are both the method and criteria for corrective advertising as well as the framework.

Corrective advertising is deemed appropriate when a firm conveys misinformation in ads. Most recently, firms have been left to their own devices as advertising experts decide how the correction will be made. For example, (and, perhaps, not too far in the future) soup companies currently advertising their products as health and fitness foods may have to add somewhere in their ads that most commercial soups are very high in sodium. Within 5 years, they may have to demonstrate that 80% of a sample of soup buyers would answer "yes" to the question, "Is soup high in sodium?" (i.e., recognition). Recent evaluations of this approach (Armstrong, Gurol, & Russ, 1983; Mazis, McNeill, & Bernhardt, 1983) have certainly suggested that this type of corrective advertising has, at best, very minimal effects on recall and recognition. Less seems to be known about the effects of such an approach on actual purchases by a segment desiring a specific product (soup) for a specific purpose (health).

This author seriously questions: (a) leaving corrective advertising to the firm; (b) relying on embedded messages (see chapters 2 and 6) to produce effects; (c) using recognition or recall data to demonstrate effects; and (d) failing to demonstrate differential sales impact. An approach is advocated here that is proconsumer (that could also eventually help the firm), insists on the more efficacious use of the media by the government or neutral third-party, and has a clearer behavioral-focused framework.

Elements of a Behavior Systems Approach

A behavior systems approach can embrace the points noted at the end of the prior section. The elements of a behavioral systems approach include:

1. An analysis of *cognitive* processes but with more emphasis on interactions with other levels of analysis.

2. An analysis of *person* variables including knowledge, wants, needs, skills, life-style, resources, and demographic factors.

3. An analysis of specific *behaviors* (i.e., type, duration, intensity, frequency), competing behaviors, and obstacles to correctly performing behaviors.

4. An analysis of *setting* variables with some contributions from environmental psychology.

5. An analysis of *incentives* including tangible and nontangible, short- and long-term reinforcers. Such an analysis indicates motivation for change.

6. An analysis of the *information* environment that includes information provided in store displays, ads, and an array of other media.

7. An analysis of *institutional* factors that drive firms to act in particular ways or individual people to continue to follow certain food selection patterns.

The major dependent variable in these analyses is the behavior of consumers and other actors in the marketplace. Note that the levels of analysis are best thought of as interactive. However, exact mechanisms and degrees of interaction are not yet specified, indicating that the analyses are more contextual and not systems. Finally, because this is a paradigm of behavior influence, the overall approach is overlayed with perspectives and techniques from communications and social marketing.

A number of basic tenets are accepted from the cognitive perspective. Choices are seen as potentially influenced by the manner in which they are framed (e.g., potential outcomes and how the probabilities of outcome are described; Kahneman & Tversky, 1984). For example, stating one possible choice as a reduction in an undesirable effect may in some instances, sway choice toward that direction then when such information is presented as a gain in positive outcomes. However, as the author has argued elsewhere (Winett, 1984), it is not accepted that such dramatic shifts as demonstrated in the laboratory can be duplicated in real life because of the many other influential factors. The effects of changes in decision frames have rarely been demonstrated outside the laboratory (Winett & Kagel, 1984) despite such claims (Slovic, Fischhoff, & Lichtenstein, 1984).

It is accepted that there are cognitive limitations that preclude rationale decision-making based on full knowledge. Notions of "bounded rationality" and "satisficing" are seen as the appropriate alternative to utility maximization that assumes the careful weighing of all alternatives and picking the alternative that completely satisfies (March & Simon, 1958). Of considerable importance is the study of heuristics that people use to make decisions within bounded rationality, i.e., ways of dealing with large inputs and cognitive limitations. It is not accepted, however, that understanding of such processes provides the key to unlock mysteries of behavior in the marketplace.

Two quotes from Slovic et al. (1984) indicate both the acceptance and value of the cognitive perspective, as well as the overriding concern that has been discussed here:

> Bounded rationality, in the form of difficulties in probalistic thinking . . . , ill-defined and labile preferences, information processing limitations, and the presence of potent and easily manipulatable decision frames provides a rather startling contrast to the presumption of rationality upon which much economic and regulatory theory is based. (p. 236)

> Scientific evidence regarding the prevalence and impact of cognitive biases in market decisions is lacking. (p. 236)

An additional problem exists if the perspective noted in the first quote is fully accepted. If opinions and choices are so easily manipulated by the manner of how information is framed, how are information remedies developed to overcome such limited cognitive ability, appropriate heuristics, and responses to decision frames? The position almost suggests a game without end as one information remedy is framed in one way to overcome pre-existing biases, but creates other biases in its place. In the "labile" world described by Slovic et al., rational intervention does not seem to make sense.

Bridge from Cognitions to Behavior

One of the major difficulties faced by cognitive positions is to make the bridge between cognitive processes and actual behavior. This was done in a well-known article by Wright (1979) that is discussed later for its demonstration of a media-based approach to change in in-store behaviors. The bridge that is provided by Wright (1979) is the "concrete action plan":

> A crucial aspect of a behavioral change program is inducing people to actively reflect on their personal action plans. Mental action planning is assumed to be a distinctive type of activity in short-term memory (STM) in which one conceives of oneself enacting a sequence of physical acts that have a goal, and perhaps, a concrete context, i.e., the time, place, occasion, pertinent objects, and people are defined. An action plan in this view is similar to general concepts like a "behavioral script." (p. 257)

Social learning theory (and other persuasion theories) is used as the basis for explaining the process by which messages advocating particular action exert influence. According to Wright (1979):

> The initial response the message elicits is attention to the action recommendation. Given this, the receiver is prompted to initiate personal action planning in STM, entailing verbal or imaginal restatements of the recommended action, self-instructions about its performance, and evaluation of the expected consequences. As a result, an action plan is stored in long-term memory (LTM). Later, when some environmental cue triggers the plan's retrieval from LTM, the plan is enacted. In this view, one may think about the attributes of action affects, the consequence of an act, or even one's global evaluation of an act without engaging in personal action planning. So action planning is an important intervening activity for translating these types of thinking into overt action. (p. 257)

Clearly, different behavioral influence theories place different emphases on mental action planning. For example, some positions emphasize preparing a favorable belief system, and therefore, advocacy messages basically seek to change beliefs (see McGuire, 1981). A social learning approach will give more attention to provoking instances of new action planning (Bandura, 1977a). This will serve as a catalyst to the storage and retrieval of action plans. As Wright (1979) explains it:

> The message is seen as a means to directly stimulate an action planning episode of the sort that heightens the plan's storage and retrieval probability. Our concern is with the characteristics of a mass media message that effectively accomplishes this latter goal . . . assuming that an advocate identifies a well-defined target setting in which to encourage the target action, inducing storage of an action plan that includes a rich accurate description of that setting should benefit the advocacy. Retrieval will be cued when an aspect of the stored plan's setting is encountered. A

> plan with many details of the triggering setting explicitly defined increases the chance that one of these details will serve as the retrieval cue when the setting is encountered compared to a plan with very few contextual details defined. (p. 257)

What is particularly appealing about Wright's position is the interconnections made between cognitive processes, information, communication variables, settings, and behavior. But, what can be done to start the chain of activities, to start new action sequences? Recall that much information search is internal and that many consumers appear unmotivated to seek out new information. In order to start the process, stimuli need to: (a) be obstrusive; (b) be repeated; (c) show problems in old approaches; and (d) make people encounter appropriate settings.

The burden of meeting these four points falls on the advocacy message that also must be constructed with the realization that for many settings people have routine action sequences. People also have a number of other, and perhaps, more urgent cognitive tasks to perform. This point suggests not placing extended messages in busy and complex settings such as large food stores that provide a host of stimuli and distractions. This has been a major and largely unsuccessful approach to modifying food purchases. What may be successful are multimedia communication approaches that will first arouse interest, attention, and model action plans in a relaxed nondistracting setting and then use highly distinct cues and prompts within the target setting to activate the action plan.

Wright (1979) then discussed the process by which communications, particularly those using modeling, can start the sequence from thinking to action:

> Direct evidence that active thinking about actions per se is important to future enactments come from studies of modeling—the process by which people learn to enact behaviors by observing other people perform those behaviors. Observers who attempt to actively produce in STM verbal or visual restatements of the modeled action sequence, to rehearse their performance of those actions, or to give self-instructions about implementing them in the future show a strong tendency to later enact the actions than do those who passively observe or are distracted from planning while watching. (p. 258)

It is important in modeling approaches to have observers think of themselves performing the action. In addition, attributes of the model (similarity to observer; active coping) and context (showing appropriate settings; having the models receive reinforcement) are important. However, the most critical event is being able to prompt the "action planning episode" in the appropriate setting, within reasonable time proximity of the advocacy message.

Part of the art and science of designing messages that will promote behavior change entails understanding medium and content variables that will promote appropriate STM and LTM storage of action plans. One of the major difficulties is to do this within a mass medium, such as TV spots. Wright postulated that in order to increase the performance of particular target actions, the following elements needed to be part of the message: (a) Use of concrete language describing the context; (b) A verbal recommendation to follow specific actions; (c) Visual display of the action sequence enacted in the target setting.

> The assumption is that the more concrete the action recommendation, the greater chance that the action sequence will be actively coded and rehearsed by the viewers, stored and retrieved in LTM, and retrieved in the target setting. (Wright, 1979, p. 258)

These points from Wright fit well within the effective elements and variables of media approach shown in Table 1.3 of chapter 1. Wright also reviewed research that indicated that more concrete stimuli enhanced performance on various learning tasks. Visual and other concrete stimuli increase the probability of coding into LTM. Given an appropriate cue in the setting, recall can then be triggered from LTM. The modeling literature also supports this position. Performance via modeling is enhanced when the action, objects, and setting are displayed and when verbal and imaginal rehearsal of modeled behavior are emphasized (Bandura, 1977). Also, showing multiple models and (similar) settings can enhance generalization. Finally, the message itself can properly organize and frame the information, use mnemonics, and promote self-instruction.

In addition to these points, a message must be explicit and memorable (perhaps justifying commercial jingles and catchy phrases) to overcome highly routine action sequences in frequented settings. For example, for most people, food shopping follows some well-worn sequences performed one to two times per week. Further, in a store or similar setting, there is little immediate feedback that a new action sequence paid off. In supermarkets, it may not be apparent that following unit price guidelines led to a lower grocery bill, or that certain new choices were healthier than prior ones. Such potential reinforcers must be shown in the message, i.e., models reinforced. Finally, messages must be delivered frequently enough, or at an opportune time, so there is not a great time gap between the message delivery and the target behavior.

All these aspects of message content and format are noted to make this point: Whereas behavior change may be cognitively mediated and cognitive strategies (i.e., information) may be used to change behavior, the success of such an approach depends upon intimate knowledge and depiction of behavior and setting.

A BEHAVIORAL SYSTEMS APPROACH TO CHANGING FOOD-BUYING PATTERNS

The prior sections devoted a considerable amount of time to argue that a strictly cognitive focus, or a cognitive focus that does not take care to analyze and carefully depict behavior and environment, is deficient. In this section, a behavioral systems approach to changing food-buying patterns is developed. The goals are purchase of healthier products (explicitly defined) at a lower price. There are, however, several restrictive guidelines that will be followed:

1. The emphasis is still on information remedies rather than, for example, environmental design or powerful consequence strategies. As an antecedent strategy, it is expected that an informational approach will not be potent as far as individual consumer behavior change, but practical for mass aggregate change.

2. Feedback is construed as a "self-regulatory" information strategy that can be fitted into a retail store's operation.

3. Manipulation of retail store environments to any significant extent will probably be precluded. For example it probably would be politically infeasible to have extremely large signs to prompt people to buy less meat products (Wilbur, personal communication, June, 1984), or to put all low-priced products in one place, or to design the floor plan so that it is easy to see and pick up "healthy" products while difficult to do the same for "unhealthy" products.

Cognitive Processes and Person Variables

The analysis starts with cognitive processes and person variables. Much of what has already been stated for message development holds, but now is the appropriate time to add specific points to the principles and some historical background on the development of contemporary information strategies by government to influence food purchases.

In December, 1969, the White House Conference on Food, Nutrition, and Health (1970) proposed that:

> Information about nutrition properties which are significant to consumers in relationship to the use of a given food in the daily diet should be required to be made available to consumers. Insufficient data are available to show what nutritional information is significant for various foods or what type of nutritional information is meaningful or useful. (p. 121)

In response to this conference, the Federal Drug Administration (FDA) was given the duty of developing a nutrition labeling program with the cooperation of the food industry, nutritionists and consumer groups (Heimback & Stokes, 1982). The FDA began investigations, which continue today, as to what information should be available on what label format. Note that the mission was immediately transcribed into finding the appropriate label, even though it is certainly unclear if the label is an effective information medium. However, this has been a customary FDA duty and approach. Further, the FDA has never been given the charge of developing and implementing large-scale consumer education programs (Schucker, 1983). In the last 15 years, the FDA has done a number of studies on label formats (e.g., Gersin Associates, 1983; Hackleman, 1981), and continues to do frequent surveys on consumer awareness of labels, knowledge of nutrition and nutritional concerns (Heimbach, 1981a, 1982; Schucker, 1983). These surveys partly serve as formative research data and are illuminating.

The consensus from these surveys is that:

1. Today, labels seem to be generally understood, at least by higher SES groups (who may need the information the least).

2. Details of the labels and terms remain unclear. For example, consumers tend not to know the difference between saturated and polyunsaturated fat; the descending order of ingredients remains unclear. When terms such as ''sodium'' are understood, it is generally not known how much per day is required.

3. There seems to be more interest by specific consumer segments in risk avoidance (e.g., high calorie food) than in health benefits.

4. Most consumers' knowledge of nutrition is poor.

5. It is unclear how nutritional labels influence actual food selection.

When labels are used alone, they fail a critical test for information remedies—labels appear to be ineffective. Other approaches in concert with labels appear necessary (Heimbach, 1982; Schucker, 1983).

It can be tentatively concluded that a more obstrusive approach than food labels alone is needed to meet the goals of cheaper and more nutritious food selection. The typical food store provides a wide array of stimuli so that simple obstrusive markers in the store (chapter 6) or general shopping heuristics may be needed to successfully process information in this environment. Further, consumers appear to have minimal knowledge of nutrition, may at present be more motivated by risk avoidance than gain, and their shopping action sequences may be quite routinized. This last point takes the discussion to the next level of analyses—behaviors and settings.

Behaviors and Settings

In this analysis, the focus is on behaviors in a specific context; the type, duration, intensity, and frequency of behaviors; competing behaviors, and obstacles to performing correct or optimal behaviors. In particular, how the physical environment enhances or restricts key behaviors is of interest. In the present example, recall that the focus is on shopping behaviors in large supermarkets. Unlike the analysis of cognitive and person variables, which was supported by survey data from the FDA, the analysis at this level is mostly ''armchair'' and must be substantiated in the field if truly effective information remedies are to be developed. The analysis, thus, will put forth some testable assumptions.

One assumption of approaches that use small signs and labels is that people will eventually notice, read, comprehend, and use the information to modify purchases. Stimuli that are small and relatively unobstrusive, particularly in large stores with thousands of products and other stimuli, require slow-paced behavior allowing for surveillance, stopping, and reading. These behavioral requisites appear unmet by modern food shopping behavior. For example, the prevalence of dual-earner families today suggests that there is little time for leisurely food shopping (Winett, Stefanek, & Riley, 1983). The behaviors allowing for optimal food selections (quality, content, price) compete with the behaviors emphasizing quickness in completing shopping. In order to accomplish shopping quickly, several heuristics may be used alone or in combination: lists (complete or partial), budget limits, selection of known brands, and following the store floor plan. The analogy here is to "bounded rationality" and "satisficing." This is not the optimal way to shop, but it is a reasonable way to reduce stimuli and options to a manageable number, and balance the demands of shopping with the problem of limited time. One assumption that must be assessed is that such hueristics are systematically used and, perhaps, differentially by population segments.

Modern food stores are large, contain thousands of product signs, and messages, and they are often impersonal. People will be encountered who are not known and the modern store requires little, if any, real interaction between store personnel and shopper. The goal of the store appears to make it possible for the customers to flow through the store at a relatively even pace. Background music, special lighting, and wide aisles may be used to enhance the pleasure and flow of shopping. Special displays with new products or sales may be placed in strategic places to lure the shopper into trying a new product, switching brands, or simply buying on impulse.

Lee and Zelenak (1982), in their book on consumer economics, described in detail how supermarkets are specifically designed to increase seemingly unnecessary purchases. They noted the special use of aisle-end displays, shelf-extenders, dump racks, tower displays, island displays, and snack racks. The average store has 14 to 20 special display areas where traffic is 15 times greater than in other part of the store. Likewise, the displays and items at checkout counters such as magazines, gum, and cigarettes are designed and selected to assure last-minute impulse buying. Fancy packaging and special in-store displays (reminders) seem to increase impulse buying. In fact, Lee and Zelenak reported that 70% of the sales of beer, candy, crackers, cookies, snacks, frozen foods, magazines, health and beauty aids are purchased on impulse!

Additional ploys are used to lure a customer into a store. *Bait advertising* is a term that suggests that the advertised special item may only be available in small supply or, perhaps, not at all. Apparently some stores still follow this tactic, although these stores can be subject to investigation by the FTC. "Loss-leaders" carry few, if any, ethical and legal overtones. This practice involves placing one or more possibly insignificant or nonselling items on sale at a much reduced price. It is a lure to get consumers into the store where probably nothing else is on sale.

Consumers are not completely defenseless in the face of store designs and tactics developed to increase impulse buying. However, in answer to a question raised eariler about consumers' use of heuristics to resist these lures or to "satisfice," Lee and Zelenak noted that 60% of food shoppers do not use a list. Of the remaining 40%, only half of these use partial lists.

Contrast this portrayal of food shopping behaviors and settings and tactics used to lure consumers to the behaviors and settings required to make food labels and unit price information (indicated by small tags on shelf) truly salient! The effort to collect, comprehend, and compile contents and costs of products is high in a setting not conducive to such behaviors (Russo, personal communication, February, 1984). Studies of the use and effect of such information, for example, unit price labels, indicate some limited initial impact (e.g., saving consumers 1% on food costs; Russo, 1977), and perhaps, some increased use now more than 15 years after their introduction (Aaker & Ford, 1983). Alternative store displays, i.e., formats such as those comparing products' contents and prices, may slightly increase savings to consumers (Russo, 1977; but see Goodwin & Etgar, 1980). Obstrusive, specific markers (chapter 6) also promote sales shifts. However, these shifts, although economically meaningful on an aggregate level, may not be very meaningful on an individual level. They certainly do not seem to be the type of shifts associated with changes in food selections necessary for yielding health outcomes. Therefore, another testable assumption here is that only a small percentage of shoppers stop to read labels or examine unit price tags.

Another proposition subject to empirical test is that a better approach to altering food selection patterns may be to arm the consumers with education and specific information *out* of the store. The educational component seems important because studies have consistently shown that consumers lack basic nutritional knowledge. For example, Goodwin and Etgar (1980) tested special in-store displays comparing the nutritional contents of food. They concluded that their effort was unsuccessful because consumers did not understand the nutritional information on the special displays! Messages, following Wright's formulation, may be effective if they are delivered via TV as PSA's, *if* they can be properly targeted. The spots would have to accurately depict shopping behavior and settings and develop simple alternative behaviors and heuristics that can be recalled and used by the shopper once in the setting.

Wright (1979) tested out an approach along these lines to activate label readings, particularly warnings, on antacids. Brief spots (30 seconds) were viewed within regular TV shows and shoppers were later unobstusively observed shopping for antacids. Different types of messages were experimentally compared. The type using modeling and concrete action plans increased the time used by consumers to examine warning labels. The modeling/concrete action spots were enhanced by in-store displays, yet they had an important effect when the displays were not present.

A similar approach was taken by Gorn and Goldberg (1982) with children in a study performed in a day camp. Nine 30-second messages were inserted into 30-

minute videotape programs. In some conditions, these messages urged eating fruit or moderating sugary foods. Other conditions involved candy commercials or no commercial messages. Later, children were given a choice of picking orange juice or Kool-aid, or fruit or candy. The fruit and moderating sugary food commercial promoted appropriate shifts in snacks choices of about 10% to 20%.

The work on energy conservation by the author is also consistent with this approach. TV programs using modeling and clearly depicted action plans viewed in group settings out of the home, or in the home, were effective in promoting changes in energy conservation practices over at least several months in the home setting (Winett et al., 1982; Winett et al., 1983; Winett et al., 1984).

Thus, one conclusion is that the behaviors, competing behaviors, and settings involved in food shopping may require educational and informational interventions that are delivered outside the store. However, such a third-party approach delivered as PSA's over TV (or in a similar format) can only be effective if all the tools and concepts of social marketing and communication are used in message development. The messages must be frequent and incisive enough to create attention, comprehension, and action plans to override the effects of other commercials. This point is presented by Gorn and Goldberg (1982):

> A number of networks and local stations have been persuaded to introduce occasional public service announcements emphasizing a balanced diet. These messages must be aired frequently and continuously if they are to be effective. An occasional PSA or fruit commercial aired against a barrage of candy messages is not likely to change children's snack behavior. (p. 204)

Gorn and Goldberg added that these healthy eating spots must be made so that their quality is on a par with junk food commercials and that the informational strategy must be part of a program to change food selection at home, in school, and the community. Thus, the major assumption is that well-developed and delivered TV spots could alter food product selection patterns to a larger extent than current in-store materials and media.

Incentives

An analysis of incentives includes incentives for individual consumers or groups of consumers to change food selection patterns, and for firms to act in ways to enhance or hinder pronutritional and economic buying patterns of consumers. From the perspective of nutrition and health, there may be few incentives for consumers to change purchase practices because knowledge of appropriate nutrition appears limited. Further, consumers may be interested more in avoiding certain ingredients (e.g., sugar) or types of foods (high calorie) than in shopping for the goal of good nutrition. Because knowledge of nutrition is limited, selections made to optimize avoidance of certain products may be faulty. For example, consumers may avoid high-sugar cereals with the assumption that white sugar and honey are really different as far as assimilation and health effects. Or the consumer may buy "low-calorie" foods not realizing that they are almost as high in calories as regular similar products, may contain many additives, and be high in fat content. It appears that education is needed to create the incentives to appropriately choose certain products over others.

Most consumers will have, as a prime incentive, saving money for altering food purchase patterns. A family of four on an intermediate budget spends more than $6,000 per year on food purchases in a supermarket (Russo, personal communication, February, 1984), and additional money on meals eaten out and snacks bought at vending machines. For many families, including middle-class families, expenditures for food represents a sizeable part of net income; food expenditures are probably only second to housing expenditures.

Although it would appear that consumer motivation to save money on food is high (and, verbal reports support this; Russo, 1981), competing behaviors and the setting militate against shopping in a way to save money. Recall that the concern for economy may be matched by the concern for time. For example, it may be possible to carefully plan each shopping trip, slowly examine every product, go to several stores, and so on. The savings of such an approach may amount to $30 per week (Lee & Zelenak, 1982). However, this approach could take several hours. The resource of money competes against the resource of time. If the analysis is correct, for most shoppers time is limited. It would appear better to expend extra money by staying in one store and shopping quickly then to expend extra time that is often unavailable time. For many people, "time is money."

When a shopper does follow certain rules or heuristics, the feedback available from newly adopted practices may be nebulous. Food and other household purchases in supermarkets can vary somewhat each week so that actual savings may be unclear. Prices on fruits, vegetables, and some other products are also seasonable, and food prices most often continuously increase; therefore, varying needs and prices usually preclude a stable baseline or benchmark for comparison purposes. Unless a consumer assiduously studies items, prices, and total expenditures over time, the effects of modified behavior are probably indiscernible.

This conclusion is quite counter to numerous ads for different supermarkets that claim that consumers can readily see savings when shopping in (their) particular store. It is conjectured here that savings between stores may be rather minimal compared to what could be saved by shopping judiciously within almost any supermarket.

However, as noted, developing effective information feedback on food purchases has many difficulties. Similar obstacles had to be overcome in developing effective feedback strategies on energy use. For example, day-to-day energy use does not provide meaningful feedback unless the energy use is represented in relationship to weather conditions and expected consumption during such conditions. Further, feedback has to be given frequently, be made explicit, and relate to particular goals if it is to be effective (Winett & Kagel, 1984). It may be possible to meet such criteria in supermarkets. The overriding assumption is that many consumers are shopping with large knowledge gaps. Educational and feedback approaches may fill this gap and change shopping practices.

What are possible incentives to firms and individual supermarkets to provide consumers with information and feedback? The primary benefits are to increase store loyalty and purchase of particular product lines, such as store brands, where the profit margins may be greater than for other brands. Russo (1981) noted that:

> If consumers find product information useful, they will be more confident in their ability to make a satisfactory purchase decision. This confidence will be translated into a willingness to complete the purchase rather than to move on to some other store in hopes for a better range of products or better prices. Thus, increases in the marketshare of private labels and the proportion of completed sales are two examples of short-term dollar benefits to retailers as information providers. (p. 165)

Russo described the task at hand as one of picking approaches and interventions where benefits are greater than costs for both retailers and shoppers. One example is shelf tags for unit pricing, which, as noted, helped consumers somewhat, but also helped retailers with inventory control. Perhaps, other approaches that are more potent and still beneficial to consumers and retailers can be developed. Such an approach will be discussed at the end of the chapter. However, this may be a situation where third-party information interventions are needed because neither the buyer nor the seller may be willing to pay for the information, but significant externalities, i.e., healthier consumers, more competitive market, may develop.

Information Environment

Because much has already been said about the information environment, only several summary and additional points are made here. The major point is that current effots to supply nutritional and price information appear to use some of the least effective formats, i.e., labels, shelf tags. Pervasive and expertly developed print, audio, and visual media are used to increase consumer demand for products (or promote brand shifts) that often are at odds with nutritional and cost-cutting goals. Yet to be developed and tested is a state-of-the-art media approach that is truly consumer-oriented. Although some benefits may accrue to firms who take a pro-consumer stance, it is most likely that a large-scale information approach must be undertaken by government.

An approach that has been advocated here entails out-of-store modeling and feedback in the store after purchases (see the following). But, can this approach be successful? Can it compete with all the other seller-related information?

Conceptually, there are commonalities between modeling and feedback that suggest effectiveness. Both procedures present extremely specific and salient individual information in a concrete, vivid, and easy-to-remember way. Their common elements, format, and medium form the core of a rudimentary "information technology" for information and consumer behavior change (Winett & Kagel, 1984).

Other information approaches, particularly to create more competitive prices, have been tried. They have consisted mainly of publishing the prices of the same or similar products offered at different stores (Devine, 1978; Greene, Rouse, Green, & Clay, 1984). Generally, the results have shown some lowering of prices and some shifts in store loyalty. However, that system depends on a constant updating of prices that can be costly. Legal complications are introduced if there are any mistakes in price quotations (Greene et al., 1984). Also, given limited external search, it is not clear how long consumers will follow price lists. Suggestions to present prices on interactive TV systems may aid search processes, but some of the limitations remain as above; also, consumers have not quickly used such systems (Weaver, 1983).

It may be simpler to present consumers with a set of easy-to-remember rules and guidelines (i.e., given the concerns above and those of "information overload," Engel & Blackwell, 1982). But can this be effective? In the author's work, it was found that one showing of a videotape program was sufficient for information and behavior change; multiple programs were unnecessary. (see chapter 2). Similar results in the health area have been found by Evans et al. (1981; prevention of smoking with adolescents), Mielke and Swinehart (1976; simple health practices for adults; see chapter 2), and to some extent, in other studies on TV and prosocial behavior developed from a social learning perspective (Rushton, 1982). (The well-known Stanford projects use an array of media and other approaches.) Concerns with what Lau, Kane, Berry, Ware, and Roy (1980) have called "dose" and "duration" of a campaign may not be that critical if psychological, communication, and marketing principles are followed, and if the information is simple, but sufficiently compelling to provoke "high involvement" (Engel & Blackwell, 1982; see also Singer, 1980). However, well-controlled field experiments assessing the impact of the approach advocated here are yet to be done.

Institutional Factors

Institutional factors can be addressed at the population level, collective firm level, and governmental level. At the population level, it must be understood that food selections are tied into longstanding patterns, rituals, and cultural myths. To use but one example, many men think they are only "real men" if they eat meat and potatoes every night, followed by a large dessert, and later, by several beers. Certain subcultures and ethnic groups by tradition and habit prefer foods that may be detrimental to health if consumed in large quantities. For example, highly processed, fatty and salty meats are a mainstay for some ethnic groups. Many families and their friends spend a considerable amount of time sitting around the kitchen table talking, socializing, and eating. Rarely are such groups only eating celery sticks! Other seasonal occasions such as barbeque cookouts and picnics have their usual food arrays. Rarely in these settings are cottage cheese and fruit the main attraction!

These points are made to emphasize that food selection and eating patterns are closely tied to culture, settings, and routinized and ritualized behaviors. Failure to appreciate this point will lead to unrealistic expectations about potential change and unrealistic strategies for change. It seems more appropriate (and probably efficacious) to carefully assess culture, settings, behaviors, and beliefs, and plan media change strategies based on these assessments. For example, given some new concerns about appearance, "real men," after seeing an appropriate model, may be willing to reduce their usual meat and potatoes meal to three times per week with other reasonable "substitutes" in between. However, the typical softball and barbeque event may be impenetrable, and it may be counterproductive to attempt change in that setting. Thus, a social marketing perspective embraces an analysis of cultural influences.

At the collective level of the corporation (and, the individual retail store), the bottom-line must prevail. Any approach that may reduce profits will be resisted. In addition, any strategy that can potentially limit the profits of certain producres and distributors will also be resisted because these firms will pressure the super-market chains. This was the case when Giant Foods developed its first in-store displays and their materials to persuade consumers to buy less high calorie/high fat foods. Partly as a result of these pressures, the in-store media was much less than incisive and the entire approach was unsuccessful (National Heart, Lung & Blood Institution, 1983; Wilbur, personal communication, June, 1984).

It may be that if food-selection patterns are just shifted, then profits will remain steady. However, pressures from certain producers and distributors are inevitable. It is impossible for food patterns to meaningfully change without some producers and distributors gaining and others losing. The individual indus-tries could survive with reduced demand for their products if they produced less and charged more. For example, egg consumption has significantly reduced in the last 15 years (Matarazzo, 1982), but there is no evidence that the egg industry is bankrupt.

Corporations adopting a proconsumer stance may profit by increasing custom-ers and store loyalty. As far as developing heuristics to help consumers save money, some corporations may profit here even though certain consumers may be spending a bit less on each shopping trip. For example, retail food and drug industries were surprised in the late 1970s on how well "generics" did in the market. Generics often come directly from the distributors. True generics do not have any brand label and brand names have been the cornerstone of advertising since the late 1800s (McEnally & Hawes, 1984). Thus, their success is counter to advertising myths.

To counter the sale of generics, many corporations have developed their own private brands, "neogenerics," positioned to compete with the generics. Thus, to compete for price-conscious consumers, corporations have developed their own lower priced private brands. On private brands, at least for certain items, the profit rate for the individual store and corporation may be greater than for national brands (Russo, personal communication, February, 1984). Also, buyers of private brands and generics appear to show greater store loyalty (McEnally & Hawes, 1984). Further:

> Buyers of generics tend to be concentrated in middle income, large households that are price conscious and predisposed to select lower-priced alternatives. (p. 81)

Thus, stores that offer lower priced product lines may profit by attracting consumer segments that spend the most for groceries. Although the relationship between the sales of generics and store brands must be further assessed, the present analysis suggests some potential for profit for pro-consumer stores.

A case has been made that at least the educational component and some specific aspects of the informational component of an overall approach to nutrition and consumer food selection will have to be supported by government. Presently, consumers appear unwilling to directly pay for such information service and it is probably best construed as a "public good" with potentially considerable positive externalities accruable to individual consumers and competitive corporations. Thus, it appears justifiable for government to be involved in nutrition and food selection information campaigns ("remedies"). If a government chooses to do this depends to a large extent on its political stance.

Conservative governments generally are not disposed to support proconsumer positions. Consumerism is usually associated with "liberal" governments. However, a strong case can be made that provision of supplying information is highly compatible with neoclassic, conservative economics. More specifically, what is called for is using more information to make the marketplace more competitive as far as price and quality of goods. Basically, the provision of more information has also been justified within the frameworks given in Beales et al. and Mazis et al. discussed before. Information remedies are not regulatory approaches in the usual sense (such as may be advocated by a more liberal administration), although the use and meaning of certain terms may be regulated.

The typical dilemma for government is how to provide information remedies that do not favor one interest group over another, and adhere to the "free choice" doctrine. The opinion here is that this is an impossible task. To satisfy the criteria of no-favoritism and free choice has resulted in information constructed and delivered in the most ineffective way. The use of measures of recognition and recall is consistent with the position of simply "informing", but not "persuading" consumers. It can be argued, as some have (Pertschuk, 1982), that over time the mere "availability" of information will eventually leave its mark. It seems clear that little labels or embedded messages are bound to be ineffective. It may not be possible to effectively inform consumers without also being persuasive.

A classic case of the extremes that seem to be dictated to make information nonsalient (and nonavailable) was reported in a study conducted in Canada by Anderson and Clayton (1982). In this study, an attempt was made to promote the purchase of energy-efficient refrigerators compared to frost-free energy-inefficient refrigerators. However, government regulation required energy use and cost data to be located on the inside hinged wall of the refrigerator! Further, when refrigerators are typically on display, at least some of their doors are closed.

It may be impossible to separate the provision of information from behavior influence (Winett & Kagel, 1984). In order for information to be noticed, attended to, comprehended, and stored by any meaningful consumer segment, its content and format must meet some minimal requirements that have been discussed throughout this book. When these requirements are met, it is likely that the information will not only "inform" but also influence behavior. If the information does not have the qualities to influence behavior, then it probably will not even inform. "Consumer effectiveness" has to be one criterion for information remedies (Mazis et al., 1981).

This position forces government to take a stand with information remedies. If nutritional levels are to be changed and buying patterns altered to accomplish this goal, if consumers are to be instructed on how to buy the highest quality products at the lowest price, then some corporations and individuals will benefit and some will lose. This is not to suggest that government needs to be an adversary of business. Production and marketing strategies to deal with food product shifts have been discussed as well as approaches that can help corporations that are proconsumer enjoy increased profits.

OUTLINE OF ONE BEHAVIORAL SYSTEMS APPROACH

The approach to be outlined here integrates points made at the beginning of the chapter on information search, third-party information sources, and least restrictive interventions with the points developed in the sections on behavioral systems. These points are summarized in Table 7.2. The focus of the "information remedy" will be on enhanced nutrition and buying for quality at the lowest price. Currently, nutritional knowledge appears limited, thus affecting food product selection. Much food selection may not be optimal with respect to price. A dense concentration of ads in various media may further steer consumers away

TABLE 7.2
Key Points in a Behavioral Systems Analysis for Effective Information
Remedies for Nutritional and Economical Food Purchases

Cognitive processes & variables	—Limited nutritional knowledge, risk avoidance, need for more incisive information forms given complex behaviors and settings.
Behavior & setting	—Time constraints, numerous products, store design and sale tactics for consumer purchase control; arm consumer with strategies before enter store.
Incentives	—Knowledge creates incentives for consumers; time versus money; within versus between store tactics; incentive of store loyalty for firms.
Information environment	—Need information technology to counter ads; modeling and feedback; properly developed information can be effective.
Institutional factors	—Change within cultural constraints; shifts and reproportion food preferences; consumer services brings more loyal consumers; third-party sources of information following effective media guidelines.

from economic, nutritional purchases, confusing the name of particular stores with economic food purchases, as opposed to particular consumer purchase practices. Store environments are designed to encourage impulse buying. When current information environment and store design heavily weight market transactions on the side of the seller, there is a market imbalance that results in a misallocation of resources.

Effective information search processes could help to rectify this situation. However, most consumer search is passive, limited, and mostly internal. Unbiased external information sources are not used that frequently and appear to be constructed so as to yield, at most, minimal effectiveness. A case can be made for intervention via third-party sources of information. The approach, however, must be done in such a way as to assure incentive compatibility, consistency with First Amendment consideration, and effectiveness in delivery. In addition, a least restrictive approach emphasizing removing restraints on information flow and enhancing information flow must be followed.

A behavioral systems information remedy can have these components:
Media

1. *General Education.* Sound nutritional and concomitant food purchase practices must be emphasized. Likewise, general knowledge about the marketplace, ploys to increase sales, consumer rights and responsibilities need also to be addressed.

2. *Specific Information.* This component can focus on specific shopping heuristics (e.g., lists, record keeping), strategies to avoid impulse buying, how to

use unit price information, and how to gradually change food selection and eating patterns can be emphasized.

It is envisioned that educational and informational messages can be developed as 30- to 60-second TV PSA's. They must be expertly designed and use modeling and other important formal features to assure attention processing, memory, and later activation. Different versions of the same basic messages need to be constructed so that characters and context are compatible with audience characteristics. Needless to say, PSA's must be shown frequently during prime viewing times and there must be control of the timing of the PSA's so that different versions of the PSA's can be properly targeted. This approach, therefore, demands the full integration of psychological, communication, and social marketing knowledge and technology.

One caveat is introduced here. Except for Wright (1979), positive outcomes from only one or minimal exposure to prosocial/prohealth programs have been the result of viewing entire intact programs not short PSA's. Thus, considerable pilot-testing of PSA's is needed.

In order to further bolster the media components and to aid the process of incentives for the industry, two other components can be added:

1. *In-Store Displays.* These displays can parallel the PSA's and change over time. For example, one display can be large and explain unit pricing—another can show the benefits of shopping lists and have sample forms available. Small, but obstrusive tags can point to specific products (e.g., low fat).

2. *Purchase Feedback.* Universal product codes allowing automatic computer-based checkout and fully itemized bills are becoming more common. It is expected that such systems (given increasing computer memory) can be more refined and provide feedback on the contents of food purchased, suggestions of ways to alter purchases, and individually tailored feedback on purchase changes, and cumulative and immediate expenditures. That is, nutritional and price feedback can be provided. Individual feedback can be accomplished through individual code numbers and individual selection of goals.

For these two components, corporations can benefit by their proconsumer position via increased, steady customers. Considerable pilot testing of these procedures is also needed and care must be taken that this approach does not inadvertently lead to other market failures. For example, it would be counter to the spirit of this approach if in-store procedures could only be instituted by very large corporations, driving small corporations or the handful of remaining "Mom and Pop" stores out of business. Thus, compatible with a behavioral systems approach and information and regulatory remedies, are careful experimental and cost-benefit analyses prior to large-scale implementation.

The approach outlined here is quite different from prior information campaigns and remedies. It is based more on an analysis of shopping behaviors and settings than on information processing per se. It attempts to be reasonably persuasive, motivational, and powerful, and its most salient outcome measure is sales data. It attempts to help consumers by providing information, heuristics, and plans so that consumers can shop in a most nutritionally sound and economical way.

8

Future Directions: Information Technology/Behavioral Systems for the Public Good

Information is powerful. When properly framed, formulated, and targeted, information, particularly through the visual media, can have strong effects on beliefs, attitudes, and behaviors. This is the major message of this book. A framework of behavioral systems was developed that provided a way to understand information impacts, and at the same time served as source for concepts, principles, and strategies for effective information in diverse media. However, rather than just reporting on behavioral science technology, a number of political considerations and values involved in information development and transfer were also addressed.

The purpose of this final chapter is to review and better articulate the framework of this book, as well as issues of politics and values. A number of directions in both technological and ideological spheres are discussed.

FRAMEWORK

Throughout this book, the term *framework* was purposely used to describe behavioral systems, and not terms such as *theory* or *paradigm*. The framework was seen as an amalgamation of social learning theory, behavioral analysis, communications principles, and social marketing. It is a working, evolving approach, and I have no illusions as to its theoretical integrity or conceptual boundaries. However, I believe the approach has been useful when attempting some multi-level analyses, predicting effects of particular types of information and media, and for designing information interventions. Here, I review the components of the framework with attention directed to areas of strengths, weaknesses, and future developments.

Social Learning Theory

To many readers, particularly psychologists, it may appear that behavioral systems can be subsummed under social learning theory (SLT). SLT has been evolving since the 1960s into a sort of meta-theory for the behavioral sciences. It is apparent here that some of the social psychological, communication principles are now part of SLT, and it is possible that diffusion theory can be seen as most basically the study of modeling by near-peers. However, SLT seems weak at this point on multilevel analysis and a true systems approach. If, and when, SLT expands on those two fronts, it may well achieve the status of a meta-theory.

The most critical contributions of SLT to this book's framework are conceptual and practical bases for the transcription of environmental events to cognitive processes to behavioral outcomes. Most cognitive positions seem to leave the person lost in thought and assume some direct linkages between cognitive processes and behavior. On the other hand, more extreme behavioral positions neglect the person's role in interpreting the environment or, indeed, shaping the environment. Modern SLT integrates nicely both cognitive and behavioral positions.

Perhaps this book has relied too much on one SLT principle and strategy, modeling, at the expense of using other aspects of the theory. For example, little or no mention was made of self-efficacy expectations as both an integrative and central facet of behavior change (Bandura, 1977b). However, when practice and feedback is not part of an intervention as is the case with most visual media, then modeling becomes the prominent way to induce self-efficacy and behavior change. But, this point shows a danger in not using the entire SLT.

Many communications (e.g., prosocial TV programs) and new media ventures (e.g., social skills training using videodiscs) have apparently understood the principle of modeling and, in some cases, reinforcement and successive approximation. However, they have not appreciated SLT as a broad approach. Otherwise, these interventions would show more focus on practice, feedback, and environmental constraints to behavior change. The full use of SLT in information innovations is one important future direction.

Behavior Analysis

Several facets of behavior analysis formed an important basis for the framework of this book. Indeed, some may say, with justification, that behavioral systems equals behavior analysis. Principles and strategies particularly used from behavior analysis were reinforcement contingencies and the insistence on fairly fine-grain experimental analyses. Positive and negative contingencies were often examined as they related to both immediate use of an innovation (e.g., computer networks, electronic newspapers) or the actual enactment of long-term behavior change (e.g., physicians as preventive health counselors; adoption of energy saving practices). These examples were quite compatible with behavior analysis. However, behavior analysis needs to expand to multi-level analyses where incentives to change may have varying values and strengths at different levels (e.g., see Wahler & Graves, 1983), and to analyses of more complex settings. For example, in chapter 7, an admittedly armchair approach was taken to analyzing shopping behaviors in modern supermarkets. The incentive analysis may have been aided by some inputs from environmental psychology (Fisher, Bell, & Baum, 1984).

Behavior analysis approaches have as a strength micro-incentive analyses; a weakness is that the microanalysis has often missed the forest for the trees, i.e., the larger systems in which incentives are embedded. This is the major area where the behavioral systems framework attempts to depart from traditional behavior analysis.

Early exposure to behavior analysis often leads to a reverence for intensive, fine-grain experimental investigation. Perhaps this reverence can be pushed too far. Certain problems are difficult to study experimentally, and valuable correlational data may be dismissed out of hand. However, many problems and issues in information innovation and transfer can be researched experimentally in field settings, but have not been so studied. I was amazed when I was told (by reviewers) that our first venture into studying the efficacy of special cable TV programs was possibly one of the best TV experiments ever done (Winett, Leckliter, Chinn, & Stahl, 1984). After reviewing much of that literature, I have to immodestly agree with that assessment.

Many questions in communications and information technology *can* be investigated with field experiments. It is hoped that this book has made this point enough times so that one potential impact here is on the methodology used in information technology studies. However, those of us schooled in using field experiments must develop more expertise (and appreciation) in other research methods that can be integrated with experimental methods.

Communications

This book possibly overrelied on the study of formal features of media that promote attention, comprehension, and memory, at the expense of emphasizing other important developments in communications. For example, Rogers and Kincaid (1981) have certainly made the case for turning efforts in communications research to the study of actual instances of information transfer. Their network approach that focuses on reciprocity and confirming and disconfirming new information is a major advance in the field. It is also consistent with systems and multilevel analysis perspectives. Their work was reviewed (chapter 3), but mainly as a critique of their research.

Instead, Wright and Huston's (1983) work on formal features of the media was emphasized throughout the book. This was done because their research provided an important link between characteristics of a medium, cognitive processes, and behavior change. Their approach and studies also were very pivotal in the discussion of prosocial TV. Recall that Singer and Singer (1983) have often criticized TV as a passive medium with many of its formal features curtailing attention, comprehension, and memory. Wright and Huston's research sharply disagrees with the Singers' point of view. It is also critical in countering claims by commercial interests that certain content (violence) must be retained to hold interest. Context may be as, or more important, to retain interest, and thus, content may vary considerably.

Many more studies need to be done that can articulate general principles pertinent across media, but that also may interrelate principles and findings with the developmental stage. Such studies can be invaluable for designing prosocial programs and new media.

Social Marketing

In doing research for this book and for several recent studies, I have truly become enamored with social marketing as an overall approach to planning, designing, implementing, and evaluating programs. As a recent convert, I may be overzealous in my appraisal of social marketing. I have tried, though, to present it fairly, covering both its strengths and weaknesses.

I see its strengths in its external framework that delineates and integrates the four key marketing variables: product, place, price, and promotion. The sin qua non of marketing is designing specific programs for specific audience segments. We are just starting to see efforts, for example, in health promotion, that are taking the tailoring notion seriously and attempting to use all the variables in a coherent way. This is an exciting step and could lead to a degree of effectiveness that has been unknown in the social and health arena.

At the same time, I have to be very cautious with this prognosis. Social marketers are often called in to approach the most difficult problems and segments. The forces propelling adverse practices that they try to counter (e.g., alcohol abuse) are usually strong. The possibility of success may be very slim. The large number of efforts that will probably fail may convince others that the entire approach is ineffective.

Then, too, there is much that needs to be developed in social marketing. There are few documented campaigns that have used the entire framework. In fact, the Stanford Heart Disease Prevention Program appears to be the only well-known effort that has seriously conducted formative research within the framework and altered product, price, place, and promotion variables based on this research (Solomon, 1984). Most efforts seem to have equated social marketing with promotion, which, in turn, is often equated with advertising. For example, recent efforts to promote safer, nonalcoholic driving in teenagers are well-targeted messages, but they are simply ads based on fear-arousal. No other marketing principles seem involved, and the effort, although upbeat and interesting, will probably be unsuccessful.

A final major weakness of social marketing is the overreliance on self-report measures and a simplistic hierarchy of effects model. A strong penchant has been shown to emulate the commercial marketers use of various surveys and the like on interests, needs, and preferences as a way to predict responsiveness to the product. This approach may (or may not) make sense in the commercial sector when products are readily available and where use of a product is widely sanctioned. I do not think it makes much sense in the social/health arena when there may be constraints to performing what often are counternorm behaviors (for example, not drinking alcohol). Instead, what seems needed are behavioral assessment methods for use in social marketing. As an example, in planning nutrition campaigns, I need to know not only about reported food preferences and nutritional knowledge, but also a great deal about supermarkets and shopping behaviors (see chapters 6 and 7). Considerable on-site observations seem appropriate here.

Thus, in the future I expect to see a much broader, but more exacting and effective social marketing approach. At the same time caution is warranted, for as long as social marketing is most frequently used in very difficult situations, it will, at best, be marginally effective.

GAINING ACCESS

The major points from the prior sections are that the behavioral systems framework provides one basis for effective information interventions, but that given the strong forces wittingly or unwittingly opposing some social and health behavior change efforts, these interventions are not likely to be effective. One problem in the United States is that in a real sense most time on "public airways" is not public. That is, except for public radio and TV, both with very small market shares, radio and TV are controlled by commercial interests. In simplest terms, the major purpose of most programs is to hold listener/viewer attention for the commercials. This is not to denigrate the media. Some programs are of good quality and are entertaining and informative. However, for any program to be regularly on the media, it must have a very substantial commercial backing.

This point is best exemplified in TV. Many critically acclaimed programs (e.g., "Taxi") have been dropped because of low Nielsen ratings. This means that few households are tuned into the program, yielding a smaller audience for the sponsor (i.e., the real customers). The network, based on the lower ratings, can only charge a reduced price for each commercial, but the sponsor, in turn, might not want to invest resources to reach only a small audience. A larger audience satisfies both the network and the sponsors.

To some, these points may illustrate consumer sovereignty at its best. The ratings represent consumer choices which then dictate the available products in the media marketplace. To others, this is not the case. The consumer has not been offered the full array of media possibilities. Choices are merely permutations (spinoffs) of prior programs. Rarely are there available resources to create alternative programming at a techical quality equal to more typical network fare. It can also be argued that media should not simply be available to serve large commercial interest, but to serve the public good. For example, it is not written in stone that TV's mission is to expose the public to all kinds of food choices regardless of nutritional quality. TV may be used, although it rarely is, for teaching the public about good nutrition.

In order for social and health programs to viably compete in the "free-market" of ideas, there needs to be some basic changes in media access, particularly for TV. Some of these changes entail regulatory approaches (see chapter 5) that may have to wait for a new political climate to become acceptable. In particular, the FCC, since 1980, has been dedicated to deregulation under the supposition (or pretense) that there is no reason to protect fairness and diversity given the plethora of new media. New media does not equate to easy access, fairness in presentations, or diversity in messages and images. Perhaps, when some of the effects of deregulation and the "free-market" approach are realized and there is a strong, coherent countervailing political force, regulation of the media may ascend the political agenda.

I list three possible regulatory approaches and one "free-market" approach to increase access and diversity:

1. *Public Service Announcements.* PSA's could be a viable way to reach the public with diverse messages. However, at present, affiliates are only bound to place PSA's in time slots not already sold for commercials. Thus, the PSA for family health that appears at 2 a.m.! The inability to target a PSA is an extremely strong drawback that *can* be rectified. Regulations could call for a certain amount of time at every commercial break being set aside for PSA's. Rules could also be established so that there is equity in gaining time for PSA's. Manoff (1985) has expanded on this idea with his designs for a public service TV time bank.

2. *Public Access on Cable TV.* Presently, local groups can gain access to cable systems, although deregulation has made such access less than guaranteed. Regulatory policy can make access rules more clear-cut and equitable. It would then fall to the responsibility of local groups to develop programs of enough importance and interest to attract some segments of the local audience.

3. *Limits on Political Commercials.* Invariably after every campaign, there are calls to limit the time and money spent on political commercials, particularly

those on TV. Clearly, one mechanism is to put a cap on political spending. Another approach, favored here, is during a preset time to provide free time to all viable political candidates. This is both analogous to the proposal for PSA time during the prime time and the noncommercial time given to political debates.

4. *Start Alternative Stations.* One way to make alternative programs and messages available is to start a new cable station. For example, it may be possible to charge a $10–$20 annual subscription to a consumer-oriented cable TV station. However, it is not clear how much resources are needed for such a venture, or the potential market. Most cable stations (e.g., Lifetime) only draw a very small market share, but some (ESPN, CNN) are apparently increasing their share.

The one commonality of these proposals is to provide mechanisms, however minimal, to bypass the current stranglehold of large commercial and political concerns and the networks in controlling programs, ideas, and messages. The basic objective, which is consistent with democratic principles, is to provide access for many views and opinions to be seen and heard. Doubtless, if some of these proposals were enacted, the author and some readers would be aghast at some of these new messages. Undoubtedly, we would be pleased with some others. But most basically, there would be greater pluralism in the world of ideas.

Effective Counter-Messages and Campaigns

Gaining access is obviously critical to delivering effective messages and mounting campaigns. The other aspects are assuring that the messages themselves are as effective as possible and also striving to develop more comprehensive campaigns. The first discussion here is on message development because many social and health campaigns focus only on promotion, essentially emulating commercial ventures. The likelihood of success of this approach is marginal, but if it is done, these promotional activities should at least follow some of the guidelines detailed here.

I use as an illustration recent spots about drunk driving directed toward teenagers. I use these spots, not because they are poorly produced or ill-advised, but because they are well-done and well-targeted. The ads appeared on radio stations popular with teenagers, and have been placed (at least in the author's media market) at high listener times. The spots are produced by the Department of Transportation and the Ad Council.

With a background of Michael Jackson music, we hear three male teenagers bantering about their evening and women. They are joyous and feeling no pain. Their car is started up and sets out at a fast speed. After several seconds, the two passengers start urging the driver to slow down. Their pleas are ineffective. After the last plea, the driver shrugs off the plea, and in a loud, crescendoing voice, says, "I am indestructable." This is immediately followed by sounds indicating that the car has crashed. An older, male voice-over then says, "If you don't stop a friend from drinking and driving, you can kill a friendship."

The ad is well-done, well-targeted, and will probably increase awareness. I do not think the ad will affect the prevalence of drunk driving or efforts by teenagers themselves to stop their friends from drinking and driving.

Note that the ad appears to be based on the assumption that knowledge and fear arousal will eventually influence behavior. As was noted before (chapter 1 and 2), evidence does not support this assumption (Leventhal, Safer, & Panagis, 1983). What may be more effective is an approach following modeling and behavior analysis principles. I do believe that the promotional/segmentation approach is good, although I am not convinced that having a spot simply sound like another musical interlude prompts attention, for example, Bettman's concept of "interrupts." Nor does having a star support the message necessarily make it effective.

Social learning and behavior analysis principles suggest a message that: (a) models *effective* pleas and responses to the driver's rebuttals; (b) directly tells listeners what to do and what not to do; (c) what constraints are likely to arise and how to handle them (e.g., suppose no one else has a driver's license?); and, (d) ends with positive outcomes. These steps are also consistent with McGuire's (1981) communication model and the analysis of effective and ineffective media detailed in chapter 1.

These same points relate to effective "information remedies" discussed at length in chapter 7 on consumer behavior and chapter 6 on health. In those chapters, it was seen that information remedies, particularly corrective ads, are not very effective. The corrective message ("Listerine will not prevent colds") may be lost in a nonsensical barrage about the perils of "onion breath." Consistent with the points made about the drunk driving spots, I would like to see information remedies follow Wright's (1979) concrete action plan, and more generally the modeling-behavior analysis approach (Winett et al., 1985). In a word, I would like to see social and health messages created in such a way that they at least have a chance to be successful.

However, to become most effective, social and health campaigns must drop their "ad mentality." Social change and health promotion does not equate to ads. Some commercial ads are effective because they *do* raise the level of awareness of a product brand, but the ad is *only one part* of well-orchestrated marketing campaigns. The product is designed for particular segments; it is generally accessible without much effort, and its use is generally socially sanctioned. If social/health campaigns are to be effective, they must make use of all the marketing variables in an integrated way. For example, an effective anti-drunk-driving campaign may need to mobilize community and organizational forces (McAlister et al., 1982), so that the product is highly salient in the community (and possibly part of a "health product-mix"); there are multiple times and places to learn about the dangers of drunk driving and the skills involved in avoiding it (e.g., role playing important strategies; Evans et al., 1981); interest and support is high enough that the social price for not drinking is lowered, and where there are multiple promotion strategies (Solomon, 1984). The full use of the marketing framework establishes the environment where conceptually sound and well-produced spots can be effective.

The Proinnovation Bias and Equity Considerations

This last section reflects points made in the diffusion chapter (3) and the new media chapter (5), and are the same ones particularly well made by Rogers (1983). It took many years for diffusion of innovation researchers to acknowledge this point—not everything new is automatically good. Any innovation will have some positive and some negative impacts. Computers have given us incredibly broad and quick access to all manner of information. At the same time, realistic concerns about invasions of privacy have been raised. Computers have also created some exciting careers and jobs and taken the drudgery out of some work. Other work has also become more routinized and impersonal; a large low-paid service sector appears to be part of the information age (Levin and Rumberger, 1983), and the distance between the resourceful, educated elite, the "haves," and the resourceless, ill-educated masses, the "have-nots," may be widening (Penniman & Jacob, 1984).

For too long our reverence of technology has blinded us to its perils—a theme of a number of contemporary writers. The information age is at its first dawning. Perhaps it is still soon enough to insist that information technology be scrutinized before its introduction on technical, equity, social/behavioral, and public interest criteria.

References

Aaken D. A., & Ford G. T. (1983) Unit pricing ten years later: A replication. *Journal of Marketing, 47,* 118–122.

Ader, R. (1981). *Psychoneuroimmunology.* New York: Academic Press.

Anderson, C. D., & Claxton, J. D. (1982). Barriers to consumer choice of energy efficient products. *Journal of Consumer Research, 9,* 163–170.

Antonovsky, A. (1979). *Stress, health, and coping.* San Francisco: Jossey-Bass.

Armstrong, G. M., Gurol, M. N., & Russ, F. A. (1983). A longitudinal evaluation of the Listerine corrective advertising campaign. *Journal of Public Policy and Marketing, 2,* 16–28.

Ashworth, W. (1982). *Nor any drop to drink.* New York: Summitt Books.

Atkin, C. K. (1981). Mass media campaign effectiveness. In R. E. Rice & W. J. Paisley (Eds.), *Public communication campaigns* (pp. 265–279). Beverly Hills: Sage.

Bandura, A. (1977a). *Social learning theory.* Englewood Cliffs, NJ: Prentice-Hall.

Bandura, A. (1977b). Self-efficacy: Toward a unifying theory of behavior change. *Psychological Review, 84,* 191–215.

Beales, H., Craswell, R., & Salop, S. C. (1981). The efficient regulation of consumer information. *Journal of Law and Economics, 24,* 491–539.

Beales, H., Mazis, M. B., Salop, S. C., & Staelin, R. (1981). Consumer search and public policy. *Journal of Consumer Research, 8,* 11–22.

Benham, L. K. (1972). The effect of advertising on the price of eyeglasses. *Journal of Law and Economics, 15,* 337–352.

Benham, L. K., & Benham, A. (1975). Regulating through one profession: A perspective on information control. *Journal of Law and Economics, 18,* 421–447.

Bennion, J. L. (1982). Authoring videodisc courseware. In M. DeBloois (Ed.), *Videodisc/microcomputer courseware design* (pp. 67–88). Englewood Cliffs, NJ: Educational Technology Publications.

Berkman, L. F. & Syme, S. L. (1979). Social networks, host resistance, and mortality: A nine-year follow-up study of Alameda County residents. *American Journal of Epidemiology, 109,* 186–204.

Bernstein, G. S. (1982). Training behavior change agents: A conceptual review *Behavior Theory, 13,* 1–23.

Bettman, J. R. (1979). *An information processing theory of consumer choice.* Reading, MA: Addison-Wesley.

Bittner, J. R. (1980). *Mass communication: An introduction* (2nd ed.). Englewood Cliffs, NJ: Prentice-Hall.

Bloom, D. N., & Novelli, W. D. (1981). Problems and challenges of social marketing. *Journal of Marketing, 45,* 79–88.

Bork, A. (1982). Educational technology and the future. In M. DeBloois (Ed.), *Videodisc/microcomputer courseware design* (pp. 3–24). Englewood Cliffs: NJ: Educational Technology Publications.

Brandt, R. C., & Knapp, B. H. (1982). Interactive videodiscs authoring concepts. In M. DeBloois (Ed.), *Videodisc/micocomputer courseware design* (pp. 89–100). Englewood Cliffs, NJ: Educational Technology Publications.

Brenner, M. H. (1973) *Mental illness and the economy.* Cambridge, MA: Harvard University Press.

Broderick, R. (1982). Interactive video: Why trainers are tuning in. *Training/HRD,* November, 46–53.

Bronfenbrenner, U. (1979). *The ecology of human development: Experiments by nature and design.* Cambridge, MA: Harvard University Press.

Brown, L. R., Flavin, C., & Norman, C. (1979). *Running on empty.* New York: Norton.

Campbell, D. T. (1969). Reforms as experiments. *American Psychologist, 24,* 409–428.

Campeau, P. L. (1974). Selective review of the results of research on the use of audiovisual media to teach adults. *AV Communication Review, 22,* 5–40.

Cantor, M. G. (1980). *Prime-time television: Content and control.* Beverly Hills: Sage.

Caporeal, L. R. (1984). Computers, prophecy, and experience. An historical perspective. *Journal of Social Issues, 40,* 15–29.

Cassel, J. (1974). Psychosocial processes and "stress": Theoretical formulations. *International Journal of Health Services, 4,* 471–482.

Catalano, R., & Dooley, D. (1983). The health effects of economic instability: A test of the economic stress hypothesis. *Journal of Health and Social Behavior, 23,* 133–147.

Catalano, R. A. (1979). *Health, behavior, and community.* New York: Pergamon Press.

Chen, M. (1984). Computers in the lives of our children: Looking back on a generation of television research. In R. E. Rice (Ed.), *The new media: Communication research and technology* (pp. 269–286). Beverly Hills: Sage.

Cohen, S. (1983). Social support, stress, and the buffering hypothesis: A theoretical analysis. In A. Baum, J. E. Singer, & S. E. Taylor (Eds.), *Handbook of psychology and health* (Vol. 4, pp. 272–295). Hillsdale, NJ: Lawrence Erlbaum Associates.

Coleman, J. S. et al. (1966). *Medical innovation: A diffusion study.* New York: Bobbs-Merrill.

Collins, W. A. (1982). Children's processing of television content: Implications for prevention of negative effects. *Prevention in Human Services, 2,* 53–66.

Comstock, G. (1980) *Television in America.* Beverly Hills: Sage.

Comstock, G., Chaffe, S., Katzman, N. McCombs, M., & Roberts, D. (1978). *Television and human behavior.* New York: Columbia University Press.

Cousins, N. (1979) *Anatomy of an illness.* New York: Norton.

Cousins, N. (1983) *Healing heart.* New York: Norton.

Cronbach, L. J. (1975). Beyond the two disciplines of scientific psychology. *American Psychologist, 30,* 116–127.

Crosby, L. A., & Taylor, J. R. (1981). Effects of consumer information and education on cognition and choice. *Journal of Consumers Research, 8,* 43–57.

Cunningham, A. J. (1981). Mind, body, and immune response. In R. Ader (Ed.), *Psychoneuroimmunology* (pp. 609–618). New York: Academic Press.

Czeisler, C. A., Moore-Ede, M. C., & Coleman, R. M. (1982). Rotating shift work schedules that disrupt sleep are improved by applying circardian principles. *Science, 217,* 460–463.

Dance, F. E. X. (1967). A helical model of communications. In F. E. X. Dance (Ed.), *Human communication theory* (pp. 37–52). New York: Holt, Rinehart & Winston.

Danowski, J. A. (1982). Computer-mediated communication: A network based content analysis using a CBBS conference. In M. Burgoon (Ed.), *Communication yearbook-6* (pp. 905–924). Beverly Hills: Sage.

Day, G. S. (1976). Assessing the effects of information disclosure requirements. *Journal of Marketing, 40,* 42–52.

Devine, D. G. (1978). A review of the experimental effects of increased price information on the performance of Canadian retail food stores in the 1970's. *Canadian Journal of Agricultural Economics, 26,* 24–30.

Devine, D. G., & Hawkins, M. H. (1972). Implications of improved information on market performance. *Journal of Consumer Affairs, 6,* 184–197.

DeBloois, M. L. (1982). *Videodisc/microcomputer courseware design.* Englewood Cliffs: NJ Educational Technology Publications.

DeFleur, M. L. (1966). *Theories of mass communication.* New York: McKay.

Deutsch, K. (1966). *The nerves of government.* New York: Free Press.

Dimmick, J., & Rothenbuhler, E. W. (1984). Competitive displacement in the communication industries: New media in old environments. In R. E. Rice (Ed.), *The new media: Communication, research, and technology* (pp. 287–304). Beverly Hills: Sage.

Dizard, W. P. (1982). *The coming information age: An overview of technology, economics, and politics.* New York: Longman.

Dolce, P. C. (Ed.). (1976). *Suburbia: The American dream and dilemma.* New York: Anchor Books.

Donohew, L., & Tipton, L. (1973). A conceptual model of information seeking, avoiding, and processing. In P. Clarke (Ed.), *New models for communication research* (pp. 74–83). Beverly Hills: Sage.

Dozier, D. M., & Rice, R. E. (1984). Rival theories on electronic newsreading. In R. E. Rice (Ed.), *The new media: Communication research and technology* (pp. 103–127). Beverly Hills: Sage.

Durlak, J. A. (1979). Comparative effectiveness of paraprofessional and professional helpers. *Psychological Bulletin, 86,* 80–92.

Eisler, R. M., & Frederiksen, L. W. (1980). *Perfecting social skills: A handbook for interpersonal behavior development.* New York: Plenum.

Engel, J. R., & Blackwell, R. D. (1982). *Consumer behavior* (4th ed.). Chicago: Dryden Press.

Ester, P., & Winett, R. A. (1982). Toward more effective antecedent strategies for environmental programs. *Journal of Environmental Systems, 11,* 201–222.

Evans, R. I., Rozelle, R. M., Maywell, S. E., Raines, B. E., Dill, C. A., Guthrie, T. J., Henderson, A. H., & Hill, P. C. (1981). Social modeling films to deter smoking in adolescents: Results of a three-year field investigation. *Journal of Applied Psychology, 66,* 399–414.

Fairweather, G. W., & Tornatzky, L. G. (1977). *Experimental methods for social policy research.* Elmsford, NY: Pergamon Press.

Felner, R. D., Jason, L. A., Moritsuger, J. & Farber, S. S. (Eds.). (1983). *Preventive psychology: Theory, research, and practice.* Elmsford, NY: Pergamon Press.

Fielding, J. E. (1983). Lessons from health care regulations. *Annual Review of Public Health, 4,* 91–130.

Fine, S. H. (1981). *The marketing of ideas and social issues.* New York: Praeger.

Fisher, J. D., Bell, P. A., & Baum, A. (1984). *Environmental psychology* (2nd ed.). New York: Holt, Rinehart & Winston.

Fitzpatrick, R. M., Hopkins, A. P., & Howard-Watts, O. (1983). Social dimensions of healing: A longitudinal study of outcomes of medical management of headaches. *Social Science in Medicine, 17,* 501–510.

Flay, B. R., & Cook, T. D. (1981). Evaluation of mass media prevention campaigns. In R. E. Rice & W. J. Paisley (Eds.), *Public communication campaigns* (pp. 239–264). Beverly Hills: Sage.

Flowers, J. F. (1979). Behavior analysis of group therapy. In D. Upper & S. Ross (Eds.), *Behavioral group therapy* (pp. 33–62). Champaign: Research Press.

Fox, K. F. A., & Kotler P. (1980). The marketing of social causes: The first 10 years. *Journal of Marketing, 48,* 24–33.

Frankenhauser, M. (1979). Psychobiological aspects of lifestress. In S. Levine & H. Ursin (Eds.), *Coping and health* (pp. 147–178). New York: Plenum.

Freedman, J. C. (1984). Effects of television violence on aggressiveness. *Psychological Bulletin, 96,* 227–246.

Friedman, M., & Friedman, R. (1979). *Free to choose: A personal statement.* New York: Harcourt, Brace & Jovanovich.

Fuchs, V. R. (1975). *Who shall live?: Health, economics, and social choice.* New York: Basic Books.

Farquher, J. W., Fortman, S. P., Maccoby, N., Haskell, W. L., Williams, P. T., Flora, J. A., Taylor, C. B., Brown, B. W., Solomon, D. S., & Hulley, S. B. (1985). The Stanford Five City Project: Design and methods. *American Journal of Epidemiology, 63,* 171–182.

Gagne, R. M. (1965). *The conditions of learning.* New York: Holt, Rinehart & Winston.

Gagne, R. M., & Briggs, L. J. (1974). *Principles of instructional design.* New York: Holt, Rinehart & Winston.

Gailbraith, J. K. (1983). *Anatomy of power.* Boston: Houghton-Mifflin.

Galbraith, J. K. (1973). *Economics for the public purpose.* Boston: Houghton-Mifflin.

Geller, E. S., Paterson, L., & Talbott, E. (1982). A behavioral analyses of incentive prompts for motivating seat belt usage. *Journal of Applied Behavior Analysis, 15,* 403–415.

Geller, E. S., Winett, R. A., & Everett, P. B. (1982). *Preserving the environment: New strategies for behavior change.* Elmsford, NY: Pergamon Press.

Gerbner, G. (1956). Toward a general model of communication. *Audio-Visual Communication Review, 4,* 171–199.

Gersin, R. P, Associates, Inc. (1983). *Food and drug administration design of food package information formats.* Washington, DC: Author.

Glaser, R., Kiecolt-Glaser, J. K., Speicher, C. E., & Holliday, J. E. (1985). Stress, loneliness, and changes in herpes virus latency. *Journal of Behavioral Medicine, 8,* 27–43.

Glasgow, R. E., & Rosen, G. M. (1978). Behavioral bibliotherapy: A review of self-help behavioral therapy manuals. *Psychological Bulletin, 85,* 1–23.

Goldfried, M. R. (1980). Toward the delineation of therapeutic change principles. *American Psychologist, 35,* 991–996.

Goodwin, S., & Etgar, M. (1980). Alternative organization formats for nutritional information: Processing and policy normative perspectives. In R. P. Bagozzer (Ed.), *Marketing in the 1980's: Change and challenges* (pp. 412–415). Chicago: American Marketing Association.

Gorn, G. T., & Goldberg, M. E. (1982). Behavioral evidence of the effects of televised food messages on children. *Journal of Consumer Research, 9,* 200–205.

Gottlieb, B. H. (1983). Social support as a focus for integrative research in psychology. *American Psychologist, 38,* 278–287.

Granovetter, M. S. (1973). The strength of weak ties. *American Journal of Sociology, 73,* 1361–1380.

Greene, B. F., Rouse, M., Green, R. B., & Clay, C. (1984). Behavior analysis in consumer affairs: Retail and consumer response to publicizing comparative food price information. *Journal of Applied Behavior Analysis, 17,* 3–22.

Gross, L. P. (1971). Can we influence behavior to promote good nutrition? *Bulletin of the New York Academy of Medicine, 47,* 613–623.

Grossman, M. (1972). *The demand for health: A theoretical and empirical investigation.* New York: Columbia University Press.

Hanlon, J. J., & Picket, G. E. (1984). *Public health: Administration and practice* (8th ed.). St. Louis: Times Mirror/Moshy.

Harris, R. J. (1983). *Information processing research in advertising.* Hillsdale, NJ: Lawrence Erlbaum Associates.

Hayes, S. C. (1983). When more is less: Quantity versus quality of publications in the evaluation of academic vitea. *American Psychologist, 38,* 1398–1400.

Hackleman, B. C. (1981). Food label information: What consumers say they want and what they need. In K. B. Monroe (Ed.), *Advances in consumer research* (Vol. 8, pp. 477–483). Ann Arbor: Association for Consumer Research.

Heider, F. (1946). Attitudes and cognitive information. *Journal of Psychology, 21,* 107–112.

Heimbach, J. T. (1981a). Defining the problem: The scope of consumer concern with food labeling. In K. B. Monroe (Ed.), *Advances in consumer research* (Vol. 8, pp. 515–521). Ann Arbor: Association for Consumer Research.

Heimbach, J. T. (1981b, June). *What to say on the food label.* Paper presented at the Institute of Food Technologists, 41st Annual Meeting, Atlanta, GA.

Heimbach, J. T. (1982). *Public understanding of the food label information.* Washington, DC: Food and Drug Administration.

Heimbach, J. T., & Stokes, R. C. (1982). Nutritional Labeling and Public Health: Survey of American Institute of Nutrition Members, Food Industry, and Consumers. *American Journal of Clinical Nutrition, 36,* 700–708.

Heller, E., & Swindle, R. W. (1983). Social networks, perceived social support and coping with stress. In R. D. Felner, L. A. Jason, J. Moritsuger, & S. S. Farber (Eds.), *Preventive psychology: Theory, research, and practice* (pp. 179–193). Elmsford, NY: Pergamon Press.

Hersen, M., & Barlow, D. H. (1983). *Single case experimental designs: Strategies for studying behavioral change* (2nd ed.). Elmsford, NY: Pergamon Press.

Hiemstra, G. (1982). Teleconferencing: concern for face, and organizational culture. In M. Burgoon (Ed.), *Communication yearbook-6* (pp. 874–904). Beverly Hills: Sage.

Hilkie, J. C., & Nelson, P. B. (1984). Noisy advertising and the predation rule in antitrust analysis. *American Economic Review, 74,* 367–371.

Hirsch, B. J. (1980). Natural support systems and coping with major life changes. *American Journal of Community Psychology, 8,* 159–172.

Hirsh, B. J. (1981). Social networks and the coping process: creating personal communities. In B. H. Gottlieb (Ed.), *Social networks and social support.* Beverly Hills: Sage.

Holt, R. R. (1958). Clinical and statistical prediction: A reformulation and some new data. *Journal of abnormal and social psychology, 56,* 1–12.

Hovland, C. I., Lumsdaine, A. A., & Sheffield, F. D. (1949). *Experiments on mass communication.* Princeton: Princeton University Press.

Israel, K., Hendricks, W., Winett, R. A., & Frederiksen, L. W. (1983, December). *Formative research involved in the development of health-risk appraisal interventions with current medical practices.* Paper presented at the Association for Advancement of Behavior Therapy World Congress, Washington, DC.

Jemmott, J. B., & Locke, S. E. (1984). Psychosocial factors, immunologic mediation, and human susceptibility to infectious disease: How much do we know? *Psychological Bulletin, 95,* 78–108.

Johnson, B. M. J., & Rice, R. E. (1984). Reinvention in the innovation process: The case of word processing. In R. E. Rice (Ed.), *The new media: Communication, research, and technology* (pp. 157–183). Beverly Hills: Sage.

Johnston, J. (1982). Using television to change stereotypes. *Prevention in Human Services, 2,* 67–81.

Johnston, J., & Ettema, J. (1986). Using television to best advantage: Research for prosocial television. In J. B. Bryant & D. Zillmann (Eds.), *Perspectives on media effects* (pp. 143–164). Hillsdale, NJ: Lawrence Erlbaum Associates.

Kahneman, D., & Tverskey, A. (1984). Choices, values, and frames. *American Psychologist, 39,* 341–350.

Kaplan, R. M. (1984). The connection between clinical health promotion and health status: A critical review. *American Psychologist, 39,* 755–765.

Kaplan, R. M., & Bush, J. W. (1982). Health-related quality of life measurement for evaluation research and policy analysis. *Health Psychology, 1,* 61–80.

Katz, E., Blumer, J. G., & Gurevitch, M. (1974). Utilization of mass communication by the individual. In J. G. Blumler & E. Katz (Eds.), *The uses of mass communication* (pp. 215–232). Beverly Hills: Sage.

Katz, E., & Lazarsfeld, P. F. (1955). *Personal influence.* New York: Free Press.

Keegan, C. A. V. (1982). Using television to reach older people with prevention messages: The Over Easy experiment. *Prevention in Human Services, 2,* 83–91.

Kellner, D. (1982). Network television and American society: Introduction to a critical theory of television. In D. C. Whitney & E. Wartella (Eds.), *Mass communication review yearbook* (Vol. 3, pp. 417–427). Beverly Hills: Sage.

Keppel, G. (1982). *Design and analysis: A research handbook* (2nd ed.). Englewood Cliffs, NJ: Prentice-Hall.

Kiecolt-Glaser, T. K., Garner, W., Speicher, C., and Penn, G. M., Holliday, J., & Glaser, R. (1984). Psychosocial modifiers of immunocompetence in medical students. *Psychosomatic Medicine, 46,* 7–14.

Kiecolt-Glaser, J. K., Glaser, R., Strain, E. C., Stout, J. C., Tarr, K. L., Holliday, J. E., & Speicher, C. E. (1985). Modulation of cellular immunity in medical students. *Journal of Behavioral Medicine 8,* 117–124

Kiecolt-Glaser, J. K., Glaser, R., Willinger, D., Stout, J. C., Messick, G., Sheppard, S., Ricker, D., Romisher, S. C., Briner, W., Bonnell, G., & Donnerberg, R. (1985). Psychosocial enhancement of immunocompetence in a geriatric population. *Health Psychology, 4,* 25–41.

Kiecolt-Glaser, J. K., Ricker, D., George, J., Messick, G., Speicher, C. E., Garner, W., & Glaser, R. (1984). Urinary cortisol levels, cellur immunocompetency, and loneliness in psychiatric inpatients. *Psychosomatic Medicine, 46,* 15–24.

Kiecolt-Glaser, J. K., Speicher, C. E., Holliday, J. E., & Glaser, R. (1984). Stress and the transformation of lymphocytes by Epstein-Barr Virus. *Journal of Behavioral Medicine, 7,* 1–12.

Kiecolt-Glaser, J. K., Stephens, R. E., Kipetz, P. D., Speicher, C. E., & Glaser, R. (1985). Distress and DNA repair in human lymphocytes. *Journal of Behavioral Medicine 8,* 257–264.

Kiesler, S., Siegel, J., & McGuire, T. W. (1984). Social psychological aspects of computer-mediated communication. *American Psychologist, 39,* 1123–1134.

King, A. C., Winett, R. A., & Lovett, S. B. (1983, December). *Stress management and the dual-earner family: Applying a social marketing approach.* Paper presented at the Association for Advancement of Behavior Therapy World Congress, Washington, DC.

Klapper, J. T. (1960). *The effects of mass communication.* New York: Free Press.

Kleinmuntz, B. (1984). Diagnostic problem solving by computer: A historical review and the current state of the science. *Computers in Biology and Medicine, 14,* 255–270.

Knowles, J. H. (1977). The responsibility of the individual. In J. H. Knowles (Ed.), *Doing better and feeling worse: Health in the United States* (pp. 53–71). New York: Norton.

Kotler, P. (1984) Social marketing of health behavior. In L. W. Frederiksen, L. J. Solomon, & K. A. Brehony (Eds.), *Marketing health behavior* (pp. 23–39). New York: Plenum.

Kotler, P. (1975). *Marketing for nonprofit organizations.* Englewood Cliffs, NJ: Prentice-Hall.

Kotler, P. (1982). *Marketing for nonprofit organizations.* (2nd ed.). Englewood Cliffs, NJ. Prentice-Hall.

Kotler, P., & Zaltman, G. (1971). Social marketing: An approach to planned social change. *Journal of Marketing, 35,* 3–12.

Laczniak, G., Lusch, R., Murphy, P. (1979) Social marketing: Its ethical dimensions. *Journal of Marketing, 43*, 29–36.

Lamb, M. E., & Sagi, A. (Eds.). (1983). *Fatherhood and family policy*. Hillsdale, NJ: Lawrence Erlbaum Associates.

Laswell, H. D. (1948). The structure and function of communication in society. In A. Bryson (Ed.), *The communication of ideas* (pp. 57–79). New York: Harper.

Lau, R., Kane, R., Berry, S., Ware, J., & Roy, D. (1980). Channeling health: A review of evaluations of televised health campaigns. *Health Education Quarterly, 7*, 56–89.

Laudenslager, M. L. (1983). Coping and immunosuppresion: Inescapable but not escapable shock suppresses lymphocyte probferation. *Science, 221*, 568–570.

Lazarsfeld, P. F., & Merton, R. E. (1971). Mass communication, popular taste, and organized action. In W. Schramm & D. F. Roberts (Eds.), *The process and effects of mass communication* (pp. 237–251). Urbana: University of Illinois Press.

Le Duc, D. R. (1982, Autumn). Deregulation and the dream of diversity. *Journal of Communication,* 164–178.

Lee, S. N., & Zelenak, M. J. (1982). *Economics for consumers*. Belmont, CA: Wadsworth.

Leventhal, H., Safer, M. A., & Panagis, D. M. (1983). The impact of communications on the self-regulation of health beliefs, decision, and behavior. *Health Education Quarterly, 10*, 3–29.

Leventhal, H., Safer, M., Clearly, P., & Gutmann, M. (1980). Cardiovascular risk modification by community-based programs for life-style change: Comments on the Stanford Study. *Journal of Consulting and Clinical Psychology, 48*, 150–158.

Levin, H. M., & Rumberger, R. W. (1983). *The educational implications of high technology*. Stanford: Stanford University Institute for Research on Educational Finance and Governance, School of Education.

Levin, H. M. (1983). *Cost-effectiveness: A primer*. Beverly Hills: Sage.

Levy, A. S., Mathews, O., Stephenson, M., Tenney, J. E., & Schucker, R. E. (1984). *The impact of a nutrition information program on food purchases*. Unpublished manuscript, Center for Food Safety and Applied Nutrition, Food and Drug Administration, Washington, DC.

Levy, S. M. (1983). Host differences in neoplastic risk: Behavioral and social contributors to disease. *Health Psychology, 2*, 21–44.

Liebert, R. M., Sprafkin, I. N., & Davidson, E. S. (1982). *The early window: Effects of television on children and youth* (2nd ed.). Elmsford, NY: Pergamon Press.

Liem, R., & Ramsay, P. (1982). Health and social costs of unemployment: Research and policy considerations. *American Psychologist, 37*, 1116–1123.

Lovelace, V. O., & Huston, A. C. (1982). Can television teach prosocial behavior? *Prevention in Human Services, 2*, 93–106.

Lovins, A., & Lovins, H. (1981). The writing on the wall. In R. Haugh (Ed.), *Communications in the 21st century* (pp. 41–60). New York: Wiley.

Maccoby, N., & Solomon, D. S. (1981) Heart disease prevention: Community studies. In R. E. Rice & W. J. Paisley (Eds.), *Public communication campaigns* (pp. 112–127). Beverly Hills: Sage.

Maletzke, G. (1963). *Psychologie der massenkommunikation*. Hamburg: Verlag Hans Bredow-Institute.

March, J. G., & Simon, H. A. (1958). *Organizations*. New York: Wiley.

Matarazzo, J. D. (1980). Behavioral health and behavioral medicine: Frontiers for a new health psychology. *American Psychologist, 35*, 807–817.

Matarazzo, J. D. (1982). Behavioral health's challenge to academic, scientific, and professional psychology. *American Psychologist, 37*, 1–14.

Martarazzo, J. D. (1983, August). *Behavioral immunogens and pathogens in health and illness*. Master lecture delivered at the annual meeting of the American Psychological Association, Anaheim, CA.

Maynes, B. S., & Assum, T. A. (1982). Informationally imperfect consumer markets: Empirical findings and policy implications. *Journal of Consumer Affairs, 16*, 62–87.

Mazis, M. B., & Staelin, R. (1983). Using information-processing principles in public policy making. *Journal of Public Policy and Marketing, 2*, 3–14.

Mazis, M. B., Staelin, R., Beales, H., & Salop, S. (1981). A framework for evaluating consumers information regulation. *Journal of Marketing, 45*, 11–21.

Mazis, M. B., McNeill, D. L., & Bernhardt, K. L. (1983). Day-after recall of Listerine corrective commercials. *Journal of Public Policy and Marketing, 2*, 29–37.

McAlister, A. (1981). Antismoking campaigns: Progress in developing effective communications. In R. E. Rice & W. J. Paisley (Eds.), *Public communication campaigns* (pp. 143–156). Beverly Hills: Sage.

McAlister, A. (1982). Theory and action for health promotion: Illustrations from the North Karelia Project. *American Journal of Public Health, 72*, 43–50.

McAlister, A., Pekka, P., Saeanen, J. T., Tuomilehto, J., & Koskela, K. (1982) Theory and action for health promotion: Illustrations from the North Karelia project. *American Journal of Public Health, 72*, 43–50.

McCombs, M. E., & Shaw, D. L. (1972). The agenda setting function of mass media. *Public Opinion Quarterly, 36*, 176–187.

McEnally, M. R., & Hawes, J. M. (1984). The market for generic brand grocery products: A review and extension. *Journal of Marketing, 48*, 75–84.

McGuire, W. J. (1981). Theoretical foundations of campaigns. In R. E. Rice & W. J. Paisley (Eds.), *Public communication campaigns* (pp. 67–83). Beverly Hills: Sage.

McLeod, J. M., & Reeves, B. (1981). On the nature of mass media effects. In G. C. Wilhoit (Ed.), *Mass communication review yearbook* (Vol. 2, pp. 245–282). Beverly Hills: Sage.

McQuail, D., & Windahl, S. (1981). *Communication models for the study of mass communication.* New York: Longman.

McQueen, D. V., & Siegrist, J. (1982) Social factors in the etiology of chronic disease: An overview. *Social Science in Medicine, 16*, 353–367.

Meehl, P. E. (1954). *Clinical vs. statistical prediction.* Minneapolis: University of Minnesota Press.

Mendelsohn, H. (1973). Some reasons why information campaigns can succeed. *Public Opinion Quarterly, 37*, 50–60.

Mielke, K. W., & Swinehart, J. W. (1976a). *Evaluation of the "Feeling Good" television series.* New York: Children's Television Workshop.

Miekle, K. W. & Swinehart, J. W. (1976b). *Evaluation of the "Feeling Good" television series: Summary.* New York: Children's Television Workshop.

Milavsky, J. R., Kessler, R., Stipp, H., & Rubens, W. S. (1982). Television and aggression: Results of a panel study. In D. Pearl, L. Bouthilet, & J. Lazar (Eds.), *Television and behavior: Ten years of scientific progress and implications for the eighties* (Vol. 2, pp. 138–159). Washington, DC: U.S. Government Printing Office.

Morris, E. K., Higgins, S. T., & Bickel, W. K. (1982). The influence of Kantor's interbehavioral psychology on behavior analysis. *The Behavior Analyst, 5*, 159–174.

Murphy, P. E. (1984) Analyzing markets. In L. W. Frederiksen, L. J. Solomon, & K. A. Brehony (Eds.), *Marketing health behavior* (pp. 41–58). New York: Plenum.

National Heart, Lung and Blood Institute (1983). *Foods for health: Report of the pilot program.* Washington, DC: National Institute of Health Publication, No. 83-2036.

Navarro, V. (1976) *Medicine under capitalism.* New York: Prodist.

Newcomb, T. (1953). An approach to the study of communicative acts. *Psychological Review, 60*, 393–404.

Newell, A., & Simon, H. A. (1961). Computer simulation of human thinking. *Science, 134*, 2011–2017.

Newhouse, J. P. et al. (1981). Some interim results from a controlled trial of cost sharing in health insurance. *New England Journal of Medicine, 305,* 1501–1507.

Newsweek (1985, April 1) p. 59.

Nollen, S. D. (1982). *New work schedules in practice: Managing time in a changing society.* New York: Van Nostrand Reinhold.

Novelli, W. D. (1984). Developing marketing programs. In L. W. Frederiksen, L. J. Solomon, & K. A. Brehony (Eds.), *Marketing health behavior* (pp. 59–89). New York: Plenum.

Olson, M. H., & Primps, S. B. (1984). Working at home with computers: Work and nonwork issues. *Journal of Social Issues, 40,* 97–112.

Osgood, C. E., & Schramm, W. (1954). How communications work. In W. Schramm (Ed.), *The process and effects of mass communication* (pp. 67–78). Urbana: University of Illinois Press.

Paisley, W. J. (1981). Public communication campaigns: The American experience. In R. E. Rice & W. J. Paisley (Eds.), *Public communication campaigns* (pp. 15–40). Beverly Hills: Sage.

Palmblad, J. (1981). Stress and immunologic competence: Studies in man. In R. Ader (Ed.), *Psychoneuroimmunology* (pp. 229–258). New York: Academic Press.

Palmer, E. (1981). Shaping persuasive messages with formative research. In R. E. Rice & W. J. Paisley (Eds.), *Public communication campaigns* (pp. 227–238). Beverly Hills: Sage.

Pearl, D., Bouthilet, L., & Lazar, J. (Eds.). (1982). *Television and behavior: Ten years of scientific progress and implications for the eighties* (Vol. 2). Washington, DC: U.S. Government Printing Office.

Penniman, W. D., & Jacob, M. E. (1984) Libraries as communicators of information. In R. E. Rice (Ed.), *The new media: Communication, research, and technology* (pp. 251–268). Beverly Hills: Sage.

Pertschuk, N. (1982). *Revolt against regulation: The rise and pause of the consumer movement.* Berkeley: University of California Press.

Picot, A., Klingenberg, H., & Dranzle, H. P. (1982). Office technology: A report on attitudes and channel selection from field studies in Germany. In M. Burgoon (Ed.), *Communication yearbook-6* (pp. 674–692). Beverly Hills: Sage.

Piven, F. F., & Cloward, R. A. (1982). *The new class war.* New York: Pantheon Books.

Presser, H. B., & Cain, V. S. (1983). Shift work among dual-earner couples with children. *Science, 219,* 876–879.

The price of cleaning up toxic wastes. (1983, March 13). *New York Times,* section 6, p. 20.

Prochaska, J. O., & DiClemente, C. C. (1983). Stage process of self-change of smoking: Toward an integrative model of change. *Journal of Consulting and Clinical Psychology, 51,* 390–395.

Rappaport, J. (1977). *Community psychology: Values, research, action.* New York: Holt, Rinehart & Winston.

Rice, R. E. (1982). Communication networking in computer-conferencing systems: A longitudinal study of group roles and system structure. In M. Burgoon (Ed.), *Communication yearbook-6* (pp. 925–943). Beverly Hills: Sage.

Rice, R. E. (1984a). Development of new media research. In R. E. Rice (Ed.), *The new media: Communication, research, and technology* (pp. 15–32). Beverly Hills: Sage.

Rice, R. E. (1984b). Mediated group communication. In R. E. Rice (Ed.), *The new media: Communication, research, and technology* (pp. 129–154). Beverly Hills: Sage.

Rice, R. E. (1984c). *The new media: Communication, research, and technology.* Beverly Hills: Sage.

Rice, R. E. (1984d). The new media technology: Growth and integration. In R. E. Rice (Ed.), *The new media: Communication, research, and technology* (pp. 33–54). Beverly Hills: Sage.

Rice, R. E., & Bair, J. H. (1984). The new organizational media and productivity. In R. E. Rice (Ed.), *The new media: Communication, research, and technology* (pp. 185–215). Beverly Hills: Sage.

Rice, R. E., & Rogers, E. M. (1984). New methods and data for the study of new media. In R. E. Rice (Ed.), *The new media: Communication, research, and technology* (pp. 81–99). Beverly Hills: Sage.

Rice, R. E., & Williams, F. (1984). Theories old and new: The study of new media. In R. E. Rice (Ed.), *The new media: Communication, research, and technology* (pp. 50–80). Beverly Hills: Sage.

Rice, R. E., & Paisley, W. J. (Eds.). (1981). *Public communication campaigns*. Beverly Hills: Sage.

Riley, J. W., & Riley, M. W. (1959). Mass communication and the social system. In R. K. Merton, L. Broom, & S. Cottrell (Eds.), *Sociology today* (pp. 225–243). New York: Basic Books.

Robertson, L. S., Kelley, A. B., O'Neill, B., Wixom, C. W., Eirwirth, R. S., & Haddon, W., Jr. (1974). A controlled study on the effect of television messages on safety belt use. *American Journal of Public Health, 64,* 1071–1080.

Robinson, J. P. (1977). *How Americans use time*. New York: Praeger.

Rogers, E. M. (1962). *The diffusion of innovations*. New York: Free Press.

Rogers, E. M. (1983). *Diffusion of innovations* (3rd ed.). New York: Free Press.

Rogers, E. M., & Kincaid, D. C. (1981). *Communication networks: Toward a new paradigm for research*. New York: Free Press.

Rogers, E. M., & Shoemaker, F. (1971). *Communication of innovations*. New York: Free Press.

Rogers-Warren, A., & Warren, S. F. (1977). *Ecological perspectives in behavior analysis*. Baltimore: University Park Press.

Rothman, J., Teresa, J. G., Kay, T. L., & Morningstar, G. C. (1983). *Marketing human service innovations*. Beverly Hills: Sage.

Rothschild, M. L., & Gaids, W. C. (1981). Behavioral learning theory: Its relevance to marketing and promotions. *Journal of Marketing, 45,* 70–77.

Roy, W. R. (1978). *Effects of the payment mechanism on the health care delivery system*. Washington, DC: U.S. Dept. of Health, Education, and Welfare.

Rubinstein, E. A. (1982). Televised violence: Approaches to prevention and control. *Prevention in Human Services, 2,* 7–18.

Rubenstein, E. A. (1983). Television and behavior: Research conclusions of the 1982 NIMH report and their policy implications. *American Psychologist, 38,* 820–825.

Runyan, C. W., DeVellis, R. F., Devellis, B. M., & Hochman, G. M. (1982). Health psychology and the public health perspective: In search of the pump handle. *Health Psychology, 1,* 169–180.

Rushton, J. P. (1982). Television and prosocial behavior. In D. Pearl, J. Bouthilet, & J. Lazar (Eds.), *Television and behavior: Ten years of scientific progress and implications for the eighties* (Vol. 2, pp. 248–258). Washington, DC: U.S. Government Printing Office.

Russel, M. A. H., Wilson, C., Taylor, C., & Baker, C. D. (1979). Effect of general practitioners' advice against smoking. *British Medical Journal, 2,* 231–235.

Russo, J. B. (1977). The value of unit price information. *Journal of Marketing Research, 14,* 193–201.

Russo, J. B. (1981). The decision to use product information at the point of purchase. In R. W. Stampfl & E. C. Hershman (Eds.), *Theory in retailing: Traditional and nontraditional sources* (pp. 155–157). Chicago: American Marketing Association.

Russo, J. R., Staelin, R., Russel, G. L., & Metcalf, B. L. (1984). *Nutritional information in the supermarket*. Working paper series, University of Chicago: Center for Research in Marketing.

Ryan, B., & Gross, N. C. (1943). The diffusion of hybrid seed corn in two Iowa communities. *Rural Sociology, 8,* 15–24.

Sahin, H., & Robinson, J. P. (1982). Beyond the realm of necessity: Television and the colonization of leisure. In D. C. Whitney & E. Wartella (Eds.), *Mass communication review yearbook* (Vol. 3, pp. 481–492). Beverly Hills: Sage.

Sarason, S. (1981). *Psychology misdirected*. New York: Free Press.

Savage, L. J. (1954). *The foundations of statistics*. New York: Wiley.

Schacter, S. (1982). Recedivision and self-cure of smoking and obesity. *American Psychologist, 37,* 436–444.

Schoech, D., Jennings, H., Schkade, L. L., & Hooper-Russell, C. (1985). Expert systems: Artificial intelligence for professional decisions. *Computers in Human Services, 1,* 81–116.

Schramm, W. (1977). *Big media/little media: Tools and technologies for instruction.* Beverly Hills: Sage.

Schramm, W., Lyle, J., & Parker, E. (1961). *Television in the lives of our children.* Stanford: Stanford University Press.

Schucker, R. L. (1983). *Implementation of a revised food labeling policy: Evaluation and tracking.* Washington, DC: Food and Drug Administration.

Schwartz, G. E. (1982). Testing the biopsychosocial model: The ultimate challenge facing behavioral medicine. *Journal of Consulting and Clinical Psychology, 50,* 1040–1053.

Seekins, T., Fawcett, S. B., Jason, L., Elder, J., Schnelle, J., & Winett, R. W. (1985). *Interstate evaluation of child restraint laws.* Study in progress, University of Kansas, Lawrence, KS.

Shannon, C., & Weaver, W. (1949). *The mathematical theory of communication.* Urbana: University of Illinois Press.

Simon, H. A. (1979). Rational decision making in business organizations. *The American Economic Review, 69,* 493–513.

Singer, J. L. (1980). The power and limitations of television. In P. B. Tennenbaum (Ed.), *The entertainment functions of television* (pp. 31–65). Hillsdale, NJ: Lawrence Erlbaum Associates.

Singer, J. L., & Singer, D. G. (1983). Psychologists look at television. Cognitive, developmental, personality, and social policy implications. *American Psychologist, 38,* 826–834.

Sirgy, M. J., Morris, M., & Samli, A. C. (1985, Winter) The question of value in social marketing: A quality-of-life theory. *The American Journal of Economics and Sociology,* 14–26.

Slovic, P., Fischoff, B., & Lichtenstein, S. (1984). Regulation of risk: A psychological perspective. In R. Noll (Ed.), *Regulatory policy and the social sciences* (pp. 211–285). Pasadena: University of California Press.

Solomon, D. S. (1981). A social marketing perspective on campaigns. In R. E. Rice & W. J. Paisley (Eds.), *Public communication campaigns* (pp. 289–302). Beverly Hills: Sage.

Solomon, D. S. (1982). Health campaigns on television. In D. Pearl, L. Bouthilet, & J. Lazar (Eds.), *Television and behavior: Ten years of scientific progress and implications for the eighties* (Vol. 2, pp. 308–321). Washington, DC: U.S. Government Printing Office.

Solomon, D. S. (1982). Mass media campaigns for health promotion. *Prevention in Human Services 2,* 115–123.

Solomon, D. S. (1984). Social marketing and community health promotion: The Stanford Heart Disease Prevention Program. In L. W. Frederiksen, L. J. Solomon, & K. A. Brehoney (Eds.), *Marketing health behavior* (pp. 115–136). New York: Plenum.

Sprafkin, J., & Rubinstein, E. A. (1982). Using television to improve the social behavior of institutionalized children. *Prevention in Human Services, 2,* 107–114.

Sprafkin, J., Swift, C., & Hess, R. (1982). The changing image of television. *Prevention in Human Services, 2,* 1–6.

Stigler, G. D. (1961). Economics of information. *Journal of Political Economy, 69,* 213–225.

Stokols, D., Novaco, R. W., Stokols, J., & Campbell, J. (1978). Traffic congestion, type A behavior, and stress. *Journal of Applied Psychology, 63,* 467–480.

Svenning, L. L., & Ruchinskas, J. E. (1984). Organizational teleconferencing. In R. E. Rice (Ed.), *The new media: Communication, research, and technology* (pp. 217–248). Beverly Hills: Sage.

Swift, C. (1982). Application of interactive television to prevention planning. *Prevention in Human Services, 2,* 125–139.

Thomas, S. (1982). Some problems of the paradigm in communication theory. In D. C. Whitney & E. Wartella (Eds.), *Mass communication review yearbook* (Vol. 3, pp. 79–96). Beverly Hills: Sage.

Toffler, A. (1980). *The third wave*. New York: Morrow.

Tracy, M. (1980). Nutrition and food policy—an emerging issue for agricultural economics? *Journal of Agricultural Economics, 31*, 369–379.

Wahler, R. G., & Graves, M. G. (1983). Setting events in social networks: Ally or enemy in child behavior therapy? *Behavior therapy, 14*, 19–36.

Wahler, R. G., & Fox, J. J. (1981). Setting events in applied behavior analysis: Toward a conceptual and methodological expansion. *Journal of Applied Behavior Analysis, 14*, 327–338.

Walker, W. B. (1986). *Use of computer-bulletin boards in clinical health promotion*. Dissertation project, Virginia Polytechnic Institute and State University, Blacksburg, VA.

Wallack, L. M. (1981). Mass-media campaigns: The odds against finding behavior change. *Health Education Quarterly, 8*, 209–260.

Ward, G. W. (1984). The national high blood pressure education program: An example of social marketing in action. In L. W. Frederiksen, L. J. Solomon, & K. A. Brehony (Eds.), *Marketing health behavior* (pp. 93–113). New York: Plenum.

Weaver, D. H. (1983). *Videotex journalism: Teletext, viewdata, and the news*. Hillsdale, NJ: Lawrence Erlbaum Associates.

Weick, K. E. (1984). Small wins: Redefining the scale of social problems. *American Psychologist, 39*, 40–49.

Weil, A. (1983). *Health and healing under conventional and alternative medicine*. Boston: Houghton-Mifflin.

Wellman, B. (1981). Applying network analysis to the study of support. In B. H. Gottlieb (Ed.), *Social networks and social support* (pp. 237–251). Beverly Hills: Sage.

White House (1970). *Conference on Food, Nutrition, and Health: Final Report*. Washington, DC, U.S. Printing Office, 121.

Wigand, R. T. (1982). Direct satellite broadcasting: Selected social implications. In M. Bugoon (Ed.), *Communication yearbook-6* (pp. 251–258). Beverly Hills: Sage.

Wilbur, C. S., & Garner, D. (1984). Marketing health to employees: The Johnson & Johnson Live for Life Program. In L. W. Frederiksen, L. J. Solomon, & K. A. Brehony (Eds.), *Marketing health behavior* (pp. 137–163). New York: Plenum.

Wilde, L. L. (in press). Consumer behavior under imperfect information: A review of psychological and marketing research as it relates to economic theory. In L. Green & J. H. Kagel (Eds.), *Advances in behavioral economics, 1*, Norwood, NJ: Albex.

Wilkie, W. L. (1975). New perspectives for consumer information processing research. *Communication Research, 2*, 216–231.

Wilkie, W. L., McNeill, D. L., & Mazis, M. B. (1984). Marketing's "scarlet letter": The theory and practice of corrective advertising. *Journal of Marketing, 48*, 11–31.

Willems, E. P. (1974). Behavioral technology and behavioral ecology. *Journal of Applied Behavior Analysis, 7*, 151–165.

Willis, B. D. (1982). Learner based and media related dimensions of videodisc formatting. In M. DeBloois (Ed.), *Videodisc/microcomputer courseware design* (pp. 101–120). Englewood Cliffs, NJ: Educational Technology Publications.

Wilson, G. T., & O'Leary, K. D. (1980) *Principles of behavior therapy*. Englewood Cliffs, NJ: Prentice-Hall.

Winett, R. A. (1983). Comment on Matarazzo's "Behavioral health's challenge . . ." *American Psychologist, 38*, 120–121.

Winett, R. A. (1984). Comment on Slovic et al., "Requestion of risk". In R. Noll (Ed.), *Regulatory policy and the social sciences* (pp. 286–292). Pasadena: University of California Press.

Winett, R. A., & Ester, P. (1982). Behavioral science and energy conservation: Conceptualizations, strategies, outcomes, energy policy applications. *Journal of Economic Psychology, 2*, 223–246.

Winett, R. A., Frederiksen, L. W., & Riley, A. W. (1981, November). *Television programming as primary prevention.* Paper presented at the annual meeting of the Association for the Advancement of Behavior Therapy, Toronto.

Winett, R. A., Hatcher, J. W., Fort, R., Leckliter, I. N., Fishback, J. R., Riley, A. W., & Love, S. Q. (1982). The effects of videotape modeling and feedback on residential thermal conditions, electricity consumption, and perceptions of comfort: Summer and winter studies. *Journal of Applied Behavior Analysis, 15,* 381–402.

Winett, R. A., & Kagel, J. H. (1984). The effects of information presentation format on consumer demand for resources in field settings. *Journal of Consumer Research, 14,* 655–667.

Winett, R. A., Kagel, J. H., Battalio, R. C., & Winkler, R. C. (1978). The effects of rebates, feedback, and information on electricity conservation. *Journal of Applied Psychology, 63,* 73–80.

Winett, R. A., Kramer, K. D., Walker, W. B., & Malone, S. W. (1985, October). *Effective consumer information interventions.* Paper presented at Bell Lab's Research Conference on Telecommunications and Consumer Demand, New Orleans.

Winett, R. A., Leckliter, I. N., Chinn, D. E., & Stahl, B. N. (1984). The effects of special, brief cable TV programming on residential energy conservation. *Journal of Communication.* Summer, 37–51.

Winett, R. A., Leckliter, I. N., Chinn, D. E., Stahl, B. N., & Love, S. Q. (1985). The effects of television modeling on residential energy conservation. *Journal of Applied Behavior Analysis, 18,* 33–44.

Winett, R. A., Love, S. Q., Chinn, D. E., Stahl, B. H., & Leckliter, I. N. (1983). Comfort standards and energy conservation strategies based on field experiments: A replication and extension of findings. *ASHRAE Transactions, 17,* 188–197.

Winett, R. A., Love, S. Q., & Kidd, C. (1982). The effects of an energy technician and extension agents' home visits on promoting summer residential energy conservation. *Journal of Environmental Systems, 11,* 61–70.

Winett, R. A., & Neale, M. S. (1981). Flextime and family time allocation: Use of a self-report log to assess the effects of a system change on individual behavior. *Journal of Applied Behavior Analysis, 14,* 39–46.

Winett, R. A., Neale, M. S., & Williams, K. R. (1979). Effective field research strategies: Recruitment of participants and acquisition of reliable, useful data. *Behavioral Assessment, 1,* 139–155.

Winett, R. A., Neale, M. S., & Williams, K. R. (1982). The effects of flexible work schedules on urban families with young children: Quasi-experimental, ecological studies. *American Journal of Community Psychology, 10,* 49–54.

Winett, R. A., Stefanek, M., & Riley, A. W. (1983). Preventive strategies with children and families: Small groups, organizations, communities. In T. H. Ollendick & M. Hensen (Eds.), *Handbook of child psychopathology* (pp. 485–521). New York: Plenum.

Winett, R. A., & Winkler, R. C. (1972). Current behavior modification in the classroom: Be still, be quiet, be docile. *Journal of Applied Behavior Analysis, 5,* 499–504.

Winkler, R. C. (1982). *Rights versus duty: A social behavioral approach.* Unpublished manuscript, Perth: University of Western Australia.

Winkler, R. C., & Winett, R. A. (1982). Behavioral interventions in resource conservation: A systems approach based on behavioral economics. *American Psychologist, 37,* 421–435.

Wolfolk, R. L., & Richardson, F. C. (1984). Behavior therapy and the ideology of modernity. *American Psychologist, 39,* 777–786.

Wood, R. E. (1982). High technology: An assessment of its potential for instruction. In M. DeBloois (Ed.), *Videodisc/microcomputer courseware design* (pp. 121–147). Englewood Cliffs, NJ: Educational Technology Publication.

Woolley, R. D. (1982). Training applications: Making interactive video work effectively. In M. DeBloois (Ed.), *Videodisc/microcomputer courseware design* (pp. 149–162). Englewood Cliffs, NJ: Educational Technology Publications.

Wright, J. C., & Huston, A. C. (1983). A matter of form: Potentials of television for young viewers. *American Psychologist, 38,* 835–844.

Wright, P. (1979). Concrete action plans on TV messages to increase reading of drug warnings. *Journal of Consumer Research, 6,* 256–269.

Zifferblatt, S. M., Wilbur, C. S., & Pinsky (1980). Changing cafeteria eating habits. *Journal of the American Dietetic Association, 76,* 15–20.

Author Index

Subject Index